Chasing Montana

Chasing Montana

A Love Story

Lori Soderlind

The University of Wisconsin Press
Terrace Books

The University of Wisconsin Press
1930 Monroe Street
Madison, Wisconsin 53711

www.wisc.edu/wisconsinpress/

3 Henrietta Street
London WC2E 8LU, England

Library of Congress Cataloging-in-Publication Data
Soderlind, Lori.
Chasing Montana : a love story / Lori Soderlind.
p.   cm.
ISBN 0-299-21754-X (pbk.: alk. paper)
1. Soderlind, Lori.   2. Soderlind, Lori—Friends and associates.
3. Journalists—United States—Biography.   4. Love—United States.
5. Montana—Biography.   6. New Jersey—Biography.   I. Title.
CT275.S58875A3   2006
978.6'033'092—dc22   2005021510

Terrace Books, a division of the University of Wisconsin Press,
takes its name from the Memorial Union Terrace, located
at the University of Wisconsin–Madison. Since its inception in 1907,
the Wisconsin Union has provided a venue for students, faculty, staff,
and alumni to debate art, music, politics, and the issues of the day.
It is a place where theater, music, drama, dance, outdoor activities,
and major speakers are made available to the campus and the community.
To learn more about the Union, visit www.union.wisc.edu.

For
William and Florence,
and
Jim and Helen

This book had the generous support of my advisors and friends. Michael Scammell, a very wise man, helped me find the story. Patricia O'Toole kept me believing in it. Tzivia Gover is a literary matchmaker extraordinaire and a tireless source of encouragement. Amy Callahan shared the worst and the best moments over years of revision. Raphael Kadushin is a savvy editor with integrity, and I thank him. Suzanne Parker helped me with her poet's eye. My workshop partners offered invaluable discipline and support. Thanks to Deborah Malmud and Jon Karp for their professional counsel. I admire and respect the Soderlind family and the people of Rapelje, Montana, and thank them for their tolerance. This work never would have happened without Janis Joplin, Laura Nyro, Jack Kerouac, Thelma and Louise, the Partridge Family, Joan of Arc, Gloria Steinem, and of course, Katherine Friedrich; I thank them all for having lived and having inspired me.

This is a work of creative nonfiction. Many of the names have been changed to protect the unsuspecting. Time frames have been adjusted to create a coherent narrative.

Action is the last resource of those
who don't know how to dream.

Oscar Wilde

When William Soderlind was thirty years old, he and his wife, Florence, packed up everything they owned and moved to Rapelje, Montana. There was nothing there: no shops, no sidewalks, no houses. Not even their own house. It was 1916, and Rapelje was only an idea of a place. Red rags waved off knee-high stakes in the dirt as William and Florence arrived, having bumped their way up the long road running straight through Montana's eastern plains. They had traveled a very long way; they came to Montana from Wisconsin, where they had spent the first years of their marriage. They had never been out West before. All they'd seen of it were some paintings, possibly, and the posters that the railroads had plastered up at trade shows, trying to lure farmers to settle the plains. Maybe they'd seen a photograph of Yellowstone Park, but they had never seen Montana and they certainly had never seen Rapelje; there was no Rapelje to see.

Rapelje. Rhymes with Nap All Day.

I have always wondered why they went there. William Soderlind was my grandfather but he died, young, years before my parents met and long before I was born, so I never got to ask him why he chose Rapelje, and what it was he wanted so badly that it was worth giving up every known thing in his life for: his job, his home, Wisconsin. It's not that I don't understand it—going west, going *away*—but I wonder what he expected to find, in the midst of a wild, sprawling nothing. Dry dust sprouts lonely cottonwood trees. Antelope graze in the crabgrass and thistle. William was not a cowboy; he was a banker, with a felt hat and spats on his shoes and a three-piece suit with a watch on the vest. He looked odd in the wilderness. Maybe a business deal got him going, a scheme to get rich in the last frontier boom; maybe some railroad poster promised greatness in wide-open spaces. But when he got there and saw the earth was dry and full of rocks, not fertile ground for whatever dreams he'd brought with him, he stayed anyhow. The loans he made to farmers failed, but he stayed. The new town burned down, but he didn't leave it. The farms returned to the dust that they came from, but my grandfather stuck with Rapelje, Montana, land of great promises that never came true, far from the rocky peaks beneath a big sky that is what everyone else means when everyone else says, "Montana." That word meant something different to William; there was something in it that he wanted, and he chased after it for twenty years before he finally let it go.

You can't always figure why people do what they do. My father, a showoff, likes to say in Latin, "Nil disputandum de gustibus," which means there is no disputing taste. My father was born in Rapelje, but as a young man he worked his way backwards to the Midwest, met my mother there and married her in her parents' home, in Wisconsin, then moved even farther east to New Jersey, where I come from. It's easy to end up in New Jersey; lots of people do. Most people only dream about Montana. My mother, a small woman with wide eyes and a lively imagination, sums up William's attraction to Rapelje this way: she says, "It turned him on." Who knows why. You can't really say what might turn someone on. She imagines William in the flat dust, a miracle of dirt and sky, and she says with her eyes closed, "He loved the place." But she couldn't tell you why people love what they do any more than I could.

One thing I do know: there are very few places in the world where you get the chance to make your own town, to start from nothing and make it turn out any way you want. And I like to think of it that way: Rapelje, parched Eden. My grandparents made that enviable journey back to the Garden, only, when they got there, the garden wouldn't grow.

When I was about the same age William was when he left for the West, I wanted to move to Montana, but not because of my family ties. I decided to go with a woman named Madeleine; she was the only person I'd ever known besides my father who had actually been to Montana, and she was the first to take me there. Before I met Madeleine, the word Montana did not really mean much to me. The way my father explained it, the place was deserted and dull, nice to look at, in a way, but there was really nothing to keep you there. He had left and not returned for forty years. Madeleine's Montana was different. Madeleine's Montana was the place she would be if she could, a place where people learn who they really are, and stick with it. And because of that people in Montana had, for example, very strong hands. They got what they needed. It was a place full of bearded characters with western eyes that pierce souls when they squint just right, and barefoot women who make tea out of grass, and know about things I'd never even thought of. She stirred up a kind of Montana I had never known, and I knew right away it was what I wanted, though it was still hard to say exactly why. It seemed like a fine idea, the answer to all my disappointment with life at that time: going to Montana and staying there, with Madeleine.

People who knew my grandparents say they were happy. I'm not sure what that means. That they played bridge every Friday night? That they found a lasting inner peace? What I know is only that they, and I, once believed in something out there, somewhere, that seemed worth doing nearly anything to have. We didn't get what we expected. I have a doorknob from the bank where William worked. I took it off the door when I went to find Rapelje, with Madeleine. A long time ago, this ball turned in my strange grandfather's hand. His ruined bank stands back in the high grass now, slumped and rotting near the silos in a small town of Quonset huts, trailers, and a few caved-in houses. And the rusted knob is mine, sitting on a shelf, small salvage of lives that never really turned out like we planned them.

Madeleine and I were bound for Montana almost as soon as we met. We didn't exactly know it right away, but it was always there; Madeleine had a sort of independent, western quality that set her apart, and I was drawn to that, and it was Montana that did it. She reminded me of the way the world looked when I was a child, when everything seemed possible, like heading into a vast frontier. I had imagined a pretty wonderful life for myself as a child. My expectations were formed at least in part by 1960s pop music lyrics, sung out loud on long trips into the woods at summer camp, and the free use of words like "revolution" and "liberation," which seemed to turn up everywhere that mattered, when I was a girl.

When I grew up and started looking for my place in the world, I was surprised by what I found; the world was not an earthy, liberated, communal magic carpet ride at all. I didn't like what I stepped into but I didn't know how to change it, and I couldn't see how I could ever make a life in it that was right for me. In 1988 I was twenty-four years old, working as a reporter at a small daily newspaper in Elizabeth, New Jersey. Madeleine was a photographer there. I felt lucky to know her, because she seemed to see the world like I did, and so I felt a little less alone. The job in Elizabeth was her first, and my second; I changed jobs a few times in my first years working, hoping I could find something better. There had to be something better, but it didn't really help when I changed jobs, or apartments, which I also tried. It was not really Elizabeth, New Jersey, or my work that I was unhappy with, though I didn't especially like either. I wasn't upset over a bad relationship; I'd never really had a relationship, which actually did make me sad but the real problem was, the relationship I wanted seemed not to exist. I was looking for an entire world that had apparently been lost somewhere, and I was sort of dumbstruck, at twenty-four, when I could not find it.

But what was it? Something more than trying to get rich, and sleeping, and staying well fed until I grew old and died; I wanted something freer than that, more creative. Something that resembled the life I was promised on July 4, 1973, when I got to finger paint the word "love," in blue, on the belly of a summer camp counselor wearing nothing but a string bikini. She walked out of the woods barefoot. Her body was a canvas of soft skin. She offered herself to a line of nine-year-olds waiting for lunch, and she said we could paint anything we wanted. As far as I knew, I was signing a contract. In the time before nearly every camp counselor, guitar player, and teacher I knew quit the so-called revolution and began a long, sad journey into silence, every one of them seemed to tell me "Do your own thing." They said "Hey, if that's your trip . . ." These were important instructions that I heard a million times as they dipped my hand into the magic finger-paint pot and said: "Write your own story. Say something brave, and we'll be with you."

Turned out that I got stranded between generations, born in the last official year of the "baby boom," too young to be a rebel in the '60s but too old to feel separate from that world, and it's promises— or to mock it, as my younger friends do now. "Patchouli? Disgusting," they say. But they never saw the point, as I saw it. As a girl I wore a peace-sign medallion and fuzzy purple pants; I wore them not as fashion but as truth. I had a plastic blow-up pillow that said "Make Love, Not War," though I may have been confused about the kind of love that meant. I believed in love and I loved earnestly: I loved my pollution-hating, mini-skirted young pretty school teachers, who told us that the air was foul and we'd all get asthma when we grew up (I did); I loved my super mellow groovy cool guitar teachers; I loved their mustaches, which grew long down the sides of their chins (was it wrong that I wanted one too?); and I loved my babysitters, who had long silky hair and suede purses with fringe. I had crushes on my babysitters, and I dreamed they would all still be there for me, when I grew up enough to be their friend, and I could become part of The Movement.

What I felt as I grew older, when The Movement just sort of went away, was more than disillusioned; I felt betrayed. I went looking for my people, but I found nothing left of The Movement and no one to move with, or at least, no one until I met Madeleine.

It's true that my own childhood home in New Jersey was not quite a hot bed of revolution. And lots of things scared me: I was afraid for all the teenage runaways in TV movies, lured off by promises that didn't come true; I was sad for the singers who overdosed and died; I was afraid of drugs, and scary cults, and war, and the lady up the street who drank orange juice with vodka in it, and the girl whose father sometimes hit her. My brother was always in trouble, growing up; my father worked in the city, and he seemed to only work, and sleep; he and my mother fought in front of us but they never seemed to hug, or kiss, or make love not war. I knew about pain, but, that only made a greater case for the message that we had to do better, go back to the land and start new.

An early memory: 1969, riding with my brother in the back seat of our mother's station wagon. She yelled at us suddenly to lock the car doors. We asked her "Why?" and she pointed to the teenagers standing at a traffic light. She said those hippies would try to get in the car. She was right. When we stopped at the light, they pulled on the locked door handles. Like, hey there square family, can we join your trip? Yeah. Right on. It seemed to me like it would be fun if they got in the car with us. I wanted to know where they were going. It must have been somewhere outa sight. I turned around backwards on the car seat as we drove away from that corner, and the pack of teenagers in headbands and holey jeans grew smaller and smaller, then disappeared.

Second grade: we listened to a record in school called "Free to Be You and Me," and I wore my matching plaid pantsuits and carried my red plastic briefcase to school because I was free to be me, and I took that message seriously. I grew my hair out of its pixie, into a long, wild mess that always needed to be brushed. I asked my second grade teacher to marry me, because I loved her. She never answered. But she told my mom.

High school: the once-half-a-million-strong freak nation that had only ten years earlier descended on Woodstock had dwindled to about twelve people, all hanging outside the cafeteria at Millburn Senior High, smoking butts and carrying on the dead revolution the only way we knew how: by staying stoned nearly all of the time. I spun folksy passionate Joni Mitchell tunes on the school radio station until one day I realized I'd been left off the DJ schedule for a very long time, and not by accident. Ronald Reagan had defeated Jimmy Carter just a year before most of us could vote, we never had a chance to change the outcome, and we of the torn-jeans set bumming cigarettes and kicking snow with our leather boots were just aware enough to realize: the world as we'd known it was changing, and it was not the kind of change we had all put our faith in.

1988: a world in black-and-white, of gray-suited men and women walking down a gray concrete street, black leather briefcases dangling from hands, industrial steam making a billowing haze. Cold, coked-out, hollow: my god, who had imagined this world, and made it happen? Everything seemed dark, or shiny, or dark and shiny, like a silver Delorian car. An abrasive conservative wash had removed so much crazy uncertainty, swept out all the colorful mess I'd known and replaced it with a simpler motif: money. Neat and clean. Cosmic consciousness was dead. It had been, for years already, a new age of greed.

That year, when I was a reporter at the *Daily Journal* in Elizabeth and Madeleine was a photographer there, I took notes in my flip-top notebook while the dream of something different got away. It was a big election year. My job included covering a candidate for the U.S. Senate, with whom I rode around in a limousine, asking questions. He lost. George Herbert Walker Bush became president, assuring us that Ronald Reagan's right-wing revolution was going to survive. On election night, our newsroom was very solemn, watching the victory unfold. We had only about eight reporters, all very young, all trying to be writers and so poorly paid; we were not the people that this new revolution had been kind to. At home in my shared rental house after work, I sat before our TV and watched the world grow stranger, tallying election returns until well after midnight, all of the newly anointed in their well-pressed suits grinning and grasping at the future, and I remember thinking over and over, "This world hates my guts," and getting drunk on Heinekens.

Meanwhile, our newspaper was dying. At the bull market's height, a Texas investor had paid too much money to buy the *Daily Journal,* so it was on its way to being an investment casualty. As it turned out, the actual secret to life (and you didn't have to climb a mountain to learn this) was: buy low, sell high. "Values," once open to discussion, were now firmly rooted in profits and share price. The *Daily Journal* was apparently of very little value, and as it died, we could feel ourselves somehow dying with it. A newspaper in its death throes was alright as a place to start out and leave quickly, but actually being there seemed to be pretty pointless. Nothing you could do, no matter how good, was going to change the outcome. Maybe that had not always been so. Maybe once there was a chance, and that place had known its glory. Old guys from better days still haunted the staff, parked in frivolous jobs, editing the spring bridal page and choosing the "pothole of the week." They grew hair in their ears and smoked unfiltered cigarettes, while young "cubs" like me kept things limping on. I came to the *Daily Journal* from an even smaller dying newspaper. I dreamed of telling stories that might rock the world somehow; I wanted to write expressive stories about meaningful things, like the ones I had seen in *Life* magazine as a child, but *Life* was over, and so I settled on the modest ambition of covering the school board without getting fired. Every day I worried that I would mess up and get fired, because in the world I knew, getting fired was a regular feature. Once, the *Daily Journal*'s whole Saturday staff got fired because the county prosecutor called to say he was resigning, but no one answered the phone. It kept ringing, and ringing, but the whole staff kept typing and typing, so they missed the big story and every one of them got fired.

The *Daily Journal*'s editor in my time there was a Texan named Phil. He had red hair and a red face that grew redder as he yelled. He yelled in short, neat bursts and he yelled lots of things. Curse words. Instructions. Tips to reporters, like "Move it!" and, "Get out of here!" What he used to yell most at me was, "Don't sugar coat the news."

"Stop looking for the goddamn happy endings."

"This is a newspaper, goddamn it."

In my first years working in the world that was nothing like the one I'd been promised, I learned against my will that failure generally makes the best stories. Failure has drama. Editors always want stories about drownings, and explosions, and senators screwing their underaged aides. My job was to seek out such stories of loss, and record them. Often, finding stories of loss involved knocking on the door of a murder victim's family or turning up fraud: nailing powerful middle-aged men for abuses I could not yet imagine, much less expose. So I tried to succeed but really, I worried. At the office, I was unsure of what I was doing and afraid of being found out. It seemed that everything about me was something that should not be found out: my incompetence, my fondness for old hippies, my inexplicable little urge to sit next to a reporter named Heidi. I sat stiffly at a green desk filthy with decades of unfiltered cigarette smoke and the perspiration of an endless stream of anxious reporters, and I wanted to succeed in this hard world but, more urgently than that, I wanted to run the hell out. I sat with my legs neatly folded, runs in my nylons and itchy in my skirts, across the aisle from a sports guy with eyes stuck far apart on his head like a snake. At least one of his eyes always pointed at me. I made calls on my tan plastic phone, sorting out words through its incessant crackle, trying to discover if anything bad had happened anywhere, each day, ever ready to run toward it if it had, so that I could take notes. I would take any opportunity to run: to a story, or away from the snake, or my boss, or my inexplicable little urges, or just work in general.

By the time we reporters at these small dying papers realized what sort of a life we'd signed up for, it seemed too late to go back and be someone else. Lucky friends left for better jobs at larger newspapers; some married accountants and were never heard from again; some just went away, to curl up into quivering balls, now that they were grossly overweight from fast-food binges, and their six roommates were married and leaving the shared rental house, and their power neckties were coffee stained and hanging from the rear view mirror of rusty, uninsured, bald-tired cars that needed new transmissions.

"You need a transmission?" Madeleine would say, overhearing office chatter as she marched past, always going somewhere. "I got a transmission guy for you." She'd lean way down on her elbows on your desk and start talking, just for a moment, before standing up and moving on. She moved on quickly, like she always had so much to do. She was ready for action. She wore draw-string pants and tie-dyed shirts to work, comfort clothes, meant to inhabit awkward spaces, climb things, crawl on the ground with a camera. She was a photographer, a very physical job that provided a bonus eccentricity: spinning out of sight into her darkroom through a black revolving door. Who knew what went on in there? Secret things, special things.

"Listen," she'd say, "here's what you do." And she would tell you about her transmission guy, Ralph or Frank or someone she had found and had cut some special deal with. She'd find people like herself who were always ready to deal, and she'd start talking to them calm and matter of fact, like she had every reason to believe they would help her, as if they'd been pals since they were kids — Madeleine always talked to people like she knew them; she apparently had met the whole world on the playground when the whole world had been kids. She'd tell you, "Just go to this guy and say, listen Ralph, I need this work done but I've only got fifty dollars." This wouldn't work for you but if you were Madeleine, by the end of the day, your car patched up and ready to go, you and Ralph would be trading Grateful Dead tapes.

Madeleine was not like anyone else I knew then. There was a quality in her that defied all this grayness, this obsession with all that was bad. She was a survivor. She believed in things other people didn't see, and she saw something in me too, which amazed me. It felt as if someone else, for the first time, actually knew who I was. When we first met, she once told me, she had thought to herself, "Ah ha! There's one," which to her meant, roughly, that she had found a karmic soul friend. A karmic soul friend: it was really not okay for anyone to say such a thing in earnest, not at a newspaper, especially, but Madeleine — even the most whacked-out things she said (and there were many) came out sounding like news leads. She walked across the long newsroom wearing ankle bells, kaching-kaching-kaching-kaching, off to do work that she believed in. Anyone else, those bells would be silly but Madeleine balanced her eccentricity with her common sense. She was very practical. She could explain exactly why you had to have an IRA just as sure as she could help you clear your chakras.

If the police scanner buzzed with reports of a dead body found or a house burning down or a local waterway frothing with chemicals, I would grab my reporter's notebook and pound on the darkroom door. "News!" I'd yell, then bolt to the scene with whichever of our two photographers spun out. Sometimes, it was an old-timer named Joe, an old hair-in-his-ears guy who was like everybody's father or grandfather and who, after trapping young reporters in his car, would drill them on the progress of their lives (When ya gettin married? huh? Married? Married with babies, babies, kids, kids, kids?) or dole out advice (Hey. Girlie. Don't be such a big baby! and, Aw, don't give me that, whadda loada crap!). On the way to a story, or what seemed like it might be a story but more often than not was a lark, I would stretch out in the passenger seat of Joe's car and sigh. It was safe there, and I knew that he would be kind to me, and maybe on the way back to the office we could stop for a hot dog.

Sometimes, when the scanner erupted, I'd pound on the darkroom door, and Madeleine would spin out. She would say, "Hi." And I would say, "Hi." She would say, "Where's the fire?" and I'd tell her. Running out the door, already ten steps ahead of me, she'd call over her shoulder, "Come on, girl, let's go, let's go!"

We covered a story once at a Hillside creek where the water was foaming and green. I covered a lot of stories in the creeks of New Jersey; I wrote a lot about urban decay in all of its forms: murders, housing projects, potholes, industrial waste. New Jersey's old sewers were not designed to handle the waste flowing through them; factories hooked up to them and who knew what poured out.

Riding to Hillside in Madeleine's black Ford, with its torn leather seats and its new-used tires, I looked ahead and stayed quiet, brooding, as if deep in thought, while she raced yellow lights through concrete Elizabeth. I didn't know her well enough then to talk to her and unlike Joe, she wasn't full of questions and fatherly prods. She had slipped off her Birkenstocks and put on a pair of worn sneakers—driving shoes—and she looked ahead, smiling. She had recently cut her hair. It was a mistake, a comic nod to the corporate fashion trends of our time; she had chopped off her long braid and cut her hair jawline-short, framing her full face, her off-center eyes blinking bewildered inside a heart-shaped mane. Her crooked smile seemed to realize the whole thing was funny. We shot off on the trail of catastrophe in companionable silence, where the demeanor I'd settled on was near sulking. I think it felt sexy, though I could not have said that. Brooding quiet is a close as I ever came to feeling sexy, then: sort of mysterious, completely tense. I watched broken down Elizabeth roll by, twisting long strands of my insane blond hair around and around my chapped fingers. If I spoke I might have sounded nervous, or stupid, because I liked her. Better to keep my mouth shut, I supposed, because I knew the power of silence. At the first red light we hit we locked the doors and watched a maybe-twelve-year-old crack dealer walk up to the car, like he walked up to every car, spreading the latest urban epidemic, staring hollow through the window as I shifted in my skirt suit. It fit too tight. It was cheap and its shoulder pads made me feel broad as a barn door. We shook our heads at the kid and drove on.

At the creek, all was murder. The dead fish had begun to pile against the rocks, and water green as antifreeze stirred into a froth. The creek was a river with a name, but it had been locked into place with poured concrete walls, so now it looked like a storm sewer, a flow of waste water, that's all anyone really thought it was anymore. I walked away from the car and felt the bite of cold on an early spring day that was really not as nice as it looked. The air stunk strong of gas fumes. I tucked my notebook under my arm, turned up my collar, and lit a cigarette, as if the match would warm me. I took a drag and let the smoke out, slow, staring at the fish piling up in the water.

"Put out that cigarette, girl," Madeleine said, swatting my fingers as she marched by with her camera. "You'll blow us up." Then she started to climb down the embankment. Madeleine was a photographer, so she simply saw things. I had to find a way to understand the mess, so I had to ask questions.

I snuffed out the cigarette on a telephone pole. I asked a cop about the situation. "So, uhm, how did that green stuff get in the creek?" I queried, squinting while my hair blew over my eyes. "How many fish you think are dead?"

The cop shrugged his shoulders. He said, "A hundred? A thousand?"

The dead fish, so many of them, felt like more than I could handle. I had to learn what had gone wrong that day, just like every day, and I was beginning to see that, in fact, pretty much everything, everywhere had gone wrong. All the evidence I found, in the back alleys of dead cities in New Jersey or in the quiet, locked-up streets of nearby suburban towns, showed me that more than a few people in the world were disappointed with the way life had turned out. Day after day as a young reporter I was shaken by the reality that somehow, in America, in march-off-to-make-money America, people had become so disillusioned as to spray paint words like "Fuck you" on their own neighbors' front doors and the neighbors had grown so despairing or so poor that they didn't paint the message over; they just left the words for all to see, down in the Bayway, down by the projects, over in Newark in the razed neighborhoods and small pockets of irascible life where, eventually, I discovered Madeleine lived. I was sorry, and afraid of these horrors, and unsure how any of this could ever be made right because really, nobody cared, and really, the revolution had failed us. Madeleine was sorry too, but her sorrow seemed different. I watched her at the bottom of the creek, using her whole body to line up just the right shot. Then she stood up and looked down at the mess and shook her head. The fish were glistening gray and belly-up, pressed against the rocks.

"What are all those fish," I called down. "Trout?"

"These?" she said, and looked up at me like I was dumb. "These are carp," she said. "Big, fat, bottom-feeding carp. Some people like them."

She scurried back up the walls of the creek. "You want trout," she said, "go to Montana."

Then she smiled, looking down into her camera bag, fishing out another roll of film. In Montana, she knew (and in the car later, she told me),you climb on the rocky banks of streaming crystal water, and you fish for healthy trout, patiently, and you can toss them back or you can take them home for dinner. Montana. Madeleine said, "It's better, there."

I quit my job at the *Daily Journal* about a year after I started and went to work for a slightly larger dying paper a few dead cities to the north. Almost immediately after that, Madeleine invited herself to dinner at my house. It was the first time we planned to do something together outside of work, and she had been the one to suggest it. This was like a miracle, that someone I liked in the world apparently liked me back. It felt like things finally might be changing.

I lived with four roommates in an aluminum-sided two-family rental house in Morristown, New Jersey, with a big front porch cluttered with empty boxes, flower pots full of dirt but not flowers, stacks of unclaimed phone books, stray bicycle tires. Against the wall was a discarded car seat, on which I liked to sit on warmer nights. More furniture of dubious origins lined the walls inside. I had been living in the attic of that house for a year and shared the rest of it with four pleasant strangers; ours had been a rental house for a long time, you could see that by the black ribbons of scuff marks along the wall up the stairs, where furniture had come and gone in steady rotation. The house was a big sleeping chamber, like a modern tenement with a bath off the hall. The first floor was split into three common rooms—the kitchen, a central room with two couches turned to face a TV, and a sunny, wood-trimmed parlor that was mostly empty, and for which we had thought of no use. The parlor had a couple bookshelves in it and a section of a sofa that someone had left behind because it was too heavy to throw out. We five lived in our house "communally," but it was a distinctly '80s-style commune; none of us could afford something better, so we were bonded, or exiled, over money. That's all. There were no group roundtable discussions about revolution, no shared drugs or orgies, no experimentation, certainly no "finding ourselves" there. Our house didn't have a name like Rising Sun or Star Den, like the shared homes that broke all the rules in the '70s and which I romanticized: I thought of them as places to bake bread and share things. Our shared children didn't live with us, because we didn't have any children to share. We didn't share friends, we didn't share food, we didn't share dreams or even discuss such things much, unless we'd all been drinking and it was late at night and we all wound up home at the same time; mostly when any of us were home we just stared at the TV. We were suburban-bred, variously educated, usually employed economic refugees, inhabiting the future that an earlier generation of communal dwellers could not have imagined: the collapse of the collapse of our parents' proper world.

On Madeleine's first visit, she and I took over the communal kitchen to make a meal. It was the nerve center of that house: a cluttered box full of doors, ringed with unruly cupboards. The room was equipped both for cooking and doing laundry, with a washing machine that doubled as a counter top. Madeleine put a cutting board across the washing machine and chopped broccoli; I boiled cavatelli and sautéed onions on the brown stove, moving its one remaining knob around to work all the burners. Beneath fluorescent lights in a water-stained drop ceiling, we cooked dinner together. It was a ritual Madeleine said she thought all women should share, if they planned to be friends, because making food is a nourishing and intimate thing, and what are women to each other if not nourishing and intimate?

Rivals for the few good boyfriends in the world?

No, she said; women were more than that. Yes, she said; you've got to have at least one true girlfriend.

"Oh, I agree," I said, which was really pretty wordy for me at the time, yet still it did not convey my full views on the subject, or how happy I was to hear those words. In essence I believed, then, that all-out matriarchy was the only hope for our very sick world; I'd believed this ever since I was about ten years old and a fan of what was called "women's lib." Then I came across a book called *The Female Eunuch* at the township swimming pool's book swap rack and there it was, in black-and-white, in words almost but not quite too strange for me to understand: women had been brainwashed, turned against each other by men who were basically dinosaurs, brutal nasty dinosaurs who'd better change their god-awful behavior or die out real fast, and I mean real fast, mister; don't test me. But I wouldn't have said that to Madeleine, because I didn't want to scare her.

"Who needs boyfriends, huh?" she said as she chopped, and told me that hers had recently dumped her, and no, she didn't want to talk about it, and I was glad, because my own boyfriend trouble was not a topic I cared to discuss. In truth, I had a hard enough time even thinking about it. How could I just say, "Yeah, boyfriends, I don't want one." I was afraid to tell anyone how I felt. Male union was the mission of a grown woman's life, wasn't it? Didn't everyone want a boyfriend? Not me, and that really was trouble, because I tended to wind up with them anyhow.

Madeleine and I carried steaming platefuls of pasta to the rarely visited and nearly empty front parlor, which could be closed off with pocket doors. We shut the pocket doors and made ourselves a den away from the others—Kathy and Jonathan and Christine and Lou, all staring at the TV in silence. Closing ourselves off from them symbolized a kind of progress. We'd found something more interesting to do. Madeleine sat on the sagging lap of the old hunk of sofa, put her feet up, and opened up a can of the potent Scottish ale I had bought—an extravagance, stronger than my usual generic beverage choices, because we were new friends bonding.

Candles lit the parlor, creating a laid-back, acid-den kind of mood in what was the otherwise plain darkness of winter. That candlelit space was almost frightening in its intimacy. We were accustomed to office lighting and work talk. Now the light created a mood. Madeleine glowed and I wished I could sit close to her and I was aware of that wish and I didn't know what to do with it. I wanted her to be near me. I wanted so many things to come to me then and I was fast to believe Madeleine had all of them, because she seemed like my only hope. There was a wooden chair on the far side of the low table in that room; I looked at it but then I chose to sit on the sofa, where I parked myself with casual force next to Madeleine. She inched a little bit away and rearranged herself in her seat, and we started eating.

When my mother was a young woman, if she made a new friend in the neighborhood, she would invite her to the house for tea. She would serve her friend tea out of a china pot—a wedding gift—in the well-lit afternoon, in a living room filled with department store furniture. Their talk would have centered on their children, perhaps, or the local schools. My mother was the sort of woman who was bound to say something too honest, out of innocence, and that would make her seem vaguely wrong in her world. But, there was still the tea, and the light in the room, and good manners to make up for any indiscretions; and something about the sureness in that life makes me think sometimes that it might have been nice to be there, with them, where they knew what was proper. Was it best just to know what was proper? Rules had been established, women learned the rules, and then came a time when the rules were thrown out, and "Hey, it's your trip," you know, you could do whatever you felt like. Now it seemed necessary to conform once again, but no one had told me what the rules were. Who knew how to act, anymore? I was raised on the "Free to Be" record, which had lied.

I sipped beer with Madeleine. She sank into the couch. I felt sure that Madeleine, like me, was not particularly interested in living a conventional life, whatever that meant, and that made me feel excited, and loosened by alcohol I began to talk about it. The sooner we agreed on the kind of life we wanted to live, the sooner we might get to do it together. I know I thought that.

"I could probably live without electricity," I ventured as we stared at the candles. "Electric lights are so . . . artificial."

Madeleine tilted her head. "Well," she said. She did like her TV. She knew people out West who had learned to live without any comforts, but in New Jersey, she said, the closest you could come to living a primitive life was to be ready if it came unexpected—if the power went out, and stayed out. There could be an earthquake, or a war. Martial law or something.

"Wow," I answered. Martial law? "Guess we don't need to worry about that much, huh?"

She gave me a "reporters should know better" look.

She said, "I know people right here in Jersey who have bomb shelters."

Leftover from the fifties, I wondered? But no, that's not what she meant. All around us were these survivalists, she said. Some for religious reasons, some political, some of them were veterans who knew just how dangerous the world was, and they were prepared. They had gathered great stores of all that was needed to live under any conditions.

"I'm only up to candles, myself," I told her.

"Well," she said. "That's a start."

It was late November, and Christmas felt near. I thought I'd like to get a tree. I thought of the lights, which look nice, like candles. I ate a bite of broccoli.

"You know what I hate?" I asked.

"Don't hate," she said. "Bad karma."

"Oh," I said. "Right. Alright. Know what I wish I would never have to see again? The fake, ugly aluminum siding on this house."

"The aluminum siding," she repeated slowly.

"It's phony and ugly. People take a decent house and slap this mustard-colored tin on it. Makes the place look like some cheap cruddy box. Who wants to live like that?" I was getting drunk. I could hear in my mind the sound of knuckles on tin, rapping on the metal drum into which my life had been sealed.

"I don't know," she answered. "It saves on heating bills."

I looked up from my plate. Madeleine chewed and looked into space as if a warm house hung there, looking perfect. In shock, I wondered if I could really be friends with someone who defended aluminum siding; it seemed like a warning, which I ignored.

"I like a good seal on a window, too," she mused. "Old windows always get stuck."

There was that practical Madeleine: even candlelit dinners had their certain use, just a drill for the air raid. We'd been eating off plates in our laps but now she set hers on the low table next to her feet, stretched her arms out, and got busy lighting a cigarette. When it was lit and the first exhale was finished, she turned and looked at me. I had been watching her, puzzled, for some time. She smiled and raised her shoulders as if to say, so sue me. "I like to be warm," she said.

"Maybe I'm just a snob," I confessed. "Maybe the outer layer shouldn't matter so much, you know? Like, fashion totally sucks. People get so stupid over how to dress themselves." I sure did. I had never known how to dress, not since about the fifth grade when Sears stopped selling pantsuits. I figured if we collectively lowered our standard of dress, we'd save energy for better things. I slugged some beer.

"Maybe we should all just be naked," I said, and looked at her. Pause. I'd said enough.

"Ah, but real beauty isn't in the clothes," Madeleine told me, shaking a finger. "It's in the hair." She drilled the finger through her too-short bobbed hairdo till it thumped her head. Madeleine had spent a long time considering beauty. She had studied to be a beautician before she went to college. She had rafts of makeup in her bathroom cabinets and she had polished nails, plucked brows, painted faces galore. She'd probably seen every kind of hair, and she was as certain as she could be that hair was a sort of destiny. Mine was very long at the time, long and thick and difficult, not flat silk, not the wild frizz of, say, Janis Joplin, just long and thick and unstyled. She ran a hand through it. "You," she said, "are a beautiful person. It takes guts to have this hair."

What did that mean? Who cared? I think no one had touched me in a very long time and maybe no one ever had touched me the way she did just then, gently tugging my hair, then pushing it behind my ear just so, and talking like nothing had happened. I froze. She said: "I finished beauty school and then I left for Montana." She had been living with her boyfriend in Newark back then, in the same place she was renting again now. Her old boyfriend's parents owned the house and they rented out the ground floor. Madeleine had moved in with that boy thinking they'd get married but they were young, just eighteen years old, and he couldn't compete with Montana.

"We used to shoot guns in the basement. Target practice," she said.

"You shot . . . what?"

"Targets."

"With . . ."

"Guns," she said.

"You shot guns in your basement?"

"Sure. John thought I should know how."

She shifted on the couch, and rubbed her nose with the back of the hand that had so recently been in my hair. "We lived in Newark," she said, like that explained it. "John was very into survival."

Wait. Could my karmic soul friend be someone with a gun? I thought about that. Maybe I could like some guns. It was a practical thing, really.

"I can twirl a gun," I offered, reaching with words for her again. "In high school, I twirled a gun with marching band at football games. Funny, you know, because I hate guns, but somehow I picked them over pompons."

"Hate?"

"Okay, not hate. Not hate. I just don't like it when they kill people," I said. "Twirling them is different."

Spurred on by potent ale, I felt compelled just then to show Madeleine a picture of me twirling my white rifle. I slid off the couch and crawled to the bookshelf where I kept a photo album. The book contained many pictures of me, in various stages of adolescence, almost always badly dressed. I kneeled on the floor and flipped pages in the photo album and was alarmed at what seemed just then like a relentless march of awkward phases, and then I flipped the page over to a picture of a large, bearded man scowling in a leather biker jacket, a bandanna on his head.

"Who's he?" she said, looking over my shoulder.

"My brother," I said.

"You have a brother?"

"Yeah. I mean, I did but, he's dead."

She stared at the page. "Oh," she said.

My past came to seem, then, sad and strange, full of awful perms, blooming acne, and dead siblings, and for all the true and beautiful things I had wanted her to know about me, the evidence looked different.

She did not quiz me about my dead brother. I spared us both the heavy details. It had only been a year since he died, and I wasn't sure yet how to talk about it. So I left him in silence, and turned the pages fast to get away.

Then there it was: me in the uniform, white boots with pom-pons, saluting, with a big wooden rifle at my side. I was chubby and impossibly erect, as if what I was doing was important.

"Oh my god." That's all she said. I felt a little disappointed.

Immersed in the past, we were slow to notice how the candlelight had grown suddenly brighter. Then we smelled smoke. Across the room the little wooden table was burning; the top held a pool of wax and flames. She jumped up and yelled, "Get water," but there wasn't any water, not close enough to help, so I grabbed a Rolling Stones sweatshirt that was balled up on the floor and beat the flames down with that. I beat hard until the fire was out, and waved the sweatshirt in front of the windows to clear the smoke. When the damage was contained, I shoved the sweatshirt behind the couch where no one would find it for at least a few years, and we sat again in silence.

The candle fire was no disaster but as we stared at the singed table I felt as if it could have been. One small moment, a little too scary, had changed the whole night, made the whole scene feel a little fool-ish in the end. As she left, I wanted to hug her, but I stood holding the door open instead, not moving. She buttoned her wool coat and wound her scarf up until she had a lollipop head. Cold air pushed in past her as she carefully pulled on her gloves, waved, and then went away. I hoped the little fire hadn't ruined everything; I called her from work the next day to make sure she was okay, and that she had not been too drunk to drive home. She seemed surprised to hear my voice. She said, "I'm fine," as if nothing had happened. After that night, it seemed like we were always together.

It was hard to think of many people who might be willing to share an apartment in Newark, so when Madeleine moved back from Montana into the old place without John around, she called on her old friend Mike. He was the obvious choice, maybe the only choice. Mike was muscular and tattooed and seemed like a sort of bodyguard or bouncer; he was a short guy, but thick and stocky with a great big belly, and he had crazy frizzy sticking-out hair that made him seem taller than he was. When I saw him, he usually looked a bit mashed and unshaven, as if he'd just crawled out of bed, but mostly he wasn't around. He worked on tankers down at Port Elizabeth, which kept him up all night most nights, waiting for ships. When he came home, he slept bearish and unwakeable in his plain room on his plain, twin mattress, bare arms splayed and a thin sheet sliding off his belly to the floor. I saw him sleeping that way sometimes, through the crack in his bedroom door, a monster in a cell just off the orange kitchen.

What was this warren in Newark, where Madeleine lived with a crazy old bear? Hers was a strange world of cluttered concrete and deserted streets and I was drawn to the taboo of it. As a girl in the suburbs a few miles away, this very place was absolutely banned; I mean, it was evil, that's what I'd been lead to believe, that's what the word Newark actually meant, it seemed. I would have been forbidden to go there, but there was no need to enforce such a ban. I had had no reason to go there. There had been race riots in Newark. Furious Newark had marched up the avenues burning and looting all the stores. That's all anyone ever told me about Newark when I was a girl, living fifteen minutes away in white, wealthy Short Hills. No one talked about what a great city it had been, or what had happened that caused people to destroy the place. I assumed it had always been bad there, that it was sooty and dirty and there was nothing pretty or green. Newark was confusing, and so in Short Hills we pretended that it wasn't there.

If you dared go to Newark, as you rode through the terror of broken glass and debris, past falling-down chimneys and empty factories all littered and decayed, you had to beware. If you drove too far on any street and forgot how you had gotten there, or how to leave, and became lost in abandoned blocks of clapboard and tar-shingled houses where people stood outside listless and bored, then in the snare of those roads you would feel how small your life really was and how easy it might be to lose it. But you don't turn back, because all that strangeness has to be crossed, to get to something better; to find the truth. That's how it felt to me, daring into the crumbling streets that I had been so awfully afraid of, and then, finding Madeleine in the heart of it.

Newark! Oh chaos, oh joy. Madeleine, the free spirit, lived there. Off McCarter highway, under the train tracks, straight back beyond a row of burned-up houses and a Baptist church, there was the Ironbound, the Portuguese section, just like life after death. On Ironbound sidewalks old men sat staring at nothing and shoppers filed into Portuguese stores full of salted codfish and crusty rolls and ripe-smelling fruits. No one seemed to know about this place but the Portuguese, and Madeleine. And me.

It wasn't long before I was making the journey to Newark every weekend. I drove out of Morristown, through Chatham, past perfectly kept Victorian houses lurching up from great lawns. Children riding little bikes stopped to watch my car fly by and I flew, mostly on Saturday nights at first but then earlier and earlier; so early at last that I started showing up at her door in the morning, still sleepy, drinking strong coffee. I came bearing gifts: six packs of beer, donuts, rented movies. On East Kinney Street, with cars parked solid down the curb, Madonnas built into the tiled fronts of homes like in Lisbon, I parked right in front of her house as if a place just for me had been waiting, always. It felt good to be there: scary and good. Scary not so much for the reasons that kept people away, not for crimes waiting to happen but just because, with half the world afraid to visit, the surviving part of Newark felt a little lonely. I was terribly afraid of being lonely, even when I was not. House fronts stitched by security fencing met sidewalks in a flat line, and the gate in the chain link fence around Madeleine's home squealed madly as it opened. I walked through to the back door and knocked. What would happen if one day I walked up to her door and knocked and found I was no longer welcome? Every knocking was a risk, that I'd be left alone in a ruined world that didn't look so charming without her.

Madeleine had returned to the house she had almost married into, which, once I saw it, seemed an odd thing to do. John's parents still lived in the apartment upstairs. It took a while for me to grasp that a whole world I didn't know stretched around and behind her; she had done so much, had a life in this house and moved all the way to Montana and come back again to the beginning, full circle, but different now. It's easier to think of life in straight lines, and people as only who they are when you see them. But that's wrong. People's lives make big circles, sometimes. I asked her if it felt funny to live there, now, with John married to someone else, living, she told me, up in the Catskills. I wondered if she missed the past. But she said, "Well, you really never lose the people you love. You can leave, but you never lose them." Not even in death, she said, as if she had just looked all this up; the cosmic rulebook says that you stay together, even in silence, even through reincarnated lifetimes. Love connects you forever.

So I guess that made it okay.

To Madeleine, who seemed to understand all the rules for everything so well, important connections knew only one boundary: not time, or space, or flesh; just sex. It was important not to have sex with someone out of bounds, no matter how great your love. She didn't say all this exactly but she did make the point clear: a married person is out of bounds. Exes almost always are. Engaged people are fair game because you could be saving them from life-wrecking errors. So

I decided that the real answer to my question was that Madeleine still loved John, but they were not lovers anymore, and never would be. They were what had come to be known in our time as "just friends."

One morning I drove to Newark bearing something the florist in Morristown had called a Gerber daisy. That's what I thought he said. It was a big pink flower with a yellow center, and it was a present, because the ice-melting spring morning was so fresh and clear that it created in me an overwhelming urge to bring her a piece of glorious nature as a gift. But still, it couldn't seem too much like a present. I did not want it to seem like I was actually giving her flowers, because that would be sort of weird; I wanted just to give her a casual stroke of joy, like a seven-inch-wide hot-pink daisy I had somehow managed to pick along the road. I struggled to choose from the foliage at the flower shop, where buckets of these comic book flowers were on hand. I bought one. I tore all the paper off it as soon as I got to the car, because a big cone of paper hardly looks casual, and I drove to East Kinney Street holding the flower near my chest. I squeaked through the gate and knocked on the door and stood there holding a bewildering hunk of bright flashy love, camouflaged as a daisy, from me to my friend Madeleine.

The door swung open with the fast force of thick tattooed biceps. There was Mike. He looked at me and at the flower in my hand and let out a yowl, and giggled like a biker on acid. "Yowie! Look at that!" he said, and pointed at the Gerber daisy. "She brought me a flower!" and he hoo-hooed and smiled and his huge bearded cheeks wadded up into balls.

I saw Madeleine behind him, standing at the stove. And for an instant, it seemed as if Mike were her husband; he belonged there, with her cooking for him on the weekend in their little house. Maybe that's why they were there, together. Husband and wife, in a way. I looked at Mike and Madeleine beyond him and I wanted to run. Maybe I had misunderstood everything. Maybe I didn't know who these people were at all. Maybe they were just plain Jersey folks, big man and his hard-working woman, wearing big sneakers, trying to get by, and they struggled but couldn't get ahead and so they just hung around the house in their shorts and tank tops and ate and drank too much and had loud fights just like everyone else in this world, and this was not the place of wonder, they were not my special friends at all, and they certainly were not "just friends" to each other. Were they? "Just friends," as if there were something less to friendship than there is to . . . other things. And that other thing was sex, I supposed, and who knew about sex? Probably everyone; everyone knew everything, except me; probably sex was the main thing; probably everyone was doing it with everyone but me; sex was the sort of truth I had forever stumbled upon in such awkward moments; it seemed like the bland truth and the one fact that would finally remain when all my big pink crazy flower fantasies were over. It was all simply sex, just sex, and I didn't belong there.

I stood frozen in the doorway fearing I had done something foolish. Maybe I really had meant something with that flower. Could they tell? Mike laughed. Probably sex. Probably everyone. Probably Mike with Madeleine. I wished I had known better. I wished I'd stayed home.

"Peace, brother," I said, handing up the daisy.

"Peeeeeace," Mike yowled, dwarfing that tremendous stem in his hand. I smiled and said I'd bought it on the corner from an old man pushing a shopping cart full of them, too pathetic to ignore, what the hell, bought a flower, so, you like it?

"It's bee-u-tiful," Mike roared. "Thaaank you."

"Oh. A Gerbera daisy," said Madeleine, who knew the correct name for every strange thing. She took a glass off the shelf so that Mike could put the pink flower in water, which he did, leaving it to rot on the table.

"Where were you last night?" Madeleine poked me in the ribs with the handle of her wooden soup spoon as she stood at the stove. She was cooking lentils. "Hm? So? I tried to call you but Lou said you weren't home. I'm making you soup."

"You're making me soup?"

"Sure," she said. I stared into the pot and beany steam stroked my cheek.

"What did Lou tell you?" I asked her.

"He said you were out on a date," said Madeleine, and here she poked the spoon into my side hard enough to make me laugh.

So I told her: "A date? No. Not a date. Well, Yeah. We went to the movies."

My housemate Lou was a man fighting multiple addictions; he had a craving for anything that made him feel good. He was a handsome man, twenty-six and a carpenter, and doing less well with his addiction to sex than with most of the others. He had often invited me to come up to his room and see his new waterbed, which I did go see once. I sat on it. Lou smiled nervously and watched me, hugging his arms. Maybe, in honor of communes like the ones ours was not, maybe in that spirit I should have just fucked him. Just once, or twice. But then again, I always figured: why?

Madeleine filled a bowl with soup and handed it to me. I asked if it was early for soup but she said it was never too early for lentils. We brought our bowls to the living room and sat on the couch. Madeleine's living room was as pale as the inside of an egg, with beige carpet, beige furniture, and big windows with dusty beige blinds. I ate a steaming carrot, feeling at once warm and cared for. Whenever I stopped talking Madeleine took the handle of her soup spoon and returned it gently to my ribs, poking, and with each poke I told her more: about how I had finally been talked into a date on Friday night with the assistant sports editor my new colleagues had nicknamed

31

the Frog. I saw no harm in it, and who knew, maybe there would be magic. There was always the possibility of magic. Maybe, just maybe, that wide flat mouth would come out with something intriguing; maybe I would even want to kiss it, for I could think of stranger things happening to young women and their frogs; maybe, if I took a chance, the frog would turn out to be the human come to change my life.

"Sounds like a real hot one, huh?" Madeleine said.

"Sure," I said, rolling my eyes and eating my soup and back came the spoon to my ribs. I told Madeleine about how the frog and I ate at a loud Mexican restaurant and then saw a violent movie, attended by gum-cracking big-haired girls and their muscular boyfriends; I wore a long skirt and a T-shirt and boots, a confused outfit I'd struggled over in front of my cracked mirror for what seemed like hours before finally construing something both feminine and somewhat like me. Wild hair on my round face and a getup like Calamity Jane: I was thinking "Halloween" when the doorbell rang.

"You got all gussied up for him?" She toyed with the word gussied. God forbid I should "dress." I could gussy, though.

"Well, sorta."

"Boy," she said. "You don't do that for me." For Madeleine, in fact, my usual getup was torn jeans and a T-shirt.

Later, after the frog had come in to take a piss and then hung around ("Oh sure," she said, "you fell for that one?"), I steered him to the front hall and said, "Well, I guess I'll see you at work Monday." He stepped closer, murmuring that he had had a nice time, such a nice time, and then wham! like a hungry frog shooting flies, the frog mouth parted and the frog lips pressed onto mine and the long frog tongue went exploring.

I sat blushing like a prom queen. Madeleine dropped her jaw.

"Why'd you do that?"

"Do what?"

32

"Why'd you kiss the frog?"

"I don't know." Was that wrong? "He kissed me." It felt sort of dumb in those last few post-sexual-liberation but pre-AIDS-conscious days to just kiss someone. It seemed like you were either on your way into bed or you were not, and that's it. There'd been nothing subtle about any of the kisses I remembered, and I assured Madeleine there had been nothing subtle in my rejection of the frog.

She laughed, and then, poking the ticklish rib, she said, "Wouldn't you have rather been here, with me?"

"Yes. Was I invited?"

"You always are."

The ceiling fan in her living room hummed, taking up the smoke exhaled from our just-lit cigarettes, and redistributing it above our heads. I fumbled between my soup spoon and my cigarette, uncommitted to either course. "I don't know, I don't know," I said, for no particular reason.

Madeleine said, "I want to show you something." She flicked her cigarette and stood up. "Come into my bedroom."

I smoked and I swallowed a last bit of my soup and when I dropped the spoon my free hand stroked the length of my heavy hair. I said, "Sure." And I coughed to clear my throat.

Every time I walked past Madeleine's bedroom and the door was open, I'd peek in to see a big green peace sign hanging on the wall. I wanted a reason to see more, but it felt off limits; if the entire city of Newark was taboo, this was its locked nucleus, not a place I might stray casually. But that day, I was invited.

She had hung her pale walls with portraits of Hindu goddesses and draped her windows with long heavy cloth like shrouds. It was a sort of temple. An antique walnut bed stood in the center of the room like a tomb, only empty. She told me to sit down. I sat on the edge of the mattress and looked up. Ceiling fan. I looked down and watched as she knelt in front of me. When she put her hands on my thighs, I stiffened. Oh god, oh god. She said, "I need to get in here." Then she pushed my legs gently to the side. Whatever she wanted, apparently, was located under my feet, which I moved, and she ducked under the bed to find something.

I studied the walls: Hindu deities and blue-green goddesses smiled, knowing, and the peace sign hung as if this weren't the age of Wall Street, as if this weren't even war-torn Newark, as if this were San Francisco, or the sixties, or someplace where unabashed longing for peace and sex and love was still fashionable. If this had been twenty years before, what would we be like? Would we be urban pioneers? Would this be our crash pad to hide underground radicals? Would we permit ourselves to commit a revolutionary act right here, together, groping for some clearer definition of love, or liberation? I hoped she would ask me something completely unexpected. I was dying for her to surprise me somehow, and for this fantasy to materialize.

But, oops: I probably was wrong again. Maybe she was going to produce her big Newark gun, and shoot me. For having kissed the frog. For having thought about her in this way. The blue-green goddesses began to frown and there was Mary up there too, very Catholic.

Madeleine emerged with a large, flat box and said she was putting together a portfolio of her photographs to send out with her résumé. She opened the big box. It was full of photos. "I thought you could help me figure this out," she said. She didn't mind the *Daily Journal* so much, but old Joe was about to retire and things would change and it seemed time for her to think about leaving. So she showed me her portfolio of newspaper photos: fires and basketball games and kids marching in parades.

"You've done a lot of good work," I said, scanning the collection of car wrecks, strawberry pickers, and dog walkers. I held one up: a small child gripping a rabbit by the neck, terror in everyone's eyes. I looked at the other photographs scattered on the floor.

"I like the way you see the world," I told her.

"They're just pictures," she said.

"But," I declared, "they're your vision."

I helped her pick a dozen pieces to send around to bigger, better newspapers. She stacked those, put the rejected ones away, then buried her head under the bed again and emerged with another collection of photos, blown up into large squares.

She told me these were her projects from when she lived in Montana. She flipped a few prints and then showed me part of a project started in Bozeman, when she lived in the house with the wood stove that she sometimes talked about. It was so cold there in winter, even with the stove blazing away, that she had sometimes spent whole days in bed. Bozeman, Montana. Whenever she brought it up I'd start to tell her my dad was from Montana, but then, her Montana seemed like a different place altogether and it seemed pointless to tell her that I knew about it too. I didn't know much: I didn't really care about my dad's Montana, but I sure did like Madeleine's. When she talked about Montana, it was another world, a mystery. And there that mystery was again, in a series of self-portraits, black and white: Madeleine in the shadows of her old Bozeman house, blowing smoke, wearing a leather jacket, nothing more; Madeleine behind billowing gauze curtains, lax focus, no clothes. My friend's naked photographs in a place far away: Her eyes were crooked. Her hair was long, then; it looked like I thought it should, like the freak girls who found refuge in a cluster on our high school patio, plotting their subversive counter-cultural acts, and smoking butts. She was haughty, all hips and half-shown breasts. Free and defiant, I thought. And mortal: the woman in these photographs was already gone, replaced by someone older. In one portrait she squinted over a cigarette that she held before her dark mouth. In that pose, she tried so hard to create an image of cool that she created in the process an image of someone trying so hard to be cool. She had captured the very image of being twenty, and the sense of knowing everything, but being wrong.

I held each of the portraits trying to say all of that but I really wasn't sure what I saw, or how to say it. The leather jacket, the smoking bad girl. I stared so long and hard trying to understand all of this that finally it just seemed, I think, like I was staring at the naked photographs of my friend. She looked over my shoulder, and said at last, "Maybe I should grow my hair out."

"These are beautiful," I told her. "Send them to a magazine," by which I meant an art magazine but who knows how it sounded.

"Ha! No," she said, it was just a project she once started; she was supposed to go on taking self-portraits forever, like a record of time, and change. But she stopped, finding self-portraiture too self-obsessive.

"But, you're using yourself to say something," I said. "It's like, a memoir."

Madeleine shrugged. "I don't have much to say." She retrieved the photographs; I tried to sneak one out with an exaggerated sweep behind my back, but she said, "Oh, give me that," and I released it with mock or perhaps not so mock reluctance. Then she slid the photographs under her bed, buried again. We left, and the bedroom door closed behind us.

We returned to her kitchen to stir the lentils that still simmered, and we spoke quietly just one cracked door away from where Mike slumbered now. I watched her work. Her arm was strong and stirred firmly. Perhaps because she knew I was watching, she smiled. And then I felt something strange. I was happy. In a kitchen in terrible Newark, with a woman who seemed so unlike anyone else I knew, I felt I had found something rare: what I wanted. Everything I knew about myself and that I had wished for the world, all buried by the cold facts of my life in that time, it was all recited in this small voice inside, and it was the only truth I had to tell but it was so fragile. Even thinking was too much; like that, the moment ended.

Once, we were out together, driving somewhere in my car and stopped in a dirty and treeless place beneath an entrance to the New Jersey Turnpike. I might have felt sad in such an ugly place, but we were together and music slipped out of the car speakers, and life beyond that bubble didn't seem to matter. I was waiting to turn. She said, "You know, I love you." She was playing with the beads hung on my rearview mirror, and she smiled so that her nose wrinkled; she might have said, "You smell funny," but she said, "I love you."

The words seemed to surprise her, so she said them again, tried it in a baby voice, and laughed. "I love you; we're women, and women get to say that," she said, and I pretended that was true.

I concentrated my stare up toward the undergirdings of the Turnpike and smiled, which I thought told her, "Of course, stupid, we've been in love through countless lifetimes," but who knows what the smile really said; I was silent. I was trying to look amused, trying to look very serious in my effort to make a left turn, afraid to say anything that might cause her to take the words back. Maybe that was my chance, then, to find out what she meant by "love." But it seemed to me that my silence made it safer there, sitting in the urban infrastructure with Madeleine. It kept all the possibilities alive. If I had said "I love you too," it might have meant something different, and that moment and her words that had stunned and pleased me would have been taken back, probably, and that would have been the end of our story.

We sat there so long it began to feel as if we had all the time in the world to spend together, under a bridge, waiting to turn; we watched traffic and waited with something lurking about us as profound and speechless as the blue-green deities on Madeleine's bedroom walls, just hanging there beautiful, intense, and unremarked upon.

Why did my grandfather go to Montana? They didn't write it down; it's not mentioned in William's business letters, which sought investors to sponsor farmers in Rapelje; the "why" is not addressed in my grandmother's seven-page handwritten family history, which has become dog-eared and difficult to read, full of names and dates, but not reasons. It is as if everyone shared one motive for doing anything, and it would never need explaining. Did my grandparents seek bliss? Love? Money? Sexual freedom? I don't know. They didn't say.

What I know of my grandparents is really very little. I never met them. I know very few people who ever did meet them. What I have learned comes down through the generations in handwritten lines whose loops and curves are not easy to decipher. Mostly what is written is names, and dates, and places.

William Soderlind married Florence Longbottom in 1911. Florence was one of seventeen children in a family that grew up on a farm in Minnesota. Her parents wandered there in 1875 from Canada, where their own families had disowned them because they married for love, foolishly, and seemed to have no working plan for survival. They were cut off forever, written out of modest wills, because the choices they made seemed to foretell disaster. With forty-five cents and one team of oxen, they walked to Minnesota. They built a cabin and began reproducing manically, creating a small society of children in a vacant land, a place where the nearest neighbors lived twenty miles away. In a way, it seems as if they, like William and Florence, started their own little town, their own whole world, even, having picked an empty spot and filled it up with people. A photo, 1910: the multitude of my grandmother's family lines up like a baseball team, smiling, impressed with their abundance against so many odds.

When Florence was a girl in the frontier of Minnesota, she had been startled to see Indians peering in the windows of her house. The glass, apparently, seemed to the native people to be made for looking in as much as looking out. They must have wondered why these white folks did it, put these windows on their lives. Why would they wish to be examined in this way? Florence stopped short, to see bewildered faces looking at her day or night. Of course, she didn't want to be examined. But there she was, behind the glass.

William grew up in Minnesota not far from Florence, the younger son of Swedish immigrants. Both his parents struck out for the new world as teenagers and met each other working at a Minnesota lumber camp. His father rose through the possibilities of the new world, managing a mill, trying his hand at farming, and finally, becoming a banker in Lake Benton, Minnesota. Beyond this, William's family remains mysterious to me, a clan of Soderlinds, a common name that I'm told fills pages of the Stockholm phone directory today but sounds strange, still, in America. Florence told the only family stories that have been preserved for me, and for some reason, she neglected to say much about her husband.

It seems that saying much about anything was not something my stern and sober ancestors were inclined to do anyhow; when I think of them, they are so busy chopping and wringing and building things, and sleeping huddled between cattle during blizzards to stay warm, that there could not have been much time for conversation among them. And what they did have to say does not explain their lives the way I want to understand them, or as I might have known them, had I met them, and seen who they really were: the way they washed their plates, or sat together on the porch on Sundays, laughing, or not laughing, playing or not playing games, looking at each other with what kinds of lines around what color eyes? What did they do for fun? Did they have fun? Surely they didn't like dancing; where would they get the idea to dance? I don't know what they had arguments about, in the house in Minnesota with all the children in it; I don't know who delivered all those children; I don't know how on earth they stayed fed, how many hogs had to be slaughtered to get them all through the winter or even if they had any hogs; maybe they ate only cows, maybe they lived on eggs and chickens; maybe they grew broccoli. Florence's parents started their life together with forty-five cents and a pair of oxen. By all rights they should not have lived at all. By all rights none of us should be here, not a one; life should not have thrived on earth, but somehow life continued and they managed to get by. Eventually, it seems, they all became bankers. William's father did; Florence's father did too, when he left the farm and moved into town to work at a credit union.

When Florence was twenty-one years old, she married William. He had followed in his father's banking trade, then left Lake Benton for a position as a clerk for Mr. Longbottom. William may not have earned much, but he managed somehow to buy a dazzling Ford, one of the first models in production, and he used it to court the boss's daughter, Florence. Florence, the bright ball of light daughter packed tight into row upon row of daughters, the one who loved clothes and music and things that had shine. Her future husband's strange, wonderful autocar was polished to a shine, and when she saw it, it sparkled in her big blue eyes. William took her for long rides to win her over. He brought her flowers, and he took her places, and they became aware of all the possibilities, driving in that car.

William pulls over to the side of the road. The gearshift forms a rigid line between his knee and Florence. She shifts on her side of the car seat like a monarch, turning to him upright and laced to her chin. They are twenty-one years old. The car is humming. William finds he has nothing to say. Florence is nervous, or happy, or tired of so much quiet and she laughs, just a small rippling laugh that breaks their silence. Then William laughs with her. He knows that he wants to kiss her, to press his thin lips against the plum smiling in her round powdered face. He looks away, swivels his head on its tall collar and stares back toward the road. He doesn't kiss her. It would set them off on a complicated course and that would not be right. Instead, he gathers himself up and hurries down from his car; he runs round to help Florence step out. He scoots her up the walkway to the door of her house, he tips his straw hat, then leaves her, returning to his car to drive away.

After they married, they tried to stay in Minnesota, but it wasn't long before William quit his job, and he and Florence decided to leave. They moved first to Racine, Wisconsin, and less than one restless year after that, they set out for Montana. Montana: yes, that is where, they decided, they would find the life they wanted, and so they left home, forever. It's what their parents before them had done: quit the certain life around them to find something else, still something they could not see, or could even be certain existed. There were only promises and myths about other lives, elsewhere. But somewhere in the world was something different and better, whatever it was; that must have been what they believed, when they set out to find it. When William and Florence left home, they must have felt that way.

My father held up a picture of my mother's cocker spaniel, which was smiling into the camera with remarkable charisma. Then he put the picture in a box.

"Top that," he said.

It was Christmas, and I was home with my mother and father to celebrate, just the three of us. Christmas, like Thanksgiving and birthdays, had always been a very intimate affair at our house. Both my parents had moved so far away from their families that we had never had relatives around for holidays, or even for visits. I knew my mother's family from summers spent in Wisconsin, but I'd really never met anyone on my father's side, though I'd seen pictures in their Christmas cards each year so I knew they were out there, somewhere. My father was wrapping his last-minute presents, sitting on the edge of his bed making precise creases in Christmasy cocker spaniel–covered wrapping paper while the television pattered on about football.

"So how's your newspaper doing?" he asked.

"You mean, the new one?" I said, and he made a puzzled face. I had neglected to tell him of the latest changes in my life.

My father liked to ask me about my work. Like me, he had been a newspaper man, but he had left the world of print dailies for the corporate end of things: making plans to buy and sell little papers like the one I worked for. He slipped back into crusty-old-editor mode when we talked, but he played it with boyish enthusiasm, nothing like the beady-eyed seething brute variety of editor I had always worked for.

"The new one?" he repeated, confused, having just received more information than he could handle while simultaneously manipulating tape. "What happened now?"

"It was awful. I mean it Dad, that last job was so awful I quit. I was totally burned out. Totally."

"Gotta be on fire to burn out, kid."

"Well, alright, not burned out, just, you know, it's okay. I have a new job. I'm still a reporter."

"A reporter," he repeated the word, listened to it as he kept taping paper. He liked the sound of "reporter." He liked words.

My father had been a reporter. That was hard for me to grasp, but I'd seen a picture for proof: 1953, a skinny Dad with all his hair, wearing wingtips and a baggy suit, taking notes in the center of a gaggle of milk-faced midwestern fashion models he'd been sent to interview. Until I started working for a newspaper myself, I had thought of my father, mostly, as a "businessman," an unpretty word that fit every father I knew in the world where I grew up. He wore a suit and went away to an office somewhere. His personal mythology included the fact that he had been born in Montana. That, too, had seemed improbable but once again there were pictures to prove it: Dad standing with his two brothers and sister, in overalls two sizes too big for a boy with always more brains than brawn. The blank eastern plains of Montana spread out beyond the picture frame.

My father made his way out of great, big, improbable Montana as a young man, pushed forward by World War II and those brains of his and a string of jobs that formed a path to New Jersey, where I found him. He was a reverse pioneer. There was nothing Montana left about him, from what I could see; certainly, not in the way I had come to understand the word Montana. I looked at him to see if it was there: his eyes were blue as big sky and they teared up sometimes, when he thought about sad things, or when he listened to a certain recording of "Danny Boy." Not that he was Irish. He'd made a normal suburban life and faded into it so completely that it was hard to believe he had once lived without electricity or plumbing. We had both become reporters, but his romantic, ink-stained newspaper world did not exist any more, not really, just like his Montana, a dusty, ranching place, remained distant and unknown to me. I had my own Montana now, the one my friend Madeleine had lived in; it was a land of far away wild things, a place I imagined but I'd never seen. It seemed like a place my father wouldn't recognize.

He finished wrapping the present and he said, "Let me show you something." From his sock drawer he produced a well-thumbed ledger, black and smaller than a deck of cards. Down one of two neat columns on a yellowing page, in exact tiny letters and numerals, he had outlined my progress at the North Jersey newspaper chain, neatly noting promotions or raises and the dates on which I had changed jobs.

"What's yer new paper?" he said.

"The *Herald and News.*"

"How much ya making?"

"Eighteen thousand," I was sorry to say.

He wrote that down. He flipped pages to where his own jobs and earnings were recorded, beginning with the faint little scrawl of his first job in Minneapolis, 1952. His finger slid down a couple years; he produced a calculator and worked some magic and flipped pages back again to my life until I understood what he was doing. My father had adjusted his income for inflation to compare it with mine at parallel moments in our lives. His calculations showed that our very first jobs had paid us each the same, miserably, and that our lives had developed at an even pace: we had earned raises at equivalent rates, changed jobs at restless intervals.

"Ha," he said. "Look at that."

I looked: my salary three employers into my career matched his, three jobs down the line. And so we ambled on, shades of each other. I was turning into him. I felt panic boring at my solar plexus. I looked up from the tiny ledger to the grin on his pink face; his smile showed a gold-rimmed bridge, the handiwork of a rough dentist in Montana back when Dad had just returned from the navy after World War II.

"What are you saying, Dad?"

"Oh, nothing, honey. Just sort of eerie. Keep up the good work, maybe you'll be a big shot someday, too, like your old dad."

An ache gripped my throat as I stared down at the numbers, so tight that I was unable to say, "No, Dad, I will never be a big shot like you. Don't you see? I'm going to start a commune in the wilderness. I'm going to raise goats. You live in Short Hills. You have just finished wrapping a Christmas present in paper that looks like Mom's cocker spaniel—and the gift inside is a framed picture of Mom's cocker spaniel. It's clever but I'm different, see? I'm *different,* the truth is I am nothing like you. I've smoked out of giant bongs, Mr. Wall Street. I've walked barefoot down empty Main Street near dawn when you were sleeping, and I knew I was an immortal piece of an all-loving God I felt it, and aaargh! I did not risk my life walking on thin ledges in the dark, trying for a closer look at shooting stars, just to wind up sedated and suburban and the angels, Dad, the angels and the stars and all that shit say my life isn't the same as yours, it never will be, Dad, it *can't* be, don't you see?"

That's what I thought, but it was a bit complicated to say. My father had the muting force of statistical evidence on his side. Facts declared that my life would proceed in the usual manner, into struggle and disappointment and money-earning and child-rearing, long nights of staring at team sports on TV, chugging down the road to its inevitable finish.

After five years of newspaper work, my father had landed a job at the *Wall Street Journal,* the capitalist tool, the engine of mass conformity with its bland columns of text unchanged day after day, a newspaper that had amassed (he liked to remind me) an enormous rack of Pulitzer Prizes. He thrived there; success in my life would never look like his. It was the one difference between my father and me that seemed certain. But I didn't like to say that, either.

"Okay, Dad," I finally said, "I guess, you know, if you were once struggling like me, then things will turn out okay. Right?"

"That's right," he said. Like it was simple. My father and I carried our last-minute gifts downstairs.

Stockings were hung for each of my parents, for their dog, and for me. My brother's stocking was gone; it disappeared when he did, along with most of the rest of his things. That Christmas in 1989, after I had quit my job at the *Daily Journal* and become friends with Madeleine, was Christmas number two past the death of my older brother. He had been twenty-six years old and three hundred pounds and his tattooed biceps were thicker than my thighs when he died, and then, when my mother finished cleaning out his room, there was barely a trace left of his once-mighty being. What I noticed most was the silence. The house was so quiet without him; he had always lived there, had never grown up and left home like everyone else we knew did. He just hung around the house and rode his motorcycle to and from jobs until he got fired, or he went out to bars to hang out with his biker friends. When he was home he sat on the couch upstairs all day, making strange noises while watching TV and talking to biker chicks on the telephone. He was not like the rich suburban guys who buy Harleys and pretend to be bad. He was a member of the Pagans, an actual Hell's Angels sort of biker, the kind that call themselves "1 percenters" to distinguish their contempt for 99 percent of the rest of us. Big and bearded and swaddled in leather, he'd roar up the prim streets of Short Hills, New Jersey, at four in the morning waking neighbors, belching home from parties or meetings of his club, intoxicated and wild-eyed and disturbing.

How someone like him could sprout from the suburbs was a matter of general amazement; he was a local celebrity. He was also a huge worry to our parents. When we were teenagers people used to ask me about him. They wanted to know why he was a biker, as if I had an answer like, it's a medical condition, or he got the idea from a book. It's just who he was; you couldn't stop it or fix it. He could be mean, but I had seen him cry at things like Disney movies, and the death of King Kong; he was shocking to see, so out of place in the world we lived in, but I knew him, and I learned to like people who could wait before just deciding to hate or fear him. My brother Steve was an impossibility, a menace roaring through the streets, shaking the neighborhood from its slumber day or night with his rude message: I'm here, I'm here, I'm here and I don't give a fuck if you like it. He had never tried to hide who he was.

The year before he died, I rode with him on Christmas Eve, out on the back of his bike through the winter wonder of Short Hills. We were going to get cigarettes. I clutched the sides of his leather jacket and hid my nose in his back as he opened the throttle and we lurched up and down the dark streets, cold, looking at the Christmas decorations strung up bright on huge houses filled with sleeping kids, in their Silent Night, and over the wail and belch of his Harley I heard my big, bearded brother cry out, "Ho, ho, ho," and I thought, "Yes. There is a Santa Claus."

Two Christmases later, my parents and I exchanged the peculiar things we tend to choose for presents, like nose hair clippers, flea market china, underwear. Mom unwrapped the dog photograph Dad gave her and laughed and called her dog over to see. Dad hoarded his books. I put on my new socks. Surviving scraps of wrapping paper were folded and put away for next year. Present opening concluded at noon.

My mother asked, "Are you going to church with me today?"

"No," I snapped. I thought to myself, "Church? Church? You call that a church? That place where the ladies stroll around in mink stoles and look each other up and down and all those Mercedes in the parking lot, how can that be church? Christ was born in a manger, Mom. Goddamn it, he suffered. And I can't pray in that place knowing I might bump into someone from high school who makes six figures in a law firm and just looks at me like, 'What do you do?' Doesn't ask, just looks. Of all the places I could go I would not choose church, not church, because no God I know would be there, and my God is staying home with me."

What I said was, "No, I mean, actually, sorry. I think I'll stay here though."

"Oh," my mother said. "Well, okay. How about you, Jim?"

"No," he said, not looking up from his new *Farmer's Almanac.*

We regrouped in the dining room to eat a turkey at four o'clock, uncommitted to a truly early supper, and yet, hours from dinner time. We formed a triangle beneath the chandelier.

"Why do we eat early on holidays?" I asked.

"Everyone eats early on holidays," my mother said.

"But, why?"

"I hated it when I was a teenager," she said.

"Why do we do it?"

"If we had thirteen people at the table I'd have to invite a friend, to make it fourteen. Thirteen was the number at the Last Supper, you see."

"But why do we do it?" I said.

"My mother never made turkey," my father said as he jabbed the bird with a knife.

"And you ate early, right? Around two?"

"We ate roast beef."

"I'm not saying I mind eating early, I just want to know why we do it."

"My family never ate roast beef. It was always turkey. My mother put it in the oven at 6 a.m."

"Why so early?"

"That way it would cook in time."

"But why?"

"To eat early."

"Mom. Why the fuck did you people eat in the middle of the day?"

There was a pause. We didn't really fuss over curse words, having lived so long with a biker, but they did have a certain focusing effect. She said, "People needed to get home before it was dark, because the roads were not very good back then. So we ate early."

"Aha," I said. "But, we're not going anywhere."

Another pause.

"No one ever said you had to eat with us," my father said.

"I'm just pointing it out. I'm not saying I mind."

"I don't care when we eat," said my mother, "you're the one who said let's eat at four."

My father finished carving, my mother recited our annual prayer, and midday eating was about to commence. I asked my father, "Hey Dad, what was Christmas like in Montana?" and I imagined his family in a ring around a decorated pine tree that had sprung up in the bare, frozen earth, like a miracle, but beyond that I wasn't really sure. He said, "Well," and then the phone rang. The dog barked. My father winced; he hates noise. My mother shot up to answer the phone, which turned out to be ringing for me. She called me loud from the kitchen as if I were six rooms away. I got up and said, "'Scuze me."

My parents began eating turkey in the candlelight while, in the kitchen, I cupped the phone the way I'd learned as a teenager.

"Merry Christmas," the voice across the wires said brightly. "Get lots of toys?"

It was Madeleine. She was not having dinner in the middle of the day. I wondered what she was doing: probably sitting somewhere by a fire, probably sipping a glass of wine, probably I could join her, wherever she was, if I could just get out of where I was.

"Hey, where are you? I'll call you back in an hour," I said with obedience. "My mother hates phone calls at dinner."

"Oh, you're eating," she said. "I'm sorry. We ate at noon."

I rushed Madeleine off the phone and returned to the table, and we three ate in near total silence, glancing off at our Christmas tree as we chewed.

"Who called?" my mother finally asked.

"A photographer from work," I said, staring at my plate.

"You have to go to work?"

"No, I mean, from my old work. She's just a friend." The plates we ate on were our "good" china, inherited from my father's mother, Florence. As food receded the floral pattern came into focus: delicate, old-fashioned, gold rimmed. Lush pink and blue flowers sprawled across the center. These plates had ringed the table in Florence's home in Rapelje. They must have been exotic, there.

My friend Madeleine had lived in Montana. I thought this and the world I sat in became strange. Montana. I had only vaguely considered the place before I met her. Now I felt like I knew it better than my father did: it was a faraway place, most of all, and I had started to think I belonged there, because it seemed so hard to be where I was.

"My friend Madeleine went to college in Bozeman, Dad," I said. "Is that where you went?"

"Not Bozeman," he said. "Missoula. That was in the mountains, not like where we lived when I was a kid."

Mizzoohlah. Where the hell was Missoula, Montana? Could this Missoula be like the place Madeleine knew, or the places I imagined with rusted, wood-burning stoves, and men with long beards thick as lamb's wool, places beneath the stars and the bolting up mountains where your hair drapes long like Jesus or Mary as you stand in meadows, breathe crackling air, drink pure water from springs beside boulders? My father was clean-shaven and bald. His father had been clean-shaven and bald. Their Montana was no Montana at all. Dad told and retold only about nine stories of being a child in Montana, of ever having been anyone but who he was when I met him, when he stood holding the infant me against the shoulder of his charcoal suit as my mother took a picture. He carried me home to my big brother and our four-bedroom house in the suburbs, with a commuter train and good public schools and a script we had been perhaps willing, at first, but ultimately unable to follow. He settled, and I grew, and began the long journey from diapers to becoming his clone, apparently. But I knew I couldn't do that.

"Rapelje, right Dad? That's where you were born."

"Yes," he answered. "Rapelje. Four grain silos. Know what that means?"

"Pretty big town."

"A regular San Francisco. Four silos at the depot means you're really in the big time."

I said, "Do you ever sort of miss it, Dad?"

My father laughed, barely, and took a drink of water. I like to think he wanted to say yes; yes, of course, his heart was still full of Rapelje. But my father is not the sort of man to say that; he's not one who misses things. "What's to miss?" he finally said. "There's nothing there." And our dinner continued in silence.

The editor of the *Herald and News* in Paterson was a Vietnam veteran whose knees hadn't worked right since the day a shell hit his convoy and blew up everyone but him. That's what people said. Combat-wounded Walter had had the good sense to sit on sandbags and he survived to one day scuttle about a newsroom snarling his motto: "People are scum." At his newspaper, if a story was filed without any scum in it, then the reporter hadn't looked hard enough, because anyone who looked hard enough at anyone else would see scum, alright.

Walter was obsessed with taking down the mayor of Passaic, New Jersey, where nearly every day reporters found more evidence linking that scum to the mob. Walter raged in editorials, placed accounts of the mayor's misdeeds on every front page, even started a coupon campaign. ("Clip and send this coupon to the state attorney general: We want an indictment! Now!") One day a large dead fish wrapped in the *Herald and News* was delivered to the front desk, addressed to Walter with regards from the mayor. Walter held it up by the gills like a trophy.

I had gone to work for Walter just before the holidays, and I covered Clifton, where at Christmas, baby Jesus was discovered to be missing from the crèche at city hall. I was all over that story: some scum stole Christmas, I told Walter. Some baby-Jesus-thieving scum. And thank god, too, because frankly I had not found many good stories in two months on the beat.

It turned out that baby Jesus was just being repaired and was back in the manger the next morning. My story was over. Christmas came and went, and I returned to my anxious search for any bad thing in Clifton that I could write about. What I needed was a murder. An impeachment. Anything. I was failing to find failure and I feared for my job. The best I could come up with was something like the bitter fight over soccer that erupted at a city council meeting one evening. Neighbors surrounding the soccer field accused the adult soccer players of urinating on their lawns. The soccer players, mostly Hispanic, argued that they were surrounded by bigots who thought soccer was a sport for illegal aliens, and that they had been unjustly maligned. The council listened to the soccer-playing immigrants and the home-owning neighbors, calculated which group had more influence at election time, and made an easy decision. The city cancelled soccer. I wrote a story about the city council scum and then I fled the gray office for a dark watering hole with three televisions hanging from the ceiling. Madeleine was waiting for me at the bar.

"Why don't I ever get to write stories about civil rights marches or something cool like women astronauts?" I wondered out loud. "I'm so sick of this bullshit."

We drank beer in long gulps. She said, "You know what you need?"

A big hug, I thought to myself.

"You need a vacation."

Then she told me how much she missed being in Montana. "I think I'm gonna try and get back there every year. It's good."

"I've never been to Montana," I said.

"Are you kidding?" she asked. "You must have been to Montana."

"Never."

"But your dad's from there. What's his town called again?"

"Rapelje," I said. "Rhymes with nap all day."

"Rapelje," she breathed out slowly. "Oh man. Rapelje. What's the population? Fourteen?" I didn't know, then, but it was more like forty.

We sat in this undistinguished bar, anonymous and nowhere, ten years before the millennium, twenty-one years after Woodstock, an innocuous point in time. The first George Bush was president; Abbie Hoffman had given up the fight and killed himself. Madeleine smiled and blew smoke in the air and told me of her friends in Montana, who could do things like make goat cheese and sleep outside for weeks without tents, they hunted for food, they could defend themselves. Their lives were so much more, well, *alive* than ours.

I remembered that Madeleine had told me about her old boyfriend John and his guns and I started to see a pattern. "They're survivalists?" I asked.

"Some of them," she said.

"What do they expect to survive in Montana? Blizzards?"

She shook her head slowly, lit a cigarette, and passed the pack over to me. She paused and glanced up at a TV. It must have been clear to her by then that I didn't really know anything. "More like, nuclear war."

I answered, "Oh." But, what could that mean? Why would anyone bomb some place like Montana, and anyhow, who could seriously imagine surviving nuclear war? Who would want to? Back then, so many warheads were pointed at us, fighting seemed futile. I told her: "All things considered, Madeleine, if the bomb comes, I plan to die." And that was a funny thing, because I once planned to save the world by explaining to everyone just how silly destruction was and simply clearing up all that nonsense. Not even thirty, and instead of saving anything, I planned to just go ahead and die.

Madeleine exhaled busily and pushed her empty beer glass forward for more. She said at last, "See, that's just the thing. They're counting on you to give up. They want everyone to give up. That way, they win. See?"

I looked into my beer. Why was there always a they, and why didn't they ever want something good for me?

Madeleine said, "It's just different in Montana. It's better there. When the rest of the world falls apart, that's where I'm gonna go." She took a drink and pushed on: "You learn to survive so nothing can beat you, see? Nothing. It's your life, girl." She slapped the bar. Madeleine looked hard at me with uneven eyes across a blunt nose, willing me to know what she knew: You fight for it. It's possible to have the life you want, see? We shouldn't even be sitting here bitching. She told me you don't ever just die. You learn to hunt elk and stay warm in winter. You have to see the little places to understand. Like Rapelje. Maybe you think a place like Rapelje should be dead and gone by now, but there it is, determined.

"I'm going to take you to Montana," she said. "You need to know."

We drank another round in the bar ringed with neon beer signs and TVs, and with that round we became a bit less troubled by the world and more enamored with it again, because threatened as it was, the world still contained places that refused to die, like Rapelje, and we could go there any time we wanted. Now and then Madeleine paused to issue a dreamy, throaty, ha-ha-ha, and say, "Rapelje!"

"Have you ever even seen it? Even in pictures?"

"Well, sort of," I said. "You can't really see much in the pictures. But my grandparents spent a lot of years there." In the flat, gray plains, they started that town. They got there first, before anyone, I said, and we contemplated that: How visionary. How incredibly bold. What survivalist fucking radical pioneers they must have been. And soon we became enamored with them and the details we invented for their lives: My grandparents, explorers, or some kind of fed up free spirits who went to go find paradise. Why did they go there? What did they expect? And why did they name paradise "Rapelje"?

Every few minutes we'd both say it: "Rapelje!"

By the time it was midnight and we tripped out of our seats at the bar, she was in love with this important new word, Rapelje—three elegant syllables and the hope of rebirth. We stepped outside, onto the sidewalk with the midnight traffic gushing by, and I shoved my hands in my pockets and slouched beneath the weight of destiny, smiling a little, thinking bold thoughts about going west with Madeleine and saying quietly: yeah, it would be better there. I looked at my shoes and played with my car keys but hope urged Madeleine up; she hopped up and down, and soon she was waving her arms above her swinging bobbed hair, chanting with joy, chanting with irony: "Rapelje, Rapelje!" and landing feet first in the heart of Montana. Don't you see? Snow drifts six feet deep in winter, lose your car till it thaws, lose the cows if you leave them too long in the million-acre fields because those are your cows, damn it, *those are your cows,* and no one will save them if you don't. Parched earth in August cracking like chapped lips and thirsty just like we were, beautiful thirsty Rapelje, Montana, something I understood then to be so much better, so much nobler than our world; where the hell was Rapelje and why had I never been there?

"Rapelje!" Madeleine hollered in the dark parking lot beside a buzzing road, where at last she hugged me and hopped while she held me and laughed. She'd quite suddenly, surely, made up her mind. "Yes yes yes," she said. "Let's go, Let's go. We have to go to Rapelje, Montana."

"Okay," I said.

It's worth noting that as we made this vow to save our dull lives, we were also standing on the verge of driving home drunk, or half drunk anyhow, with that young feeling of immortality that snuffs out one's common sense. I didn't have much use for common sense. I was looking for something more like . . . Rapelje.

I left with the glow of Madeleine's enthusiasm but for weeks after that I did not believe we could really do it—go west, go see Rapelje and do all the good things we dreamed of. I loved the idea but I was only a few months into my new job at the *Herald and News* and I thought it might be tough to swing a big vacation. Work was always getting in the way of good ideas. Could I take the summer off? Was such a thing allowed? I would have to ask, which was intimidating just to contemplate. The idea of Walter staring at me while I explained to him that I needed to spend some time in Montana, where everything was better, made the whole project seem a little absurd.

But Madeleine made plans: she said maybe we could fly out, then rent a van, load it up with gear in Bozeman sort of like the fur traders and miners and homesteaders had done back in pioneer days, loading wagons with blankets, whiskey, guns, supplies, receiving great sendoffs upon striking out into the wild. We would gear up and head out to the wild places that were still out there, still waiting. Madeleine explained to me how to borrow against future vacations, or sign up for all the holiday shifts and work some overtime to get a few weeks off, but still, I didn't think I could do it. I was not like Madeleine.

Work was always busy. Crime was hitting some fascinating peaks in the late 1980s and corruption was ever-present in New Jersey. In the gray cave of our newsroom, the entire *Herald and News* city desk would turn as one, several times a day, to hear the latest screaming on the police scanner. Mechanical voices erupted over static, alerting us to crisis after crisis. "What's going on?" Walter would trot stiff-kneed from his office and growl. Just another armed robbery on a soft spring day, just another crackhead shooting up kids in the projects. The news was always bad, and Walter seemed to think that if the worst of it were laid out in print, then maybe the blight on our collective soul would at last be forced into the open where it could be stomped to death by outraged innocent people, if there were any left when we were through. Or at least, if the newspaper was doing its job, then no one would be able to continue living in self-deluded bliss like pansies, and we could start dealing with reality. It was a public service: we hunted for the ultimate low, the anti-enlightenment, some bitch-goddess high-crisis nirvana that seemed never to arrive. It was never bad enough: never enough perverts committing sex crimes on minors; never enough public officials caught telling big enough lies to be able to say that the worst was finally over. There was always another paper to fill.

"What's going on?"

"A retarded boy in Clifton had a bar mitzvah."

"Jesus Christ, call me when they let him drive. What's going on?"

"Baby in Paterson waiting for a liver transplant."

"GUB!" Walter shouted. That was not an acronym, that was just the word our editors felt best described the differently abled.

"GUB! Another GUB! What the fuck is going on?"

"Molestation charge against a grammar school principal."

"That scum."

One-word names of stories, what reporters call "slugs," were listed on the daily news budget, the same ones over and over, every day: Rape. Rob. Shoot. Slay. Rob. Slay. Knifing. Shoot. It was endless; everyone was insane. My story on an autistic boy who was sent away to a school in Kansas earned me an honor: the autistic boy article was hailed as "the best goddamn GUB story" the *Herald and News* ever ran. Who knew what that meant? It was a happy-ending story that finally made the front page, but I don't think Walter actually liked it. Most often, I just seemed to disappoint everyone, like the day I'd been sent to check out a tip that a coffin had been left overnight on a gurney in the hall of Paterson's Evergreen Cemetery. The grave it was supposed to be buried in hadn't been dug in time. The corpse inside this coffin was no ordinary corpse; it belonged to a guy who'd been hit by a bus in the act of saving an old lady. The city desk was dreaming of the headline, maybe something like, "UN-SUNK HERO," and the editors were searching for the best bad pun right up until I brought them my report. Then the room fell silent.

In the cemetery in the rain, I had found a freshly dug grave, determined it belonged to our hero and looked down; I saw what the chief grave digger explained to me were neighboring coffins, which over years of rainfall, frost heaves and other acts of nature had shifted toward the empty middle, where the new coffin was supposed to go. The hero was being held in the mausoleum until heavy digging equipment could be brought in to make room. No scandal.

Even Walter's glasses couldn't magnify his buried black eyes when he looked at me that day; had he sent Jones or McGuire to the cemetery, by god he'd have found injustice. "Well, if there's no fucking story then there's no fucking story," he finally said, and looked away. The scanner buzzed. I scratched my neck.

I was afraid, then. Of Walter, of everything. Of getting fired. I didn't really understand what was so wrong with the world: with school boards voting after midnight, with powerful people giving jobs to their friends, with heroes lying unburied in cemeteries. Everywhere you looked, and I mean everywhere, someone was doing something evil, but even if I knew this, it was not what I believed. What did I believe? Just, something different. I looked up at Walter and tried very hard to see what he meant, but I kept seeing myself getting fired instead. Walter shuffled into his office to drink black coffee and scream into the telephone. The TV above the copy desk played mute nature programs, trout fishing shows, mountain panoramas, commercials for insect repellents or fishing poles. The scanner on the city desk whined: beep, sirens, static. "Gunshots on 18th Street." "Roger," "ten-four." And then, it was clear to me what had to happen next. I quit.

Two days later I gave two-weeks notice. "I'm going to Montana," I told Walter, and then, everyone.

"You're . . . what?" they invariably answered.

"I'm quitting," I said. "I'm going to find America."

This expression and its variations seemed to annoy people. It particularly aggravated my aunt in Milwaukee, who I visited at the start of my journey. "I'm going to find America," I said. "I'm going to take my time." She rolled her eyes. She'd looked once for America; she'd even joined the Peace Corps and gone to Thailand, looking for the world, but then she found Milwaukee. She said, "Oh, please. The world is big, go find a little part of it and be happy." Then she described her long painful crossing of the arid northern highway in Montana, driving the length of hellish Route 2 in a camper van with a new baby who cried and cried; her entire Montana experience was awful, but not as awful as when she almost died in the riptide off Thailand in the Peace Corps, 1965. Ghastly awful. But awful things make good stories and she didn't know the Montana I knew and anyhow, I was going.

Others were dubious. When I told people at work that I was "going west," they said this foolishness would ruin my life. "You'll never get another job," some said. "You don't just quit jobs, you don't just get to pick up and go. You'll be sorry."

But that didn't make any sense to me at all. What was this obsession with having a job? If you didn't like your job very much and saw no future in it, then wasn't staying wrong? Of course it was.

Others, more spiteful, said: "Life doesn't come up and hand you things. You don't get to wander off just because life is tough. Life is tough for everyone, tough tough tough, so just stay here and tough it out, tough girl."

Look at you, I thought, looking at everyone: You are trapped in an endless cycle of work and sleep, back to the same thing again daily like a newspaper where nothing means anything by the next morning, your lives are pointless. Someday you'll all be dead. Then I imagined my exit from work: spinning on my desk and shouting, "I am an artiste!" and winning, somehow; having the last word and using it to say "I am taking my life back." I could do this thing: I could become who I knew I was, and not the person gravity was shaping. I had to.

In the end, pens stuffed in my pockets and files dumped in the garbage can, I walked out to my car in the usual manner and said nothing.

"Running away from home, cosmo?" Walter asked without waiting for an answer as he trotted past. But I was going with Madeleine. And Walter or anyone else didn't need to understand.

Madeleine said, "Hey, you quit your job? Wow. That's exciting. That means you gotta go out there and stay on the road just as long as you can," and she started planning. Maybe she'd get the summer off. I said, "Maybe you could quit your job, too." That's what I wanted. I felt as if I'd figured out the secret to finding a real life, the best kind of life—just leave the junk behind! Forget it!—and surely if I felt it then she felt it too: when I thought of Montana, she was always there. And if it was wrong to stay in an unhappy place, wasn't it equally wrong to discover bliss and then turn around and leave it? Why would anyone do that?

Well, no one would do it. Joy is not an amusement park. It is not a place you visit, then leave. Joy is a place you give yourself to. If the place Madeleine and I discovered together was so beautiful, would it be possible to just leave it? To just see the truth and walk away? Is that the sort of weak commitment to freedom I had quit my latest job for?

It was not. But what I also knew was that I shouldn't talk about it; if I asked with too much force, Madeleine might say she would not stay with me. If I kept quiet, anything was possible. Finally, before I left New Jersey two weeks ahead of her she said, "Well, let's wait and see." She had to cover most of July for old Joe, couldn't let him down, but after that who knew? And anyhow, it shouldn't slow me down, nothing should stop me from saving my own life. So we made our plans.

We figured I would drive on my own as far as Wisconsin, where my mother's family lives and I wanted to visit. I would meander through the Midwest for a while, spend a little time exploring Indiana and Ohio just to see what there was to see, which turned out to be cornstalks and blond hair and strip malls. In August Madeleine would fly out to meet me in Wisconsin, where I'd be staying with my aunt. From Wisconsin, we would drive together to Montana.

But wait: maybe she should just hitchhike to Wisconsin. Didn't it seem rather frivolous to fly? Flying would cost so much money. She said she thought she'd rather just try to hitch a ride.

Of course, I told her; hitching made sense. We were freeing ourselves of convention already. I pointed out that twenty-five years earlier, hippies and college dropouts and Janis Joplin hitched rides all the time, jumped into stopped cars and took off fearless into the world because, hey, it's groovy, whatever your trip is, go with the flow. Just jump a boxcar, thumb a lift, Kerouac across the continent. Why should every one of us going in the same direction have to drive?

We understood, of course, that some people—the ones who thought I was crazy to quit my job, for example, and my entire family, and all their neighbors and friends—some people with small ideas about life on earth might find this hitchhiking plan foolhardy, but we also knew that they lacked imagination. "Yes. I will hitchhike," Madeleine announced, in her pragmatic way. "It makes sense." I agreed. I pictured Madeleine in a perfect world, standing on the side of the road, blue jeans and smock top and Birkenstocks, thumb out, hippy and haughty and beautiful. She said "I'll hitch a ride" and I imagined her tossing her own duffel bag into the back of a red pickup truck with a bumper-sticker: Semper Fi, and I saw in my mind's eye Madeleine climbing into the truck next to some stranger, not a Bohemian at all but an ex–Marine with a buzz cut and an unfortunate psychological disorder discovered only after he was trained to kill, then discharged and sent home with a grudge against free spirits and a machete under his front seat, and in this fantasy Madeleine never joins me in Wisconsin because she is chopped up into little pieces.

The problem with great ideas is all those people who resist them. I said, "Hitching is probably stupid." She agreed.

So she paid five hundred dollars (two weeks take-home pay to her then, but who was counting money when everything else about our lives was now so gloriously free) and she bought a plane ticket to meet me in Wisconsin, and I left. The journey had started. We were in it together. I departed from my yellow aluminum house in Morristown one morning at six, my cat turning his back to me in the window as I pulled away ("I'll send for you, Wally! Don't be afraid!"). I traveled out slowly, across Pennsylvania, past Chicago, past Racine, up for a visit with my mother's Milwaukee family and my skeptical aunt, up to northern Wisconsin and the pine trees and the airport where I picked up Madeleine. Back in Milwaukee my mother's stern father was crossing my ruined name off his will, seeing that another loser grandchild was up to no good; in New Jersey my parents might have wondered if they had lost another child, but they were kind enough not to say so. I had no job, little money, and no idea what was coming; no one seemed to think I was doing the right thing but somehow, for once, I was not afraid of anything. It was the first time in my life that I felt I was doing what I was meant to do, and that I would be with someone I was meant to be with, and it seemed to me that if I stayed long enough, drove fast enough, stood quietly by and glowed bright enough in all my new certainty, then the promised better life I had almost stopped hoping for, in a better place and time, would finally be mine. It almost felt too good to be real, but, there I was, driving.

So what's not to love about Racine, Wisconsin? Nothing, probably. But some time around 1916, William and Florence decided to leave it for Montana. They packed up their new shiny Ford and drove out beyond everything familiar, to a place where the whole world seemed to change. They rumbled down long empty roads, past the sod and tarpaper shacks of wheat farmers in the eastern Montana plains, and the farmers stopped and waved when the car charged by. Dust churned out behind them, a plume rising higher than even the wooden grain elevators towering over the fawn-colored fields. Chicken coops stood amid craters and wind blew dirt fast across the top of short, dry grass. They had a faintly drawn map and no radio, and he drove: north and west, up the old Molt Road, two ruts and no markers for guidance, mile after mile in the hot sun with no shade, no air conditioning. William drove, and Florence clutched her first child in her lap, laughing because that was her way. Wind, and an engine humming, and a constant clunk and plunk of poor suspension and flying rocks on a so-called road that was more like a trail; with the engine shut, there was no sound at all.

"We must be lost," William growled, squinting through spectacles for some landmark in the bright outside. They were nowhere. The map had no landmarks; the road signs were scarce and vague. He opened the car door and stretched his stiff legs and got out to look around, standing in his shirt sleeves, his tie still knotted tight. He pushed his hat back. Only a post in the midst of dry dirt stood out to tell him, finally, where to turn: an arrow in the waiting fields pointed west to Rapelje.

They had spent their first year in Montana living in the city of Billings, looking for the right deal out on the open plains. They examined pamphlets and charts and prospectuses, talked to investors and tried to decide. What was the perfect place for them? Where could they go, in this whole great big state, to find whatever they were looking for?

The posters at the tractor trade shows and the newspaper advertisements back east had said:

GOVERNMENT LANDS!!

At the present rate of production Montana will soon surpass Minnesota in the growing of wheat, rye, oats and barley. You cannot AFFORD to pass up this OUTSTANDING opportunity.

In Montana, there was still mile upon square mile of land, unclaimed wealth, all waiting to be taken in the government's last active homesteading program. A thousand more stores were open in 1917 than the year before. Fifty-thousand reported filing land claims that year. And then there was this deal a Billings banker had with the Northern Pacific Railroad, which was laying tracks across the state. The railroad wanted to lure people west to live along the train route, so that one day the whole line would be surrounded by farmers with cattle and grain to send to the markets back east, by train. The federal government gave away land, to farmers, to the railroads, pushing the whole country west, and new towns grew up all along the way. Across the plains of Montana, depots and grain elevators grew up side by side, like siblings. Every depot with a grain elevator became the core of a town. And once all the bare flat land was put under plow, then it was a sure bet that Montana's grandest town would rise at the end of a spur line out of Billings. It would be a town so big and important in the midst of all this bounty that it would need four grain elevators to handle the harvest of Stillwater County. Four elevators: like fat skyscrapers downtown, marking some place with a future so bright that the Northern Pacific didn't even call it Molt, or Rye, or Wheat Basin, or some other word for grass, like all the other little towns around; this one, the railroad claimed for its company vice president: R. J. Rapelje.

"Oh, William, it's perfect, let's go."

The car engine hummed. There was their dream, out there invisible but real and they followed it to that one place of all places on the map. Driving to Rapelje: not long ago, living in the soft pocket of their midwestern hometowns, could they ever have imagined what they saw now? The sun beat into the deep crags of wild earth, antelope scattered before them. The Montana landscape exaggerates: the sky looked so wide, it could not be the same sky they knew in Wisconsin. The blue dome faded through four or five different shades until it hit a faint line of mountains on the western horizon.

When they arrived, William walked the lines of the lot marked with flags, the site of their new home in Rapelje. He would be cashier at the First National Bank. In the center of this world of unturned earth, all the farmers would gather with their livestock, and grain, and money. It was perfect. And suddenly he knew he was the most fortunate man in the whole great, wide world, soon to be a wealthy man, too, in the right place at the right time. William and Florence set up a platform tent as a temporary home, and William lit a cigar, leaned against his car, and made a list of all the things he had to do, to hasten the future of Rapelje.

August 1917: builders waited on supplies to come by horse cart, twelve a day, up slow and steady from Columbus. The town grew as William and Florence stood watching. A stiff wind blew Florence's hat hard against its chin strap, churned dust into William's eyes. She turned her head and he squinted. "It won't be long now, mother," William said to his wife, as their firstborn son made tiny bubbles on her arm. Success would require faith and imagination. In the dirt in front of the house they built, William cleared rocks with sticks of dynamite so that Florence could have a garden. She loved flowers; she grew hollyhocks and wildflowers. She would even try to grow roses there, beside the sage brush and cottonwood trees, but they didn't take well in the shadeless dirt. Builders took rocks blown up from the garden and made a fantastic stone chimney in their new house, so big and lovely that for generations neighbors admired it, they all said how grand it was. They would talk about it still, many years later, long after it was gone, even after there was no one left living who had actually seen it, or seen anything like the first year in Rapelje.

The government carved up the West. Homesteaders were doled out parcels of 160 acres, quarter lots. On a patch the size of these, Rapelje's streets and shops and houses were plotted by businessmen who would prove up their claim not by farming, but by making a town. The town would be nineteen blocks square. Five blocks were set aside for park land, so that even as this world grew up, there would always be some open spaces.

September: William walked to his new bank. Above the door, words were brightly painted: "First National Bank of Rapelje, Farm Loans." The door creaked open on tight new hinges; when it slammed shut, plate glass rattled in its frame. William's wingtips rocked across the plank floor and echoed. The fresh wood smelled like a forest. Behind the counter inside was the machinery that would mortgage the plains: the safe from Billings, the cash drawer that opened along smooth wooden runners, the adding machine that rang out when the handle was pulled. Outside, beyond the plate glass windows of the First National, stood miles of grass.

In 1918, one year after the building binge began, the Northern Pacific spur line was finished and new trains began delivering a great crescendo of farmers and merchants, not in a trickle but a flood. Every day when the train came, throngs gathered at the station to see what would come next. That year, Rapelje was home to three lumber companies, three garages, and a feed store; there were two hotels, four grocery stores, a shoemaker, a weekly newspaper, and a large brick school. There were three churches and a pool hall; two doctors, a drugstore, an undertaker. And there were two banks, including the First National.

Yet what sprang up so fast was easily swallowed by all that unfathomable nothing. In photographs, it feels as if no one was alive, there, even with bodies in pictures like proof. The din of boomtown dispersed into the air, like thunder that growls down off the mountains to the plains, some sunny days, rustling the silence even when there is no rain or lightning in sight. Children are barefoot in these pictures, standing in dirt roads that aim at nothing, wind-whipped, small expressions on small faces that don't speak of glory. They stand on a dirt road, or by the shed, or by the sage brush: meager props and behind or all around them, empty.

William's bank had a boardwalk attached to the front but it stopped at the ends of the building, waiting. The long, wooden sidewalks weren't there; they were hoped for. Even after the construction was done, after the trains and the people had arrived, even after the last of Florence and William's four children was born, the emptiness still looked like the wish that it was.

Rapelje. It sprang into an empire, a mirage that unfolded all at once as if fortune lay dehydrated out there, in the dirt plains. It was everything William and Florence dreamed of, and all you had to do . . . was add water.

I was on the road for three weeks when Madeleine finally flew to Rhinelander, Wisconsin, and I met her. She had a fake-fruit covered hat on, and she had started growing out her hair. The flips were down past her chin now, curling toward the middle like the bottom of a heart. When I saw her I couldn't stop smiling. We hugged each other hard and she kept hugging while she jumped up and down and I didn't want to let go but then we ran to the car and started driving. "Hey," she said, "Wisconsin is really beautiful," and I was pleased with her approval but who cared: we weren't staying. We drove north to Lake Superior, just because it was there, and then we zigzagged into Minnesota, planned a crazy route or didn't plan at all, really, for the first day of our drive, when being on the road was a new feeling for us both and we wanted to see everything: all the lakes, all the rivers, all the towns and trees and statues of dead heroes. But then we dropped down near Minneapolis and we could not bear to waste another hour. We had to point our car west and drive, just drive, for a long time without stopping and so we drove, west, west, west on the northern highway, with bare feet out the window and our big dark glasses on.

Soon, all the world that had seemed so intense and important for so long was far behind as if it were nothing, and had been nothing all along. It was taken in what seemed like an instant, and only the wonderful earth remained; there weren't even many cars around as we crossed the Mississippi in lush bucolic idyllic Minnesota, where freckle-faced farm kids ride bikes and catch bugs forever before school starts again in the fall and we drove, that summer, counting the colors of wildflowers we saw, and trees, as they thinned and gave way to brush and then disappeared altogether. In one long, hot day we drove so far that everything around us changed. Conifers parted to a sea of earth, the Badlands, North Dakota, all dirt and blue sky. And it was marvelous. It was hard to imagine life was like that, there, all the time, all that empty space there every day and just a drive down the highway, just down the road from where I, like a fool, spent so much time trying to climb over the crowds, snaking through traffic, standing in grocery store checkout lines with my heart crowded and pounding as lethargic shoppers lifted items out of their baskets, all of us resigned to lines and lives of no importance and no change; I had waited back east for everything like a soldier in endless and unhappy lines. That had been my life: standing around with an aching heart, waiting, as if what I wanted would finally be there. But no: if I wanted joy, I would have to go get it.

In North Dakota at a gas station in a clapboard shack whose chalky white paint had worn thin, we bought cartons of orange juice and some peanuts. Madeleine thanked the gas man for her change. He said, "You bet." She winked at me. "That's what they say out here," she said. "You bet." So that's what we said, too.

I played Joni Mitchell songs on the tape deck and sang along: "I'm on a lonely road and I am traveling, traveling, traveling, looking for something what could it be?" I sang the more important words louder to Madeleine, "traveling, traveling, traveling," and, "Oh I hate you some, I hate you some but I love you some," and Madeleine said nothing to me. When my tape ended she took over the show with some bootleg Grateful Dead. Sometimes when the sun and the music and the old houses and farms and the fields and the wind were all just too perfect and too beautiful, so fabulous and unburdened they made me ache until I felt sick, just sick with the wonder of this world, at some of those times Madeleine would make me pull over so she could get out of the car and dance on the side of the road, shouting "Woo Hoo!" and waving to the huge spaces in broad daylight, a bright sky full of stars that we just couldn't see. They were out there all the time, above us, even if they were invisible; the stars were watching, we believed. Madeleine sometimes hopped out to dance to a perfect song in a perfect moment and I'd say come on, come on, get back in the car, and I'd laugh, but I couldn't join her. Back at the Mississippi River, then at the North Dakota border, even on the outskirts of dusty old Bismarck, when Madeleine felt the urge to dance, I sat back and smiled and I watched her, but still, I stayed inside.

And then I started to wonder: when am I going to let myself out, just get out and start dancing?

In the Badlands I dreamed I saw bison run with wild horses where the buttes push up through the sand; we turned down side roads and Madeleine stopped the car and raised her arms to the burning sun and smiled beatific sainted smiles of joy deeper than any joy you can feel if you just stay home. By that time she was stopping us to do her ecstatic dances not just on the road but up on top of the car, on top of the *car*, for god's sake, parked on a dirt scrawl with nothing around for miles and miles and miles, and finally, then,

I felt I must act; I must get out and acknowledge the force beating in me, too; the force will not be ignored forever. Love? Was it love? Was this where all the love we'd ever felt had led us? I wanted what it was, this bliss, and I wanted it with Madeleine.

Madeleine was twirling in the sun and I checked the mirrors: no one else around us, anywhere. Okay: I unbuckled my seat belt and looked for my shoes in the back seat. A stirring rendition of a song called "Cassidy" was playing, not an ordinary "Cassidy," but louder, stronger, it sounded like some huge high school marching band was playing full tilt behind Jerry Garcia's guitar, all those drums driving rhythm out farther, farther, clinking bells and horns and this is crazy, marching bands make me cry, it's all so beautiful: I thought, just go! But wait. I can't dance if it's not spontaneous; not if I'm too, you know, formal. But then again, I thought, if I don't go now, I'll just seem totally uptight. So I'm uptight no matter what I do. Jesus. I put a sneaker on. I tied my shoes and looked at her and thought, this is it, I am going to go. Now! I bolted out the door and did a hopping lap around the Honda and started tossing my long hair round in circles Hoo HOOOO! I hopped in place, hopped in place, hopped, looked left and right until I found Madeleine, who had stopped dancing and was itching her nose. She looked up and down the road. She looked at me, hopping on the shoulder. A car whizzed by out of nowhere and honked. "Watch it," she yelled. I hopped back and did a couple jumping jacks and . . . well, the song ended.

"I'll drive now if you want," she said, and put her hand out for the keys.

The Grateful Dead sang: "Fare thee well now, let your life proceed by its own design," the quintessential song of the young journeying soul in that or any time, because it is about going off to find something, alone, imperfect and raw and alive and sprung from the dreams of a radical time. Even if in the real world my body could not move loose and free with whomever it wanted, still I danced inside, and the road before us suggested that our lives would proceed by their own perfect design until we came to the answer and the end of the story.

We drove. I thought of the word utopia then. Its meaning was vague, a concept more or less understood, I suppose. But what about the details? I imagined a mountain, rising up steep and angular so far off on the horizon that the snow on its shoulders looked pale white as ghosts, gauzelike against the sky almost like clouds, that mountaintop. Heaven. I imagined seekers of utopia streaming to the mountain like pilgrims, some walking with shepherd's crooks, with lambs. I thought perhaps utopia was thriving on the hollow inside. I thought perhaps the pilgrims were actually souls. Then I thought heaven might be the place souls go when bodies die, but enlightened souls could find it while they were still alive: peace on earth, wisdom, joy, bliss. Utopia. If we wanted, we could have all these things and life, too. Imagine.

Actually, this steep, snow-capped vision I had was Mount Rainier, viewed from Seattle. I didn't realize it at the time, but now that I've seen Mount Rainier, I know that this utopia I imagined was something I'd once seen on a postcard, stuck to a fridge, which my mind borrowed when it pictured a place where bright souls lived freely, singing Van Morrison songs in harmony on sunny days, sharing food off each other's plates. It was a paradise to which I hoped I, too, was going. Is it possible to cross this country and not believe in such a place, at least for a while?

Three days and we were still driving. Because two thousand miles is a long way to go. Three days in a car and you're an astronaut, hurtling through space observed through the glass. Heat and fresh air melted discretion from our car talk. Politeness, social distance thinned with the trees. Madeleine lit cigarettes for me while I drove. She cracked peanuts, which I ate. We turned south to go see Mount Rushmore, and somewhere in the heat of South Dakota, midday, the subject turned to sex, as sometimes happens among friends, and she started to count past lovers: More than ten, fewer than one hundred. Maybe fewer than seventy-five; she couldn't really say. I stared intensely at the highway, and she let slide a dirty laugh.

She counted: a series of one-syllable names. Rob. John. Phil. Jim. They were all men. Of course they were: the game had rules. Much as everyone seems to want to talk about sex, everyone is really only allowed to say the same thing about it, apparently. Over and over. Save the crazy stuff for movies. Up inside utopia mountain, hardy souls might light up and say, hey, you know what happened to me? And tell the truth about it, about someone they loved, or about who they wanted to have sex with and why, and how often they had done it, and if it really mattered, and why. But we were not in the mountain; we were still just in South Dakota, and like hitchhiking, some things were too dangerous to practice in the world as we knew it.

Madeleine recited three or four one-syllable male names that seemed to come out of some deep recess that it pleased her to recover, and then she stopped, and just smiled with all her teeth showing, and looked out the window at the petrified earth.

I listened to the car engine working, and didn't say anything. And she didn't ask me anything, either. Why not? Did she think I was a virgin? Because if she thought I was a virgin, I could tell her that my high school friends would never have let that happen. But now I began to wonder if there were new, more exacting standards to meet, and what it might be like to be able to say: more than ten, fewer than a hundred. Who had time for this many partners? Where did all these desirable people come from? Did one meet them in bars, at parties? Did one have sex with complete strangers? Did they do it indiscriminately, ducking behind bakery counters, between shelves in the library, sneaking off into storage rooms? Was there something going on all around that I was fully unaware of? And was more than ten, fewer than a hundred the actual standard deviation for a fully lived life? Never just one; you could never just stop at one lover or even just one time, one single time in your life to do it and say it was enough.

Had I even met ten people that I'd wanted to have sex with?

On my right hand, I counted. Forget high school; he was just a homework assignment. Who had I really wanted, and had? That maniac I met my senior year of college. His name was Steve. He drank vodka from the bottle and threw condoms full of paint at his apartment walls. He had stringy hair and sideburns and loose T-shirts with holes. Why not try Steve, I figured at the time, he seemed like the sort to have a wild free-love kind of affair with, someone I'd recall fondly on a day very much like this day and think "What wild young things we once were." I thought to myself, "We were so young and wild once," and extended a finger: one.

Steve was wild, but he didn't last long; one night he stumbled drunk into my bedroom and got sort of nasty and wouldn't go away until he had to run vomit out my window. And thinking back on Steve, if I was brave I knew I'd admit that, after all, he was really just someone exotic enough to make me forget someone else, an even wilder war story from those wild warring years. It was a secret and it haunted me but I couldn't talk about it: lamb eyes. Lamb eyes, whom I had wanted so badly that I had scared myself. I just wanted to be near her. We met in college but my college was so cruel, the fraternity boys used to throw rocks through the windows of the gay alliance leader's dorm room. Even the word "gay" scared me, because even thinking it, just generally, seemed to make you a target for a violent hatred, and I had spent so much of my life trying to be loved. Now, how could something as unpopular as this happen to me? I wondered, panicked, and yet I wanted lamb eyes. I spent a weekend with her in a Cape Cod motel and there was nowhere to sleep except together, and later when I tried to tell her about love, and her, and sex as an expression of love, and her, she said, "I don't think I love you that way."

And I felt as if I would either die right then for having said these things to her, or die later, when the front desk clerk would shoot me for talking dirty to a girl at his motel. He'd know. Everyone would know. And then I wished he would come shoot me right then: I was going to die of shame anyway. I felt sure that one didn't survive judgment errors of this kind, or if I did, why would I want to? What would I do, now, having discovered this pitiful thing about myself? I was sure I was alone, or, at least, I was too frightened to find others.

Frozen beside lamb eyes with a sheet tucked around me, I stared desperately at her; she was pretending to sleep but not sleeping. "What have I done?" I wondered, laying there for hours, and worse: "Why can't I do more?" No one I knew would ever understand this. When I dropped her off at home the next day, she sat in my car and looked at me. Without a warning she leaned over and touched my face, and she kissed me. Her hand held my cheek; she smelled of scented soap and shampoo, and then her lips opened up against mine. It seemed to go on, and on. I tried to remember everything I knew about kissing, and to kiss well. I wanted this to be a kiss that would change the world. I don't know why she did it, maybe pity, maybe curiosity, but she did it and in that moment time stopped. She never did it again. I had waited for her to come and do this again, for anyone to come and do this again, ever since then.

In the car, seven years later, I felt mortified and confused as if it had all just happened. But lamb eyes had left for the West Coast with a handsome husband years earlier and I couldn't believe I was thinking of her, just then; it would never go away. If I ever spoke of lamb eyes to another woman then surely that woman would fear I was after her, too. Worse: maybe I was. Maybe I was after every woman I ever saw, maybe I just wanted a woman, any woman, to get into my car and kiss me and get it over with, just settle this mess. But I had already decided I would never tell anyone what I wanted again until I was sure that she wanted it, too, which is hard to determine in all that silence.

Madeleine was looking at a road map, this whole conversation having apparently ended for her miles ago. "Let's stop near Sturgis," she said. "It's sort of on the way to Mount Rushmore. There's this big biker rally there."

"Sure," I said. And the extended finger that had stood for Steve curled back with the others.

We passed a field of sunflowers with their faces turned to the sun, but then that field was behind us and there was nothing, once again. I held the steering wheel tightly and ripped down the highway. I was so afraid, just then, of Madeleine. She had become enormous to me, invested with importance she could not have understood.

I rolled down my window. The air rushed in like a flood of invisible cotton, soft and edgeless. It smelled like the earth baked in sun. Oh god: it could all be so beautiful, it could, it could, if we wanted. I yelled above the radio and the wind rushing in: "Madeleine, I want to be free as wild horses, I want to live among the buffalo, I want to let my hair grow to my knees and swim naked in cold rivers. I want to live, to live, to live until I die and nothing can stop me now. I WANT TO BE FREEEEEEE!"

She sat up. "I know you do," she yelled over the wind, and she held her straw hat onto her head as the brim flapped crazy. She looked at me, and then looked ahead again. And I kept driving and kept letting the wind slap my face—ah, ah, ah—and she looked at me, and then she looked ahead again.

"Could you roll up your window?" she finally said.

"Oh. Sure." I dropped my hand to the crank and rolled it up.

She said, "You know, maybe this trip is an initiation for you." An initiation: I liked that. It was almost exactly the word I'd use to describe the night I'd spent with lamb eyes.

"Every now and then you get an initiation, where the universe hands you a choice in an instant, and if you choose right, you grow, you balance out some karma," said Madeleine, who could distill all the secrets of the universe into a kind of cosmic grocery list. She knew things. She said, "Every now and then, you fail initiations, too. But of course, you get three chances."

Of course. Three chances. Like baseball. Three is a cosmic number, like, the trinity, and the number of days before Christ rose from the dead . . .

I said, "Madeleine, how do you know this shit?"

"Well," she said thoughtfully, "I picked up a lot of it when I lived in Montana." She looked ahead for a while, then she added, "I learned about a lot of things from my church."

"Your church?" I said, and I remembered Mary hanging on her bedroom wall in Newark, up by the green goddesses, but I didn't think the Catholic Church taught what Madeleine knew.

"Yeah, well, some people call it a cult but I prefer church." She reached between the seats to the food bag behind us and pulled out a handful of peanuts. "Cult just sounds so dangerous."

Good god, I thought. And then it hit me: Why had Madeleine gone west in the first place? What had made her give up every known thing in her life for Montana, sight unseen? I had always thought it was to go to college, but why go to college there? Madeleine had joined a cult. Wow. Was there anything this woman had not done? And why did I feel jealous? As in, gee whiz, I never got to join a cult; no one even asked me, and now, were there even any cults left anymore? Not the really good cults. Not any like the Hare Krishnas hopping around with tambourines.

"I always thought I'd join a cult, but I never found one," I said.

"Well, it helps if they find you," she answered, and I fell silent. What if I was heading west with Madeleine to be inducted into the cult? Maybe our whole friendship had been an elaborate recruiting mission (like the time another friend tried to get me into Amway). She had been working me all this time because she had to meet her quota back east, she couldn't go back to her home in Montana until she got someone to go with her and join up. Wow. And the craziest part was, I kind of felt alright with that. I had this enormous desire to find a new life, to be selected by Madeleine for something better than what I already had, and maybe that meant something I had not thought of. Anyhow, I would have probably followed her anywhere, then.

She said, "When I was in Montana, everything just made sense to me. Maybe that will happen to you. Maybe you'll find yourself there."

I said, "I guess," but it bothered me that she seemed to think I needed finding. I thought I'd managed to hide that, by being quiet. I wanted just to seem world-weary, seeking a long-lost better life. But she knew there was more to it than that, and by knowing, it seemed her power grew. I was the lamb she was leading to something, to slaughter, to a spot inside the mountain of utopia, to a cult initiation ritual, to madness or freedom or just anything. I was the lamb. I made myself good and quiet for most of the rest of our ride.

The first sign I saw that said "Rapelje" on it was in a small town, Columbus, at an intersection not far off the big highway. We stopped at a gas station where we bought eight gallons of gas and two six-packs of Rainier beer for the cooler, a few postcards of mountains and flowers and some photographs of men and women from the old days, with their blank faces and long-dead eyes.

The Rapelje sign was stuck into the dirt on the side of the road as if it were no big deal, just some town. The arrow pointed north, so we drove that way, past blocks of cracked sidewalks and old houses with old cars and pickup trucks in their drives. Then the narrow road turned rough. The pavement faded into a dirt-and-gravel line scrawled out thin in front of us. There were no cars anywhere, and I could see a long way because the ground was so flat it almost disappeared. Houses drew farther back and blended into folds of grass until they were gone altogether. I could not recall ever having gone ten miles up a road without seeing any passing thing, not a car, not a person, not even a cow. It seemed as if it couldn't be right. There was nothing. The road dipped and rose. Northern Stillwater County: blank flat land, then five mountain ranges rising like a ring of blue shark's teeth at the edge of the world, as far away as eyes could see.

It was late in the afternoon on our third or fourth day of driving. A few miles up that gravel road we opened the cooler and brought out two cans of beer; it was cold and thin and drinking it in the car suited the lawlessness that had come over us. We turned up the music and rolled down the windows, did all these things in place of worrying that perhaps we had made a wrong turn, that perhaps there was no Rapelje after all, and the whole trip would turn out to be a big mistake. Where could it be? We rode for thirty miles of what seemed like forever.

"Geez," she said. "It's been a while since I've been out wandering in Montana. And you know what? It doesn't change."

"This is really nowhere," I said.

"Well," she told me, "it's Montana."

When the town finally appeared, it came as a spot spread on the horizon, a haze with a silo at the far end of the road.

"That must be it," I said.

We pulled over to look upon Rapelje. The wind continued even when the car stopped, but no other sound rose. A silo floated in the yellow space ahead, surrounded by unbroken grassland. There it was, a colorless Oz. And there I was, in a blankness for which I'd come searching, resting my eyes upon the mystery.

It seemed as if I could blink and be back in New Jersey, asking my father about this unreal place, or sitting in the air-conditioned sports bar with three TVs, just laughing about it over a beer while Madeleine and I sounded out the crazy name: Rapelje. No one ever comes here, I thought, yet there it was; there it had been all this time.

We drove closer. The haze cleared at last into small structures, old houses. The gravel scrawl became the main street of Rapelje, where a smaller road crossed it to mark the spot with an X. Our car was the only thing moving anywhere. I said, "Wow." We parked off to the side of the road, got out and looked around. Wind blew with nothing to stop it. There were a few, maybe eight, abandoned houses scattered about, made of white pine planks or shingles, with peeling green or black trim around the windows, and front porches broken down into dirt, empty of people, just a rubble of plaster and appliances piled inside the missing front doors. Even the houses that weren't falling down were empty. Farther away, casually mixed with these failed structures, stood a few more houses that looked newer, well-kept and painted, fences with gates at the edges of their yards. We walked toward them on the crossroad, looking for people.

Madeleine took out her camera and whispered, "This is wild." She had to whisper; we both did. The place didn't seem to want to be roused.

We walked. For a long time, nothing moved but us, The road was dotted with wooden carcasses, empty homes and shops in a cluster, trailing off into other structures in various stages of decay. It was evening, quiet anyway, but the place was thoroughly vacant; it was emptier, it seemed to me, for having been something once. I could feel everything that was missing, but I could only see what was there. Fifty yards away, a man emerged from a garage with a horse and walked the horse across the road. Both man and horse disappeared into a horse trailer and Rapelje was still again.

"This," I said slowly, "is wild."

Madeleine kept taking pictures. "Wild," she said.

Then I decided I wanted to be a squatter. I passed the broken buildings and I decided I wanted to live in one. It would have been all right to do that; no one would have cared, the original owners of the old homes were long gone, their property of little value and forgotten, probably the taxes unpaid for years, and the bill probably not much anyway. So it was still possible to be a homesteader, after all. Pay off the taxes and take some place over, and the rest of your life is all up to you. Wouldn't need much money. I stuck a piece of grass between my teeth and said to Madeleine, "I think I'm going to just stay here, live in that old house over there, fix it up, and write."

"Too expensive," she answered. "Think of all the money for repairs, see that floor? Rotten. The electric hook up would need to be redone completely. Probably dry rot everywhere. And there's probably skunks," she said. "I wouldn't try it."

"Hmm," I said, because really, what else could I say. Was there anything Madeleine didn't take seriously? Good god, most of my life was pure fantasy. I just wanted to live with this idea, at least for the day. Here was what remained of the world my own family had been born out of, so remote from any life I had ever known. We walked up the road past a mobile home on cinder blocks set on a little square lawn, thick and tended, the only green grass in town. Then, not far back beyond the trailer, I saw an old rusted hand pump beside a cottonwood tree.

Shock, cold and visceral: Something I knew. Something of mine. I had seen the pump in pictures, and I knew it was the pump beside what had once been a shed, in which my aunt and uncles were sent to wait one September day about sixty-four years ago while my father was born in his mother's bed. It had to be my pump, I'd seen the cottonwood tree behind it, smaller but still there, in old photographs; the house and the shed had been right there, right there beside the pump on the ground where the ashes were scattered. The ashes: all around, in the dry grass, lay scattered scraps of burned wood, ground-down ashes, and nothing more. Madeleine took my picture. The house had been burned down. "It was here," I said, trying mightily to envision it, closing my eyes and wondering how it felt to be a house, right there, what it felt like to call that rectangle of land home, for twenty years. "The house was right here and it's gone," I said quietly. I kicked the ash-dark earth. It seemed wrong that the house could be gone, just simply not there, but it was true, and so I'd never get to see it, and the loss made too much sense in that place to be truly disappointing.

"Wild." Yeah.

Across the tall dry grass was the Rapelje school, empty for summer. Near where we left the car was a cafe. The sign in the window read, "Nope." We walked along till we came to a concrete vault, each side maybe eight feet, crumbling into a grass lot as if it had once been part of something. What thing? I stood in the vault, touched its cool walls. I closed my eyes and I felt certain my grandfather had been there, had locked away money in this safe concrete place, while my father kicked stones in the road outside the First National Bank, waiting to go home to dinner.

I told Madeleine, "This must have been part of the bank." She gripped a steel reinforcement rod protruding from the concrete. "It looks more like an old jail cell to me," she said. We stood there hushed, like Rapelje, wondering.

Turns out it was neither. We found someone to talk to, a blond and ruddy-faced woman who was uncapping beer bottles in a bar inside a Quonset hut right in the center of Rapelje, where the east-west and north-south roads met. I had come to notice Quonset huts in tiny towns all along our route, as if people weren't interested in actually building at the risk of losing anymore. Quonset huts, I supposed, could be dismantled and moved. This one, with a bar inside and a large open area that looked like the town meeting hall, echoed like a pail any time anything moved. We scraped stools up to the bar and ordered two Rainiers and asked some questions about the town, about that old concrete thing, for instance: was it from a bank, or a jail? The woman at the bar squinted and said there wasn't any jail, never had been. Another man sat there, ignoring us, which seemed crazy to me, in a place so small. It was not as if this bar was in a place where anyone might stop, normally; it was not as if they ever saw anyone beside themselves or that they could possibly be sick and tired of people coming around to ask questions about Rapelje. Maybe people in very small towns just don't like strangers. But I was not a stranger; my family made this place.

My father told me to look for a bar in town with old-time signs in it, including one with the family name painted on it. It could not possibly have been this bar; he had described an old place. I asked the woman behind the counter about the old saloon I'd heard of in town and she said, "Oh, fire got it. About two years ago."

She told me she couldn't remember what that concrete vault had been, or when it landed there on the side of the road like it had, though she smiled at me and stopped wiping glasses for a moment, long enough to register just how curious I really was about this place, to be asking about some old hunk of concrete that who knew where it came from and really, who cared? She put her towel down and stood in front of me, which was as clear an invitation to talk as I was going to get.

I told her my name and she knew it: oh sure, she said, we just burned up your family's old house. Skunk nest, she said. Real nuisance. It was one of a half dozen abandoned buildings torched by the Rapelje Beautification Committee. It was a shame about the house, she told me, because it had such a nice fireplace, made of stones. People still talked about how Florence Soderlind had chosen the stones for that fireplace. People still talked about Florence; people remembered her there, how she was so lively and bright, and how she had died so young, not even sixty. This was 1989, and she was dead thirty-five years already.

My grandfather's bank, on the other hand, was still around, if indeed the bank I was looking for was the building the bartender had in mind. A historic building had been sitting in the middle of town empty for decades, and the Beautification Committee had moved it with a trailer out to the edge of town. Well, maybe that was the right bank, the bartender said, but she wasn't really sure. She started wiping glasses again. She lived in Rapelje, and I watched her with curiosity. She stacked glasses in a plastic crate behind the counter, ignoring us again.

We finished our beers and drove out to the deep weeds full of crickets by the old train tracks that had lain silent for more than fifteen years, ever since the spur line from Billings had closed. Past the tracks, I saw it: an old building with a high front, all the glass gone from its windows. The floor had started to cave in. I could see the boards hanging beneath it and the walls sloping to the middle. The false-front wood was so weathered that the paint had faded, it was all but gone. I could barely read the words: First National Bank.

Madeleine said, "Is that it?"

"That must be." We parked and walked toward the building.

"Go in," she said. "Have a moment. I'll be right back." Then she jogged off across the deep grass that grew unchallenged in fields between the old tracks and the grain elevators in the long distance. She was heading for the elevators, which were as still as the bank, and probably as empty; trains didn't pull up there anymore, but trucks did, so there was equipment hooked up to the side of the one still-working elevator, but nothing was running just then. It was evening. The last of the sun lit the tips of the brown grass yellow. Madeleine ran and dipped out of sight for a while but then I saw her head pop up from the grass folds and disappear again as the ground rose and fell.

I stepped up to the empty bank alone and watched her from the porch for a while. Then finally I stepped over dirt and broken boards through the door of the First National. I stood in the littered center of the old room thinking, "He worked here, he worked here, he worked here." I could see that someone had worked there; business papers were strewn across the floor, but now the place was just quiet and old and finished. Some of the papers on the floor had dates from the 1950s. It was an interesting old building, but it had existed without William Soderlind for a long time. It could not tell me why or how to care about him.

I thought, this is what he came here for. He stood in this room every day for years. Here. I kept saying things like this, as if a vision would come of it. I walked back to the window. Madeleine's face popped up from the grass again; she was jogging back toward the bank. I hoisted myself up to sit on the old teller's counter and waited for her. The wooden sidewalk still attached to the building creaked beneath her sneakers. She walked slowly into the bank and took in deep the smell of rotten boards and moved across the plank floor so that the scuffle of her shoes echoed. She took my picture while I sat on the counter, then while I stood in the windows, and then while I posed in the open door. The abandoned building was profoundly empty, like something someone had lost, and I felt as if I wanted something better for it, but it was too late.

Madeleine picked up a hunk of metal and with an inspired burst started to pry the rusted knob and plate from the front door. It was the only thing still unscavenged worth taking but it was so rusted that to get it off she had to slam it with a broken two by four, again and again until it finally came and she grabbed it and danced and her hair swung around. She said, "Your grandfather touched this" and gave it to me. "Keep it."

I said, "Wow." After we walked back to the car, I put it on the dashboard, like a plastic Jesus.

It was 8:30 and slowly getting dark. Even as the sky drew down, no lights came on; the shells of houses began to fade away and there were no street lamps at all. We were being swallowed in the night; we would be lost if we stayed. So we left. I looked around one last time, then got into the car, drove slowly back through that main intersection, and steered onto the gravel line south, a bit reluctantly, as if the evening had squeezed us out of town. But there was nothing more to see and so we left, just like that; that was Rapelje, there for an instant and then, gone again.

The road seemed shorter than before as we drove into Columbus, drinking two more cans of beer, then four, and folks on their front porches waved as we traveled and we smoked some more and drank another beer and passed without comment the wooden crosses stuck into the side of the winding road that marked all the places where the wild drunken drivers of Montana had crashed, and died, and we wound up, at last, in Fishtail, where my father's brother Paul and his family still lived and where Madeleine and I finally stopped for the night: our first night in Montana.

My aunt was expecting us; she had made dinner three hours before we pulled up the hill to her log cabin and parked. It was 9:30. She was keeping the casserole warm when we arrived, six Rainier beers out of Rapelje, waving our doorknob overhead and laughing and encouraging her to be thrilled about this treasure, too. She said, "Neat," but we might not have done a good enough job of explaining what an important artifact it was. She examined the rusted object through half glasses perched on the end of her nose. My Aunt Jean has loose white hair and shy features, bashful darting eyes, both friendly and distant, depending; I had only met her once before and so it was hard to know how to read her.

In the back of the long open space in her log cabin was a sort of ranch kitchen big enough for cowboy appetites, large iron pots hanging all around a six burner stove. Madeleine ran her hand over the many knobs of the stove and said, "This is what I call a kitchen." And I thought it would be the sort of kitchen Madeleine and I would have one day when we shared a home, and then I realized what I was thinking and it scared me. Then I thought about it some more.

"Gee," said my aunt, as she set the table, "it's been so many years since we went to see Rapelje. Of course, there's really nothing there."

With awe and wonder I gushed: "I know."

Fishtail is forty miles south of Rapelje on the edge of the Beartooth mountain range. I felt with sudden clarity that we had made a bad impression on my aunt and I started up a new round of beery apologies but she said, "It's okay, it's okay." All the relatives of my parents' generation conduct their lives with specificity and order, I knew this, and I knew she had expected us at dinner time. That was a literal hour, the time of dinner, which was at about six o'clock. Dinner had been warmed over and over by now. She put croissants into a basket, saying she had baked them herself and that they were better when they were eaten hot. She said she just loves croissants and she really really loves hot croissants and then she set the cold croissants on the table and said, you girls help yourselves.

My aunt called two of my cousins who lived across the road and told them I'd arrived, if they cared to come see me. A third cousin lived off in another corner of the state and I would probably not get to see him at all. My uncle was in Billings on business so I'd missed him too. But my cousin Bill arrived at the house pretty quickly, with his girlfriend Laurel. They shook my hand, firm and hardy, and they sat at the table and watched Madeleine and me eat. Aunt Jean dished out casserole and fresh corn and asked Bill and Laurel, "Do you want some?" but they said no; they'd eaten hours earlier.

Laurel, my aunt told me, was getting straight A's as a math major in college, in Bozeman, where she had just started after a few years working in a belt buckle factory outside Fishtail. Laurel had straight flat hair and eyes slightly close together over her wide nose. She smiled at me, exposing wide teeth, very strong features, very ranchy. I thought, when I live in Montana, ranchy sturdy Laurel will be my friend. Bill and Laurel lived in Fishtail in a little double-wide trailer they'd set up in the field across the road from my aunt's house. Bill worked at the Chevron mine down the road. He told me as I ate that he had come to live in Fishtail after years of wandering. When he was younger he took off to go try something different. He'd worked for geologists, searching for oil all over the country. Now he was looking for platinum. It was a goddamn miserable job, he said.

"Have some more of these yummy crescent rolls." Bill passed the basket over. "Mom loves making crescents, she'd live off 'em if she could." His blue eyes conspired with me over the importance to his mother of the evening meal and its rituals, and this made it clear that he understood my predicament, and we were friends.

I said, "So, cousin, I hear you've done some interesting things." I could really only remember that he had been what my mother had called a problem child, which was in fact interesting.

"Oh, heck, I don't know," Bill said, "let's see." He smiled and rubbed his mustache. His was the sort of long mustache that probably hung with ice in the winter if he stood outside in the bitter mountain air too long, breathing through his nose, calling the dog in from the sheep pasture or something. Bill was six years older than me. He had wide-open blue eyes and a thin, red, whisker-spotted face and he had a deep voice that said things like, "that old geezer's got a hitch in his gitalong," instead of "the old man limps," but he could turn that off any time, I knew, because he looked right at me hard sometimes like any minute either one of us was going to burst out laughing at all this bullshit. He was leathery like a Western Art greeting card but really, he could stop that any time, too, if he wanted.

He'd dropped out of college, he said; he'd been arrested down in Red Lodge for fighting in bars—the kind of fights where stools get broken over heads: you know, late nights in the long winters and some guy looks at you just so and that grizzly bear inside comes knockin' on yer inards and you just haul off. He told me about waking up with blurred vision and a bloody head in some stinking jail cell where the other drunks were still snoring. About a half hour into

the story Jean, who had seemed to shrink and then disappear altogether in her seat as Bill spoke, got up and started clearing the table.
All this running and fighting came to an end a good five or seven
years before we sat there talking. By now he had sworn off drink and
cut his hair redneck short, and I was about to find out how that happened but first he said, "Say, cousin, what do you think is worse,
them tree-huggers or them yuppies?" Them yuppies, he told me,
had even gotten to Montana. Everything was changing. He changed
too. He one day took a horse from his sister's barn and rode into the
hills for a few months to think things over.

I said, "Wow, you went up into the mountains on a horse, for
months, just to think things over?" And he lit a Winston and leaned
back and said, "You bet."

He had to figure something else out to do with his life or he
would just fight and drink until he died. So many men and women
had wandered through places like Red Lodge for the last 120 years to
fight and drink and then just die. So Bill rode into the Beartooth
Mountains and pitched a tent. He followed deer trails to find ponds,
and caught fish for dinner, and if he got too hungry or too lonely
he'd ride into Cooke City, a town full of cheap gift shops and coffee
shops and motels and bars, way up in the mountains near Yellowstone, a good place for a mountain man to get a shower and a beer.
He'd sit like an old cowboy on his vinyl covered stool in a lightless
bar in Cooke City and listen to the jukebox. Once, he left his money
on the counter and walked out into the blinking daylight and he
never walked back into a bar again. It just hit him that all those sons
of bitches were sitting there wasting time. It was time to start a life.
He was almost thirty then and he was done wasting time. He got
himself a haircut, rode back to his tent, noticed the days had started
getting short, and cold. He'd had enough time alone to know what
he needed, or at least, to know what he didn't need anymore.

Bill leaned back in his chair at the long pine supper table and folded his arms and looked at me.

The West made me feel as if it was okay to be fast friends with a person I liked, when I found one; maybe that was why Madeleine, who had lived in Montana for years, always seemed able to be friends with anyone. I smiled at Bill, and then I looked at Madeleine. She was leaning back in her chair with her arms folded and her legs bouncing restlessly, looking around the cabin walls, which were covered with photos and horseshoes and other western ephemera.

I turned back to Bill. He had lines in the sides of his eyes, like he'd been looking hard all his life. He had been into the wild places. He might even have been afraid of what he'd find if he went, but he went anyway.

I said, "What do you do now?"

"I work in the mine." He reached for a croissant and tore a piece off and chewed it. "Like every other son of a bitch from here to Absarokee, I work in the shit hole mine."

Then he said, "So, cousin, what do you do?"

"Well," I said, "not much. I quit my job."

Bill nodded gravely.

My cousin Robin arrived. Two children followed her. She stood all the way across the open living room at the front door and stomped mud or gravel off her feet. Robin was the middle cousin. She was forty, the cousin who I knew raised horses and really, really loved horses because every Christmas the family Christmas card contained pictures of Robin and her latest horse and my mother had showed me pictures, and said, "Isn't that neat?" and I had answered, "Why can't we have a horse?" prompting my mother to put the Christmas card away. Robin's two kids were in their pajamas and sneakers and she was in her horse clothes, Wrangler jeans, a plaid shirt and a rancher's hat; she loped tall in scuffed leather boots, her face saddle-colored, flat and squinting like the wind had followed her even into the room. She was it, a certain sort of real Montana, the kind you read about in western novels; she even had a knife strapped onto her belt. She and the kids grabbed croissants from the basket on the table and started eating them and she said, "It's past bedtime, gotta go, but you come back sometime, we'll ride." And thinking back on it, my heart swears that she tipped her hat and winked at me but in my head I'm sure she didn't.

Robin and my aunt went back over to the front door and started talking in loud whispers and deeply frustrated gestures, pointing at each other and the door and the children, who were chasing each other around the living room couch; I could see that the conversation had to do with Robin's children. Robin said, "Aw, come on Mom," and the answer was "No, not again, absolutely not."

Bill and Laurel didn't even turn their heads to see the commotion, Bill turned up his volume and soon I stopped hearing the furious whispers. He said, "What the heckerya gonna do with all your new freedom?"

"I dunno," I said. "I'd like to go live in the hills." I looked at Madeleine.

"Yep, you'd do well out there for a while, sure, it's a hell of a feeling out there with nothing but you and good God and Moses and his brothers and all those damn bunnies and bears."

Laurel rolled her eyes.

Madeleine said, "How far is the pass to Cooke City from here?" And she and Laurel started talking. Bill asked me some questions about newspapers, to which my answers, inspired by his, came out in such bursts as, "Oh, there's nothing like the news business, damn, it's like war: days of nothing and then bam, the enemy. It gets under your skin, it gets in your blood, newspaper ink and black coffee and adrenaline," and I probably started describing a long night spent watching an abandoned building burn down or some big chemical spill. I told him about chemicals draining into creeks through the sewers, and I added many flourishes about belly-up fish and corrupt politician scum and the way garbage piles up and landfills leech poison into the water and some days the air is so bad you can't even breathe. "Yep, lots of waste dumps in New Jersey," I probably said. "You got that right, yessir, a hell of a mess. But that's the news game for ya."

Madeleine cleared her throat and shifted in her chair.

And that's about when Bill said, "Lots of explosions up in that damn shit hole mine where I'm working now," and he started into details of worst accidents, explosions and body parts flying through the air, and I hung on every word of how he became a certified emergency medical technician so that he could learn to pull guys out of mine wrecks when they were screaming and losing their blood; until he'd learned to help them, the miners would get maimed or just bleed to death waiting on the Billings ambulance to come all those miles. Bill said that once he got trained he had to go out on calls any time the scanner screamed, not just at the mine but every time some local drunk had a car wreck going home at 105 miles an hour, and out on the Rez they don't even drink booze, hell, it's Aqua Velva or Draino or whatever pours, he said, and fast cars, fast women, fist fights, blood, that's what he was saying right about the time my aunt came back to the table and said something like, "You are going back to work tomorrow, aren't you?"

Then it was quiet.

And then some terse debate about too many sick days followed. Leave of absence. You'll get fired. Mind your business. Must work. Stop worry. I got up and had a long stretch and started walking around the room, looking at family pictures with everybody smiling and standing in front of my aunt's log cabin, Bill and Robin and their older brother Mark. They were all baby-faced in the early '60s when they were little kids. Robin on a horse jumping a hurdle at a rodeo. The photo must have been from about 1970; I wondered why it was that color film from the 1970s tended to fade into shades of orange and green. Behind me back at the table, Bill sounded like he was getting near the end of his patience and my aunt was too and there was worry about losing that job and good riddance if he did and it was escalating but finally he said, "I just came here to see my cousin. Hey cousin," he said. I turned around and smiled. "When you leaving?" In the morning, I answered. He said, "Aw shit, I didn't even get to know you yet."

I said, "Well, we have more people to see and loads of places all up and down that long highway where we need to go; we have to find whatever waits for us out there," and he nodded.

"Yup, alright you do what needs doing."

I said I'd come back someday, and he said, "You do that, any time," and Laurel smiled her big ranch smile and waved and they moseyed slouching out the door.

That's how it happened, and then the quiet followed: my aunt had a star-gazing telescope at her front window, and I noticed when I looked through that it was pointed down to Robin's house. Through the windows bodies moved, there were no drapes; two kids jumped on a bed with the TV on. I pointed the lens up and saw the stars: dense white crowds of stars that you couldn't see with just your eyes, because these stars were too far away. They were out there all the time, billions in heaven, and you wouldn't even know it. In New Jersey sometimes it seemed like there were only nine or ten.

"Wow," I said.

And my aunt had appeared beside me and she said yes, it's truly lovely, and it's so peaceful there at night with the stars, and a fire, and a book about the old west, or a foreign country, the things about which she preferred to read.

My aunt asked, "You girls mind sharing a bed? I've only got the one made up." I looked at Madeleine. My face flushed, but I thought no one could know that but me, and cool as anything I shrugged my shoulders to indicate that one bed was fine.

"I'll just take the couch," Madeleine said. She walked off to the couch with her by now well-worn edition of *Lonesome Dove,* and that was the end of the discussion.

Sun up at six and waking early to drink coffee in the dewy air. We went out to reorganize our gear in the car and move on. It was the first daylight look I'd had at the Beartooth Mountains: they shot out of a dead flat field beyond Robin's little cabin down the hill, gray granite rising from brown grass, and then they just piled up on each other and back and back and back into who knows where. "Wow," I gaped.

Madeleine set her coffee cup on the fender, bent to pour melted ice out of the cooler in the driveway, and said, "Have any good dreams last night?" which left me standing stupid. In fact, I had had a dream about her. I'd been holding that to myself, smugly, as if her presence in my dreams meant we'd slept together despite the fact she had made up a bed on the couch. In the dream we were in the car, stopped somewhere gray and dark and silent. She had told me she could read my mind. And she said she knew what I wanted. Something certain. Something real. And she put her pretty and terrifying face so very close to mine, until her lips almost brushed mine when she spoke, but then what she said was: "You can't have that dream. Not yet."

So instead I dreamed about me and her and some woods we were running through, getting chased by a huge cat with sharp teeth.

Now, in crisp daylight, she inquired about my dream and stood blowing on her coffee, waiting, holding her pretty and terrifying face over the coffee mug, tormenting me because she knew about my dream, she must have known, why else would she ask me? She could actually *read my mind.* I hurled deeper into the madness of my silence. It was no longer enough to be quiet; she could see through me and hear my thoughts—or at least, some of them. The ones I was hiding. I believed this for an instant, or a little longer, really, because at least it explained my growing attachment to her. She had invaded me. I tried to accept the disturbing notion as a good thing, really. After all, she had seen inside me but she hadn't screamed at me or anything. Maybe she was interested in my thoughts. Maybe I should think braver things, and test her. Maybe I should just get it all out there, just say, "Yo, Madeleine, why didn't you kiss me in that car?" Yeah, I could do that. My mouth formed the proper shape for the quasi-word "Yo." Nothing came out.

Madeleine gave up waiting for me and resumed her work reloading the car. I wandered around the driveway weirdly.

"I know what you're thinking," she finally said. Ah-ha, see? She did know.

"Okay then," I thought loudly. "Now we're getting somewhere." This mind-reading stuff was probably something they taught in cult school. Nothing shocked me. I thought this and looked at Madeleine with my new knowing look, the one that said I knew she knew and I knew, too, whatever that meant.

We both sat down on the front fender and lit cigarettes. "You can talk about what happened if you want."

What happened? In the dream? I thought, "God, Madeleine, do you think I can talk about this stuff? I don't." Then I got huffy and I thought at her, "Well, hell, who says it's any of your damn business anyhow, what goes on in my mind?" And I slurped coffee defiantly.

Dead bugs caked the grill of the car. Long days of traveling awaited. I said nothing out loud.

She said, "I know, I know. It's none of my damn business . . ."

I sat right up. "How do you do that?" I wondered at her.

"But, don't be sad," she said. "I mean, people have problems everywhere, even in Montana. People are people."

I leaned forward to rest on my knees, and looked hard at the gravel driveway, and thought loudly, "What do you mean, what do you mean, what do you mean."

"They're really pretty nice, you know?" And that seemed to be all she would say. I thought, "Are we having the same conversation?"

She added, "They mean well."

"They . . . what?" I finally said out loud. "They . . . Madeleine, what are you talking about?"

"I'm just saying, you know, that your cousins are nice people. Right?" she said. "People have problems wherever you go, and I'm sure they're very nice even if they've had tough lives. Sort of, well, messed up."

I stood up and kicked some gravel, and ran my hands through my hair. What the hell did she mean, my cousins were messed up? What happened to *us?* I turned to her with a pained look. And then she actually touched me. She squeezed my shoulder and shook it some. It gave me something else to think about.

"Oh, don't worry so much," she said, and walked over to put out her cigarette in the ashtray inside the car. Then she said, "You find your path to happiness, they'll find theirs. Believe it. Come on, I'm going to show you a few things."

I poured out the rest of my coffee and followed her silently. I was very confused, but that was not unusual. Soon, we were off again to find Montana.

Highways in the plains of Montana look like runways to the end of the world. Buttes and craters. Land laced with dinosaur bones.

I found a tumbleweed the summer I went west with Madeleine, I saw it on the highway. A *tumble*weed, imagine that; nothing tumbles in New Jersey but the garbage in the streets, newspapers, McDonald's cups, pink plastic spoons from Baskin Robbins scrape along, detritus of crowds rolling in the foreground of Manhattan skyscrapers.

But there it was, in Montana: a lone tumbleweed urged on by the wind down the vacant runway of the plains, grudgingly, like a puppy walked too long.

My own tumbleweed: I would keep it in my yard, at home, if I ever went home, and I would have it for a pet. On bad days I could look outside and watch this evidence roll around between the fences, and then I would remember how it felt to be in a different place, un-written on, and to be happy, seeing myself as a tumblin' tumbleweed and my life as an adventure in a world of endless possibility.

Leaving Fishtail, we drove up the switchbacks out of Red Lodge that lead dizzily up to the Beartooth pass. We pulled over to stand in summer snow above the tree line, near the clouds, up as high as the earth grows, where the rocks look like the moon. Standing at the crest so far above every ordinary thing, all the stuff below is gone— the commerce, shops, signs, sales, houses—all of it gone without being missed on the windy peak, where it was chilly that day and smelled of cold pine.

We made our way down the other side of the pass, back to the busy earth and a corner of Wyoming and Yellowstone National Park that exists every day without me, there, beneath that lonesome peak; in those lower rings we slipped into clotted traffic, among the hordes that had come to see the West and jammed up around the sight of animals. We stopped with the other cars to see a moose standing in the weeds, eating leaves, and we cheered for it because it was beauti-ful and peaceful and there. Then we got back in the car and kept going, left the watchers on the sidelines, drove off on a little blue vein of highway into Paradise Valley, which is where on impulse I pulled over to pick up that tumbleweed and threw it in the back with our gear. That day, after five or six days driving that seemed like so many more, we arrived at last in the place where part of Madeleine's heart had stayed behind, years before: in the big, free spaces where her friends were like a family—the people she loved but couldn't stay with forever because like she said sometimes, you can't always live with everyone you love, just because you love them.

The first member of her Montana family that I met was a woman named Velma. It took many turns off many roads to reach her. We found her sitting on the step outside a shed that was her workshop, weaving a wreath of dried flowers from her garden. When she saw us, she rose from her weaving and brushed dry petals from her lap. She was a thin woman in a yellow cotton tank top and baggy cut-off shorts so big that I think they must have been her husband's. When she saw us she smiled wide above her square chin and pushed back rambunctious pieces of the red-blond hair that hung akimbo from her bun. She ran to meet us across the dead grass. A big black dog followed. Velma had varicose veins on her pale legs in the pattern of wild violets, and she held out long freckled arms to Madeleine, who fell into them, and they rocked with hugs and laughter. The black dog raised his nose toward the two hugging friends and sniffed, then padded over to get a better sniff of me, then turned his head to sniff the air around us. I stood with him a while and sniffed too as the re-union bubbled on. It showed no sign of slowing. I turned away and wandered a few steps over to Velma's little workshop. Through the open door I saw a confetti of dried flowers spread on a table and hanging from the rafters, on the walls, sage and yarrow and mari-golds, roses and lavender in bunches, blue bells. There were wire cutters on the table and a little stone pipe in which to smoke dried marijuana leaves, and there were some of those there, too, in a small bag. I saw it there like a signal that I'd come to one of the far off law-less places, a zone of unconcern, much different from a visit with an aunt. I adjusted the tension in my posture, shoved my hands in my pockets and summoned my sense of mellow detachment, a mari-juana posture. Like, you know. It's cool. I wandered back around to find Velma and Madeleine, who had started walking toward the car. I followed with pronounced unconcern. We arrived at the fender with the dog hovering nearby and those two standing there still hanging on to each other, bubbling.

"Oh, we stopped in Rapelje and spent last night in Fishtail."

"Fishtail! You know you're in Montana with a name like Fishtail."

"Oh, I know it."

"You girls mind tenting in the yard while you're here? The house is so small, I think you would be happier."

"Hey," I said, slouching hard on tipped hips. "No problem." I nodded my head for a while, but they were talking and not looking at me so I got to work pulling dusty backpacks from the car. The tent was buried under our gear, and as I tugged it up, my tumbleweed fell out to the ground.

"What's that?" asked Velma.

"Tumbleweed. See?" I said, presenting it to her.

"That's a stick," she said.

"My tumbleweed?"

"Your big stick. With little branches," she said, and touched one of its skinny points, and shrugged and turned back to giggle in the direction of Madeleine, who was digging her toe into the dirt and twirling a small tight braid into her hair and smiling wide enough to reveal all of her intriguing gray teeth. Madeleine looked at the tumbleweed and then smiled strangely to Velma, looking bewildered, as if she too knew better, as if she had not been right there with me when the car stopped and the tumbleweed got in. As if we weren't on this whole crazy ride together.

Well: tumbleweed, stick. No matter; I returned it to the car and shut the hatch. Then I started playing with the mildly interested dog again until Velma and Madeleine turned to walk away, and I followed.

We carried our bags from the car and dropped them in the yard where we would pitch our blue dome tent so that we could stay a few days with Velma and her husband, Joel. The tent would be a monument to our wandering souls, two women on the road together, sleeping wherever their tent hit the ground, sunburned and barefoot and carefree, and maybe we would sit outside that tent and smoke some of that marijuana from the workshop, or who knew, maybe this isolated spot would be a psychedelic retreat out beyond the barriers of behavior and well-traveled roads, maybe Velma would produce a sheet of LSD from underneath her flower petals and we would trip in this pleasant valley for days and days and emerge changed, having received a shared vision to never leave this place, to stay and dream previously unknowable dreams. I dropped the bag of tent poles and examined the yard, studied the earth in anticipation of its change. I was ready for my world to change, forever; it was just a matter of time.

We went to work. Our tent would be a masterpiece of car-camping comfort, a Madeleine delight of elegantly piled blankets to keep the ground chill away from us, followed by foam mattress pads, and then sleeping bags laid out in two long, separate lines. I watched as it came together and I passed gear through the flaps to her on command. For the finishing touch, Madeleine called out through the unzipped mosquito netting for our packs, which later I would find she had piled up between the two sleeping bags like a little wall. And then, later, when I poked my head in to see what she had done, she would explain to me that, piled this way, all our stuff would stay dry. This wall, I would discover, was rather substantial. I would see this and ask her, "Why don't we just keep our stuff in the car?" And after thinking about it for a minute as she appeared to be concentrating very hard on her wall project, she would tell me, "We might need something." And she would look up and smile. Two back-packs, two camera bags, and a pile of books would stand between the two separate spots in which we would sleep. That would be the end of the discussion.

But this was yet to come; for the moment our tent life was a pile under construction on the yellow grass, just nylon flaps and folded blankets and cases filled with who knew what, on their way to becoming whatever we would make of them. When it was mostly done we quit working to walk around and talk with Velma.

Velma said she and Joel had once lived in a platform tent with nothing but a bed and a stove and the crickets singing all night and the stars or sometimes rain above them. They lived like that while they hunted pieces of the house they would build, doors and windows and parts found in warehouses and wrecks and dumpsters, enough parts at last to build their home and move the bed and the stove in before winter. It grew out of nothing: a sloping cedar structure with windows all around, dried flowers and weavings hanging inside and out, all the walls and high ceilings shaped by items they had made or found. Building that home in that notch of Paradise Valley had laid a foundation for their life together and now all else mattered only in relation to it. I could feel this and I craved something like it for myself. It was good there; they had made a good life. The fleeting sense of this good life around me but just outside my grasp reminded me of something; it was like slipping into a beautiful coat, then finding by surprise in the mirror a person of great substance whom you had always secretly known yourself to be. There she is, my higher self, my could-be me. Usually, I could not afford the coats that made me feel this way and had to leave them on the rack. Upstairs in Velma and Joel's house, a claw-footed tub sat in front of a window full of mountains and beside the tub room was just one other room, and in that one room were only lace curtains and a painted bureau and a waterbed. That's all. No piles of clothes, no piles of papers and half-written letters and *TV Guides* and well-read books. No carpet. No posters or mirrors. Just this simple room in a house like the cabins homesteaders made, only bigger, and brighter, with heat and plumbing and electricity. Through the bedroom window, I watched horses run at the velvet toes of mountains.

Downstairs Joel piled wood beside the stove even though it was summer because it would get cold at night. He stopped his wood piling to hug Madeleine when we came down the stairs and he shook my hand, his hand maybe twice or three times the size of mine; a real hand, his was, and I stared at it a moment before Velma said "come on," and led us into the greenhouse. They'd built a greenhouse on their eastern wall, so that when the morning sun was strongest at that dry, high altitude, it would hit the plants just so and when she was lucky, Velma could grow red tomatoes. They had managed to get red tomatoes two years in a row now, and life was good.

"We love this valley," she said. "It's so full of peace."

I wondered why it was such a suspicious noun, peace. It's stronger to say "peaceful." Peace itself as a word, as a goal, did not fit our time; too weak. And why, then, did it feel to me like this house in this valley with Velma and Joel was the last place on earth where "peace" was still in standard usage? We were so far away, there.

"You've never seen these, Maddy," Velma said, flopping down onto the sofa with a photo album in her lap. We took up sides around her and looked down: Velma's wedding pictures. Things had changed since Madeleine left Montana. She had not been to the weddings of her old friends; New Jersey was too far from this orbit. In the pictures, Velma and Joel were wearing fine clothes out by the greenhouse, next to a big barbecue in the yard; Joel had a tie on, and Velma had strung dried flowers through her hair. She wore pearls. I liked the pearls. They caught you off guard, just in case you thought for any reason that she was getting married in her yard just because no other location would have her. Wrong. There was Velma in pearls, staring ahead expectantly, ready to walk right over and marry Joel, who was standing, in the second picture, next to the woodshed. She looked as if she could have been in the garden of a country club back in Short Hills, only she was in Montana in an ivory dress, barefoot, getting married in the field next to the house she had built, and she was laughing.

"Oh, how pretty," said Madeleine, "a wedding outside."

Velma answered, "We wanted it to be fun, and anyhow the nearest church is that crazy one up on the hill so we just had our wedding in the yard." She let out a wailing little sound, "Hooo!" like a bird call.

"God, Madeleine," Velma sat up. "Do you know Bozeman is full of those people now."

Madeleine, shuffling slowly through photographs, said, "I guess they're still doing pretty well then."

"What people?" I said.

"The Church Universal and Triumphant," Velma said. "Cult people live right in this valley."

I looked at Madeleine. She winked a twitchy little wink at me.

"They've got guns up there, a frickin' arsenal, god knows what they plan to shoot with them," Velma was saying. "Did you hear, Maddy? That's what 'the family' is up to now."

"The family?" I asked.

"That's what they call themselves," Velma explained. "The family." She nearly spat the words.

Velma gathered up the stray photographs and stuck them back into her album, then shut it. She let out a hoot as she did this, perhaps for the prospect of the Armageddon she was just then imagining.

Madeleine, twirling a piece of her hair thoughtfully, looked at me and raised her eyebrows and pressed her lips as if to say, "Oh well, what can you do." And I realized we were all keeping secrets. For a moment when Madeleine's brown-green eyes fixed on mine I saw her in our old newsroom, like she was winking at me across the desk just to say hello when everything was too hectic to stop and talk but she wanted me to know that she could see me. And then there we were in Montana together, me having quit my job and brought my savings and credit cards and fantasies all the way west and ready to stay forever with her there. Maybe I was going to join a cult, even. Who knew? Who cared? As long as I did something interesting with my life, I figured.

"Do you know what they're doing with that land?" Velma asked.

"I heard they're building a bomb shelter," Madeleine answered, taking peanuts from the can Joel had set before us as he passed on his way to some other cranny of the household.

"That's right, digging a hole in the ground and filling it with weapons and breaking every zoning law in the state in the process with their plumbing and who knows what."

"The state doesn't have zoning laws," Madeleine said.

"Well they should get some," Velma snapped.

"Not on our land though," Joel called from somewhere.

"Selectively," cried Velma, and then we all laughed, and the subject changed to a guy they had known in college who was a political lobbyist in Helena now, fighting to stop a concrete company from taking advantage of Montana's friendly lack of zoning laws to build a toxin-spewing plant.

"You girls hungry? I've got some elk in the fridge," Velma said, incredibly, "but that was sort of going to be dinner."

I adjusted my posture to a nature-loving rugged back-to-the-lander slouch and said: "Geez. Elk for dinner, again?"

We sat on the sofa with coffee and homemade bread and hunks of cheddar cheese and watched a videotape of the Yellowstone forest fires, which had devoured much of the park just two summers before. "Sometimes I really miss cable TV," Velma was saying, "but at least we have a VCR. I have to drive all the way to west Yellowstone to rent movies, but at least there's that." As she put in the tape she told us, "Me and Joe like to open up the sofa, watch a movie, hit pause, make love, watch another movie, hit pause . . ." Madeleine smiled, and leaned out from the couch so she could catch a look across the house at Joel, who sat by the greenhouse reading. He looked up at her like he knew he'd been talked about, but wasn't sure what had been said. Madeleine issued a short dirty laugh, "Hemn hmm hmm," and said, "no place like a couch on a Sunday afternoon," and Joel returned blushing to his book. What privacy they had in this space! I started thinking about how you could be naked in Velma and Joel's house all the time and the world would never know; I thought maybe the only reason they were wearing clothes right then was because we were there, and clothes are for company, but usually you could be naked in that place and do your gardening and make love on the couch every afternoon, because the world beyond this place almost did not exist, and no one was ever going to come look into those big windows or knock on that screen door, and even if someone did, would it matter? Who cares? That was freedom. That was pure. I resented my clothing, my orange T-shirt and my striped shorts that buttoned too tight. I had spent a lot of time putting that outfit together, and for what? Maybe later I'd take my clothes off, what the hell, it's paradise.

The videotape began, and we watched dramatic orange flames surging to classical music and lapping up half of Yellowstone: devastation, charred wood, walls of fire high as steeples and elk and deer running running running through the woods in panic. We drank coffee and watched videotapes of the fire for the rest of that day and for dinner we made burritos from a pot of stewed elk meat. Smells of spice and meat quickly filled the house like they belonged there seasoning the cedar walls.

We would go dancing after dinner, "just the girls," Velma said, and she patted Joel on his elk-filled stomach and kissed his red hairy cheek. He said, "Don't do anything I wouldn't do," in a slow, deep voice and he smiled at Velma, his blue eyes and long dimples as thick and as deep as his voice and his hands and everything about him. We were going out dancing at a bar in West Yellowstone called the Blue Goose, where a band called Paradise was playing just like it did most every night. Velma and some friends of hers who worked the gates of Yellowstone taking entrance fees went dancing at the Blue Goose on Fridays, and so did the gold miners who had spent the entire long day in dark holes in the sides of rich mountains nearby; they all came out and piled into the Blue Goose after work to spend their paychecks, and they were glad that their town had such a hot spot because most Montana towns just had plain bars.

That evening, Madeleine and Velma embarked on an ecstatic ritual of preparation, making themselves drop dead gorgeous for the big night out. Velma searched through Madeleine's ample makeup case, a vinyl accordion-like thing that was produced on special occasions. The case contained treasures for Velma, cosmetic adornments she didn't normally wear in the country, out in the place removed from all the real and formal places, where I seemed to find little call for wearing anything at all but where she apparently missed the structure sometimes. We were fifty miles from a beauty parlor, ten miles from the nearest general store in Glastonbury, Montana, which is the Church's town so Velma ignored it, unless she was desperate for something. She had few things.

"Gonna paint your face, girl?" Velma asked me as she and Madeleine prepared to begin their ordeal, unzipping vinyl bags of makeup. I plowed through my backpack looking for matches, knowing that the safest place for me was outside, smoking.

Madeleine said, "This isn't her thing," tipping her head toward me. Velma smiled at me and said, "Alrightee."

Not making myself up made me feel slightly childish. To excuse oneself from such ritual seemed to make a woman just that much less a real woman, somehow, no matter how firmly one rejected the concept on rational grounds. My refusal to make up my face was usually spoken in terms of, "Don't believe in it. Never touch the stuff." But really, I looked like a sloppy drag queen in even the most careful makeup job: polish on my nails made my hands look like awkward meat slabs, and a coat of makeup seemed to make my facial hair sprout more distinctly, to turn me into a wax figure at Madame Tussaud's, something so obviously just pretending to be real. I despised pretending, and I despised the whole general notion of what being real looked like; trying to do this was far worse than quietly stepping outside, where I felt safe. Pretending meant telling lies actively about myself and I preferred passive lies.

Meanwhile Velma and Madeleine were twisting up lipsticks like candy and tasting various shades. They put their hair in knots and tried on big red lips and cobalt eyelids and long lashes, and started painting their as-if-by-magic long and perfectly shaped nails, and became beautiful in that deliberate and disturbing way that to me conjures up glamour girls from the early '60s, the stylish set, untouchable by anyone unless maybe you were Dean Martin. Long eyelashes batting innocence off these high-heeled, bee-hived, sexy women, not girls, some unfathomable species coaxed to the surface with little pancake sponges. Madeleine turned and looked at me, and her deep red lips smiled when she saw my expression and I shook my head and thought, "Wow, I better just get out of here."

I retrieved my favorite bright-yellow and pink Hawaiian shirt from my backpack and tried to stretch the wrinkles out; I put it on over a tank top, and went outside in the twilight to smoke as their glamorous transaction took place. I closed my eyes and saw those red lips and thought, "Oh god. Is that who she's hiding?"

Crickets in the dry grass. Stillness of late day drifting into night. Leaning my back on the pine door frame, I looked out: what mountains are those in front of me? The sun was setting behind them so that they were dark against the sky. I called to Velma as she passed by the screen door, "Hey, Velma. Are those the Absorkas?" It was about nine o'clock and the sky was light but already a lamp was on inside the house, the only lamp glowing in the valley, as far as I could see.

"Those?" Velma stepped through the door behind me. "Those are the Crazies." Her voice was high and gentle, but not fragile, and as she spoke she went to work fastening a chain of glass beads behind her neck; I felt I didn't know her well enough to help with it, as certainly a real friend would have; certainly any other woman would have, too, with the same ease Velma used to hold Madeleine's hand as she painted her fingernails. Velma's neck bent down swanlike and loose hairs fell around her face, and I wondered if I should help her but I just stood frozen and watched.

"Back in the homesteading days, some lady lived in those mountains with her husband and their kids and one winter, she went crazy and killed them all with an ax," Velma said, still fumbling with the clasp. "Crazy Lady. She wandered around there howling at night for years after that, but no one ever found her. Maybe that's just a story. The ax part is true." Velma stood a moment after her clasp was finally fastened. She looked at the mountains; I looked at her eyes, looking at the mountains. "Pretty, aren't they," she said.

"Incredible." There I went again, falling in love with everyone. I looked down.

"Yeah, we love those mountains."

Then she darted back inside and up the steps to the bedroom, and my cigarette was gone too, leaving just me and the view and the faint smell of a wood fire in the stove. After a little while, I heard Velma and Madeleine inside laughing against the spreading twilight. Whatever had been said or done was so funny that even Joel joined in, a baritone and an alto and a soprano above me, bursting out against the quiet world, spreading, then silent again.

Madeleine and I were standing in a river, trout fishing. She showed me how to send my bait drifting toward the hidden places where the trout like to float. We stood knee-deep in a wide bend of a stream rushing with mountain rain, sun beating down on us. My head was dizzy with a Rocky Mountain hangover, acquired by drinking several shots of whiskey bought for me by a miner at the Blue Goose bar. Swells of nausea rose over unquenchable thirst. In between waves I stood in the river, imagining that my head was a thin egg, easy to crack.

Madeleine said, "When I'm standing in a river, I always think of a story I know about two Buddhist monks; maybe it's something you would like to hear."

She cast her line and I watched it fly past in the direction of a low branch over the water.

She said, "There were two monks on a journey to a holy place, and their vows forbid them from performing any work on the holy day, so as they traveled they could carry no baggage."

She paused, and the river rushed, and I asked quietly, "What kind of baggage would monks have?"

"Well, conveniently, these guys were monks so they didn't have any baggage but they weren't supposed to carry stuff or make a fire or do any work of any kind on this trip."

"Why were they allowed to walk?"

"Listen to the story. The monks carry no baggage. They come to a river, which they must swim across, because it's deep. And there is a woman standing there by the river who can't swim, see. And one monk picks her up, swims across the river with her on his back, sets her down, and the two monks walk away. And so they're walking. And the other monk waits for an explanation or an apology or something and they keep walking in silence. It gets thicker and harder to take, damn silence. Loud, screaming, bitchy, awful silence, see, and finally the one monk asks his friend, 'Why did you carry that woman? You broke your vow.' And the first monk says, 'My friend, why do you still carry this woman? I set her down on the riverbank.'"

Madeleine cast her line again when she finished the story. I thought, "Wow. How many things could I set down by the river-bank, and leave there?" My hangover? My friend? The bad stuff that had happened last night? The funny ideas I had for my life? What-ever you would call the thing that was bothering me.

The Blue Goose had been crowded already when we got there the night before, and Madeleine, Velma, and I ordered beers and drank them. Then they started dancing in the dark near the band in the back of the room. I was in Montana with these two beautiful friends and I wanted to dance, too, but it was possible that everyone would stare at me and laugh. The music was loud and fast and I really wanted to dance so bad. Finally I decided I would just close my eyes and forget all the other people and just do it: Ah. Dancing. Me. I was really in Montana now, boy.

I looked up and Velma and Madeleine were motioning to me that they'd had enough and that the two of them were going to sit down. And they walked off toward the bar together with their hair up and lips on, and left me there. I didn't know if I should leave with them or not. I felt like such a follower all the time. I decided to wait for the song to end, then head for the bar when I was good and ready. When I did, they were gone. I saw through the propped-open doors that they were outside leaning on a car in the orange neon glow of the Blue Goose sign, talking to some guy standing out on the sidewalk.

I ordered a beer and drank a long, hard gulp and felt the cool of it whirl up behind my eyes with a small ache, marking the spot where a big ache would hit in the morning. Then a man appeared before me and said, "Excuse me miss but would you like to dance?" And I looked up at him, standing there so polite and formal and waiting for me. "You bet," I finally told him, and shot a smile out the door, won-dering if Madeleine could see me. I took my beer and cigarette with me to the dance floor. Me, not even all dolled up, I was dancing.

The man was clearly a miner, pale and scrubbed clean. He had his hair combed back very carefully and his long mustache similarly trimmed; he wore tight white jeans and a tight red T-shirt, redder than his red-ringed eyes, opened wide, accustomed to seeing things in dark tunnels. We placed ourselves at the foot of the stage where Paradise played and we boogied down. That man was full of energy like he'd been on his back inside a mountain all day, which of course he had been, and now he was out and free and what the hell, so was I. We wiggled like maniacs.

He leaned down and said loudly just above my ear that he was a gold miner, and that he had come up from Alabama. Then he smiled at me shyly, just enough for me to see that he probably had all of his teeth, which sort of set him above some of his less well-kept buddies. A slower song started up right away and we stood awkward and looked at each other until he put his hands on my waist, like we were at a prom. I put my hands on his biceps, which were all I could reach in the direction of his shoulders, and we kept dancing and making conversation. He told me that he loved Montana; loved it more than anything, didn't ever want to leave. He said he liked to go hunting up in the mountains, slink through the hills, silent, walk for hours until he finds some mountain meadow way back where no one goes and then sit there, maybe on a rock, maybe underneath a tree, and wait and wait until sure enough, an elk comes along with her two baby elks and he lines her up in the sights of his rifle, a kill shot for sure, and he puts his finger on the trigger and watches, but then, he doesn't shoot. He leaves her with the calves in the meadow. He gives himself something better to take home. He waits there watching until he's seen enough of her to know that this moment in this meadow is real, and those animals will still be there when he goes home empty and happy.

After hearing that story I said, "Wow, that is so great," and I danced the slow dance with him, not quite myself, more like Mrs. Miner, like this could be my life, you know, I could just come here and marry this man and dance at the Blue Goose and do his laundry while he mined for gold, why not; and if I went and had his baby he would thank me for bringing him a miracle and making his life complete, and that was all he wanted and it was so fucking simple and I could have that, if I just up and decided to. I could have a little house like Joel and Velma's, couldn't I? Now I was pleased at all my options, how big the world had suddenly become for me, how I could do anything I wanted. And I was pleased by how easily I was making friends and having fun in Montana all by myself, and I hoped hard that my friends could see it through that door, that they knew that I was popular like I just knew all the half a million people in Montana already and I fit right in, I did, I belonged there.

The music picked up again. Me and my miner started hopping circles around each other and then one of his miner buddies came over carrying shots of whiskey for us and we swallowed them down. We did two shots of whiskey like that and I lit a cigarette and he said, "WOOOOOO HOO!" I laughed, and Paradise reeled off crazy scales and wicked drums, the whole band singing and smiling down at us from behind their dark glasses in the dark back room of that bar, small, and spinning, and the whiskey shots put a hot hand around my throat to mark another place where I'd feel awful later. Then before I knew it Madeleine was on the dance floor, right next to me, in that dynamic dim wooden box of music. I smiled at her, and kept dancing, perfect and complete now with her there, and I turned back toward my miner, who was dancing the dance of the aerobics studio, and I closed my eyes in the whirl of the perfect world. Madeleine tapped my shoulder. She called my name. She called again and said loud enough so that I could hear her above the raucous band: "Put out your cigarette."

"What?"

"Your cigarette. You're burning everyone." I looked at the butt, and at her. "Put it out." Then she went back to the bar.

111

I dropped the cigarette to the floor and stepped on it.

In the morning, we were fishing in the river and we stayed quiet for a long time until she told me a story about the Buddhist monks and I just wanted to vomit.

She said, "You were certainly dancing up a storm last night. Who was that guy?"

I stared at the water. After a while I told her he was a miner who had a sensitive soul and liked to sit by himself far off in the mountains and point his gun at the elk and her calves, but then, not shoot them. She listened to me as she let out her fishing line.

"Of course he didn't shoot them," she said. "That would be poaching. You need a special permit to take the cows."

The air smelled fresh from morning rain. The river smelled even more like water than it might usually smell, a metallic odor that made me feel ill. I bent down, peered at my watery eyes, my puffy ugly face. Stupid. I waded over to the rocks on the bank, sat down, hung my head in my hands and then finally reached into the river to scoop up the pristine passing water, hoping to cure my cotton mouth or at least to finally make myself sick and get it over with but just as I scooped up the water, Madeleine screamed "NO!"

Cheeks flush, puffing hard from wading fast across the knee-deep river to stop me, she put her face in my face. She said, "An animal might have died a mile upstream and that water could be swimming with bacteria. It'll kill you." It can all turn so ugly, so fast. The water streamed out of my hands.

I brushed some water to my brow and sat back with my egg head on the rocks, thinking about the possibilities of bacteria and death in the wilderness and things going wrong. It was a pristine day, in a pristine world, and it was all very fragile, all this goodness.

"Madeleine," I said at last, "if the water could be bad, are you sure it's safe to fish here?"

She smiled in the way that pushes her closed lips up into her left cheek, and she watched her line float downstream for awhile.

"We're not going to eat the fish," she eventually said.

The rush of that river made a soothing sound, and I closed my eyes and listened. When I opened my eyes she was still just fishing. She was clearly unmoved by my suffering. She didn't care at all about me, she created walls or gaps between us, depending, and left me suffering on the other side. In a moment of clarity, I despised her.

I picked up my pole and waded back into the water. I said, "I want to go camping." Silence. I knew I had stumped her. "I thought when we said we were going to camp in Montana it meant we'd really camp, not just go sleeping in your friend's yard. I want to camp. Tonight."

And she said, "Okay."

My bait floated downstream, out of sight.

"Are you angry about something?" she asked me.

"No," I said, "I'm not angry. I just want to go camping."

We fished some more.

"If you weren't so busy pretending like you were all alone on this trip," I told her, "you might have known I wanted to go camping. We would have talked about it if you had asked me but you never ask me anything."

"What are you talking about?"

"You know what I mean," I said.

Madeleine shook her head and pulled her line in. She turned to walk up close to me and waited for me to stop fishing and look up. When I did, I could tell it was going to be bad, whatever was coming. She said in a firm voice that I had never really heard before: "Listen." And she leaned in so that her face spoke into my face. I could see little dark mascara clumps from the night before clinging to her regular eyelashes. "Listen," she said. "You need to speak your mind. If you have something to say, say it." She waited. "I don't like playing mind-reading games. I really don't."

"Ha," I said in my mind. "You started it." She looked at me so hard I might have fallen in the river, fallen right down because the tension was overwhelming, and her anger was so intimate, it was sexy. She was angry at me for the first time since I'd known her and it sort of meant we'd grown closer. We were fighting. If I could have said anything, I would have asked why she acted like she didn't love me, but how could I ask such a thing? It had to be enough that she took me on this journey and was with me. Let that be enough, I pleaded with myself. I turned to face downstream with my back toward her, and tossed my fly. I was in danger of crying.

She said, "Do you have something to say?"

"No," I said.

A fish jumped.

Silence, but for the river.

After a while the sound of the river seemed to rush over everything. We kept fishing, even though we had failed to produce a single fish over a very long time. It was worse than silence; it was the oppressive weight of the unsaid. The weight of the woman I should put down and leave at the river.

I decided to do it: I decided to tell her everything, and for it to be okay. I know it had to be done eventually; it was beginning to get hard to hold all this in and at that moment I was suffering. I wanted to confess to end the torture. I began in a small way that I hoped would not offend Madeleine. "You know," I ventured, "I've always known that I was different, but, I was never really sure what that meant. I still don't really know what it means, but, maybe I'm starting to know. You know. I'm, different." My bait floated away, and then I reeled it back.

Madeleine said nothing.

My hand was actually shaking. It was twitching, even. At the end of my twitching hand the pole was twitching too, bent by a twitch-ing fish. "Whoops!" I yelled. "Whoops! Whoops! Whoops!"

The pole sprung up and down. There was a fish on that line I'd been throwing over and over into the river. Imagine that: a fish, jerking in wild spasms until I managed to reel the thing in and pull the mad creature from the water. And there it was: a five-inch baby trout, slick and brown, eluding my grasp with a ferocious display of baby-fish life.

I pulled it up from the water, laughing at my accomplishment, and as I began examining the deep set of my hook, beyond the mouth and in the throat, its unskilled positioning gave me a fast cold shot of dread but then Madeleine was there and she said, "Hey, there's a little fighter," and took the fish from my hand.

"Aw. He's just a tiny little thing," she said. She sized him up, looked in the throat. She handed the fish back to me.

"Good luck with the hook."

I stared at her. "You're not . . . I have to do it?"

"It's your fish." She stepped away.

I peered in through fish lips white and hard as the crescents of clipped fingernails. Small bubbles formed around the hook where it was set, wedged deep into the smooth pink of the baby trout's flesh. I tugged. The tiny bubbles turned red. The hook tore free and I let the fly dangle at my side. Then I looked the fish right in its little black eyes and told it to swim hard, to be very strong. It gasped at me. I let go. I watched the fish break the surface, sink bravely into the water and disappear for a while.

"You just keep throwing the little ones back," Madeleine called over to me. "Eventually, the big ones come."

The little fish resurfaced. It was not fighting so hard. There was a brief thrashing on top of the waves that carried it along. It rolled. Its tail flipped once. Then the fish turned belly up and floated down-stream, around the bend, and out of sight.

Not another fish came, and I forgot whatever I'd been saying to Madeleine. Soon, she reeled in her line and set the hook in the cork on her rod, then waded to the shore and put her gear away. I called to her, "You don't want to fish anymore?" and she called back over, "I'm done."

She climbed up the loose rocks to the top of the bank and in a few minutes I followed and found her sitting in the sun, cross-legged in her shorts and Birkenstocks, sipping at a can of cold beer. The cold beer cried to me. It gleamed up as the long awaited answer, at last, to the hangover that had maligned me all morning, and I accepted the cure gratefully and fished a can from the cooler. I sat next to Madeleine. We drank for a while, watching the water run across rocks down the bank below.

"We could go camping," she finally told me. "We should really do it. We'll hike to a spot I know a couple miles into the woods, with a shelter of pine trees that's so thick you almost don't need to pitch the tent. Would that be fun? We'll build a fire, we can look at the stars. It's something you really should do while we're out here. But the spot is closer to Helena. I think we need to go to Helena, first. Maybe we'll camp later in the week, alright?"

"Alright."

"There might be some bears near Helena. Maybe grizzlies. We can get some gear from my friend Marcus. Maybe pepper spray or borrow a gun. He could even go with us." We sat on the rocks and she planned the whole thing, even the menus—fruit and nuts and macaroni and cheese. We'd keep our packs light, hike back to the clearing, bring fresh water in canteens, that's all we'd need. And I loved the sound of it, loved every detail as she weaved them in layers and we packed up our fishing gear, and put it away, and returned to Velma and Joel's house. There were so many beautiful places in Montana, so many possibilities and so many people to see, and we talked about them, and about the days ahead of us, as we drove away from the rushing river and the dead fish and the rocky creek bed. We pointed ourselves toward our next adventure, and after that, we never talked about going camping again.

I had a vision one clear, hot day. We were heading for a small town north of Helena. The road was fresh, and the highway north seemed smaller, and drier, than Paradise Valley Road. Fewer travel it; fewer know it is there. Brown hills rise and fall, rolling away until they turn into mountains at the horizon: short and craggy like the looking-up profiles of stern, famous men, captured and prone. We stopped at the Town Pump store to restock: beer, postcards, ice, film. I bought popsicles, blue and red, paid the acned youth behind the counter, and we ate as we walked to the car. I began driving again and then I saw it: that moment extended forever, the rest of my life was right there, in front of me, like the road.

On that road, I realized that the last nervous thoughts about what I'd left at home, my job, my cat, my life and time and everything familiar, were gone; I did not care anymore about that life or any place but where I was. It was a feeling I could not begin to believe I could feel all the real days of my life, anywhere. But there it was.

In the seat beside me was Madeleine. "Montana suits you," she said. "I've never seen you look so happy as you do right now."

Was it anesthesia? Or ether? Or the big empty sky that had filled up our car? We weren't wishing, we weren't drinking; we were just flying, at last, long and far away from everything we once knew to be hard, and fast, and real.

This is my vision: that who I see ahead of me so clearly is who I really am, real as the landscape, the sage, the sun, things that never apologize. I have no doubt and no shame, only joy to be alive amid gulches and mountains and dirt cracked like leather. I see myself out there for a long time living, not just hanging on and wary of what happens next. I can even see myself living without Madeleine, because I am so certain, in this vision, that all is well and as it should be, no matter what happens. Montana showed me that, and I understood it, but I've always been the sort who forgets things fast.

Madeleine slapped my arm and said, "Put your hands on the wheel, girl!" as I rode along clapping for the brilliance of everything. We sped north from Helena on Canyon Ferry Road with the dammed up lake to the right and a double rainbow spanning it. Incredible! Ah! We drove to the tiny town of York, crossing a bridge and the patchwork of houses by the river, past the local bar, and we turned by a bank of raspberry bushes into Marcus's driveway.

His was a red house on a block of houses, a square neighborhood set like a napkin in the lap of the mountains.

"Welcome, welcome!" Marcus said, standing with his arms open at the top of his rutted drive. His teeth gleamed through his thick beard, and hair sprouted wherever it could fit. Large dark glasses hid his eyes. He walked right to our car and hugged us both.

We had started the day in the tent in Velma's yard, waking in the broken wall of stuff that spilled around us as we slept. We packed it all up again, early. We said good-bye to Velma and Joel, and Madeleine and Velma hugged and shed tears for the long time to come in which they would not see each other. They had to say good-bye, but I was going to be with Madeleine, still, as if I were the winner after all. I waited for her by the car, feeling married.

Marcus was among the ones whom I had been told knew how to survive. Madeleine mentioned his name now and then and always said that she admired him; he was very wise. He had held court with her in bars and coffee shops and living rooms in Bozeman, talking among friends about all the things in this world that are hidden from view, and she was even brave enough to think for a while that they were in love, which was only natural. "It's hard not to love your teachers," she had said, "because when someone helps you see what the world really is, you can't help but think it has something to do with him, like he was the one who thought it all up, like he's maybe God or something."

And so I understood Marcus to be a teacher, and I hoped he might be my teacher, too. I wanted to learn how to stay in Montana.

There were pine trees all around York and it felt very small and far away, but the houses were neat like they belonged to office workers, as if there could be an office building tucked away in the nearby margins of the planet. We all walked through the ranch-style house and sat on the deck behind it.

Marcus had taught Madeleine about the types of planes the military uses, how many and why, and what types of weapons and planes were tested at the bases all around. I had never known anyone in the army, or anyone who talked about such matters with real knowledge; maybe the particulars of war were something you became aware of as a man who had come of age at the tail end of Vietnam, as Marcus had. It made sense to really understand the military apparatus if there was a good chance you would one day use it, but well-bred eastern girls ignored planes and bombs as matters not to be discussed but discretely relied upon.

A low, deep growl entered our space. "Look," Marcus pointed to the sky. "A transport plane. The only planes we see over our house are military, flying to the base near town." The plane showed up right behind him, as if this man could actually fling them from inside his head. Once you become aware of a thing, you begin to see it everywhere.

I said I didn't know much about all that military stuff.

"Well, that's what they want, isn't it," Marcus said. "As long as you know nothing about it, you'll do nothing about it."

Marcus was a youth counselor. He had been in college for many, many years before that. He had married his college girlfriend, Gina; she was from New Jersey, from a town right next to the towns that

Madeleine and I came from, which was like evidence of an underground Montana–New Jersey connection, or a virus we had all caught.

Marcus and Gina welcomed us to use their laundry room, so I went into the guest bedroom to put on some fresh clothes and piled up the dirty ones. The guest bedroom was small, with lots of mirrors and a double bed, next to which Marcus had neatly lined up our bags. Madeleine came in as I stood in my underwear. She said, "We're hot tubbing on the deck as soon as it gets dark." Then she dragged her backpack and duffle bag out the door, into another small room at the far end of the long ranch house.

I carried an armload of clothes to the washer by the kitchen. Gina was chopping vegetables, standing at the sink where a window looked out on the yard. I asked her what lured her to Montana years ago, when she was just eighteen and had never been there; why did she just pick up and move to some place so far away? How did she find the courage? Why, Gina? Why Montana?

Gina stared down at a sweet red pepper, very thoughtful for a moment until the answer came, and then she slammed her long knife once and for all onto the butcher block, looked at me with wide eyes and said, "New Jersey was sucking the life out of me." In a moment, when we were both sure I had heard and understood, she resumed chopping. In fact, I had understood so well that I really had nothing else to say to Gina.

With my laundry loaded up and tumbling around in there with Madeleine's, and dinner simmering, and nothing else to do, I went outside to play with Marcus and Gina's ducks. I chased the ducklings through the yard, to the bath tub in the garden, where they paddled and I watched them as the sun sank. Marcus came and joined me after a while, leaning against his split rail fence with his arms folded, his glasses still hiding his eyes in the dusk, and told me about the first ducks they'd brought home, Huey and Louie. They were so cute but got eaten by a lion.

"A lion?"

Yes, there was a mountain lion out past the houses in the little town of York and either that killed the ducks or maybe it was a real mean raccoon. I looked over the fence and across the road at the stiff pine covered hills, quiet and darkening and harboring wild animals, and I said, "Wow."

Madeleine had stepped out onto the deck with Gina and was now cutting her hair.

"How do you like Montana?" Marcus asked me. I said it was incredible. He smiled through his beard and said nothing more. So I said more, about how I'd probably been waiting all my life to come to Montana, only I didn't know it, and now here I was and it was about time and all there was left for me to do was to figure out how to stay. He nodded.

"I think Montana has the power to change people," I said.

"Maybe it just lets people be themselves," he answered.

He waited to hear more. He held his arms tighter; his legs were crossed at the ankle, and he listened as if I were his only concern that day, and he had all day, and the profound silence made me want to tell him everything.

"I tried to run away from home when I was seven," I heard myself say. "I got caught down the street."

He nodded. I felt stuck so he helped out with questions: "What do you do in New Jersey? How do you like that? So now, how long have you known Madeleine? Oh, I see. You two seem very close. Are you a vegetarian? Because we have a lot of great health food out here. You're not? Oh, well, I guess I thought you would be, somehow."

At last his interview wound down. We'd pretty much covered me, so I said, "Say Marcus. Do you guys have a bomb shelter?" Marcus threw his head back and made a large laughing noise. "Why?" he finally said. "Do you know something I don't?"

I felt embarrassed then, and I just said, well, all those planes that fly over. He said, don't worry, I don't think they're after me. We went inside and he opened us up some beers. It was dark in the kitchen, no lights on. I remember thinking how nice it was to own a kitchen, never mind a house. When dinner was ready we ate; at the table Marcus finally took off his dark glasses but his eyes were just as dark and hard to read. They disappeared behind crinkles when he laughed, and his head tipped back and his face crunched up so that all you could see was a nose and a whole lot of hair. We all talked until it was time for the hot tub.

Then it hit me. I wondered if we were supposed to be naked in the hot tub. No one had addressed this and I waited but no instructions came. Now the time was near. Madeleine and Marcus reminisced about their days in Bozeman and talked of friends they both knew and pretty soon it was nine thirty, and the sun had finally slipped behind the trees, and then the tequila came out. There was supposed to be a meteor shower, to make our deck sitting and sky-watching and hot tubbing even more perfect. I don't think I had ever found a place where there were so many cool things, all the right things, all in one place. It was an ultimate sort of blissed out perfection. Montana. We drank a round of tequila shots and they all started hinting that the tub time was near, saying "It's almost time," and "It's going to feel great to soak."

And gradually, I understood that I was paralyzed.

If we were supposed to go in the tub naked, why hadn't they made that clear? Were we all going to take our clothes off and hang out together? It's not like we were sitting naked on the deck. Did the rules change in the presence of water? Was I going to be the only one who did not know? Was I going to make a nudity mistake in front of everyone? Would I look just as stupid if I asked?

I wondered in silence. Colored party lights lit up the deck and music hummed: Reggae. Jimmy Cliff. Pine trees swayed. Gina lit the kerosene torches, and Madeleine and Marcus talked, feet up on empty chairs. I sat and watched them all. Then Marcus slapped his knees, stood up and announced, "It's time." The group dispersed to get ready. What were they doing? Getting naked? Putting suits on? Why hadn't I been told?

In my little room with a mirror on the closet door, I packed and unpacked clothes while the kittens, Yoda and Boho, watched. I paced, trying to decide about my bathing suit. I put it on. I saw myself in the wall of mirrors, blue flowers stretched over bunches of flesh. I took it off. Thing is, though I loved the idea of freedom, I didn't know when or where to be free, which meant I was not free at all, didn't it? Was this to be the moment in which I shed my spiritually crippling inhibitions, or would this be the moment in which I shed my clothes and walked outside naked, like in a bad dream? I put my suit on, took it off, put it on halfway.

I went out to the deck in a terry robe, stepping through the sliding glass doors with a towel and another beer and then the other three ran past me naked, throwing their towels onto the deck and leaping into the mouth of the deep redwood tub. "Ah," they said, and, "Ooh, that's nice and hot," as their feet slipped in cautiously at first and their bodies followed with conviction, sitting up to their chins in tumbling water. I went back inside and took off my bathing suit. When I came out, Madeleine, Marcus, and Gina shifted to make room for me. My body disappeared with theirs beneath the foam.

In the hot tub, we passed around more shots of tequila, hot in my throat and tingling like the air jets. We watched the sky for meteors. There are many hot tubs on many decks in Montana; this one was round, a California hot tub, Marcus called it. But when I thought of California hot tubs, I thought of swinging sex parties with champagne and women who start out in bikinis but don't end up in them.

The Montana hot tub ritual was something different from that. We were not supposed to notice the nudity. It was, like, natural. In Montana it's okay to just be yourself, your naked self; at least, that's what people in Montana believe. I hit a posture of extreme liberation. I sunk in, and then I knocked someone's knees, and then everyone shifted like dominoes until we were rearranged and were no longer touching.

"Ah, look at the stars!" Marcus said, his head tilting back and staring at the heaven. The water came up to the middle of his chest and he spread his arms out along the rim of the tub. We all leaned our heads back. "Come on, meteors!" Marcus said to heaven.

So much of Montana's sensuality is in its sky, and as the warm water caressed me I looked up into that rich darkness sequined with a billion stars, trying not to notice that as Gina strained for a better view her nipples pointed through the thundering water. I stared up.

"Ooh, I saw one," she said, looking at the stars. Her nipples peeped higher. "There!" she pointed.

"I saw it too!" Marcus said.

We stared up searching and expectant, but no more meteors came for a while, and we were looking up blankly until it felt to me like time to talk again. Warm inside and out from tequila and water, in the intimate matrix of that tub, I felt compelled to ask the wise Marcus: what is love?

"I mean, how do you know if it's real?"

He laughed. "Do you ever?"

"Well but what I mean, is it like magic? Or is it just sex? Is that how you know when you really love someone? Sex?"

Gina lifted a hand out of the water and rubbed her softened cuticles. She said, "Hmmm. I don't know," sounding thoughtful.

"I guess what I mean is, after all, is sex a fair basis for major life choices? And, would it be all right to spend your life with someone you love, but, never have sex with her? Or, uh, him?"

Now Madeleine laughed, but Marcus was looking at me. I could almost see his eyes. He was listening.

"I suppose that would be sad, wouldn't it, to love someone and never have sex. Like, you'd miss the best part," I said. "Or would you? Is that even the best part? Maybe sex doesn't even matter. Why does sex have to matter?"

"You ask good questions," Marcus said, staring up again.

I said, "Maybe what I really wonder is, why you would choose a life partner solely because it is the person you prefer to have sex with. I mean, doesn't marriage ruin sex anyhow? Do you even really feel like having sex very often?" I looked from Marcus to Gina, then back. Gina said, in a small voice, "What about children?" which was something I'd completely overlooked somehow.

Just then, I noticed a long silence. Naked in the hot tub with near total strangers, it seemed as if every second or third word out of my mouth had been "sex," and it occurred to me too late that I had committed a hot tub faux pas.

Gina and Madeleine started reaching for towels on the deck behind them. And then after a moment, Marcus stood up, too. As they stood I tried hard to look past them, like I was looking for a shooting star that had landed in the bushes. Marcus put on his robe and toweled his face dry, and then he walked back over to the tub where I was still soaking, waiting for the right time to get out: some time long enough after the others to make it seem as if I had not simply followed. Marcus leaned on the rail of the deck near me, and, still looking to the sky, he told me, "Gina is my best friend. That's why we're married." He looked up as if he was waiting for something else to occur to either him or me, or to fall down to us from the sky, and when that didn't happen he walked off and smoked a cigarette.

After a while I got out and joined the others on the deck again, each wrapped in a towel, each finishing off his or her container of alcohol. I tried to finish my beer but put it down, finally, feeling near to being sick. The sickness was becoming familiar, the natural counterpart to a near constant high. No one spoke until Marcus slapped his knees and said, "Well. Good night." And then, slowly, he and Gina stood up, collected a few empty containers and went inside to bed. Then Madeleine put out her cigarette, and she and I got up and went inside too, heading off in opposite directions through the house to our beds. I laid down, pores wide open, skin soft and red, and the two black kittens Yoda and Boho curled up on my blankets. The three of us spun gently into pure, hot tub–clean sleep.

The phone rang at 2 a.m. It was Twilight. That's Marcus's mom, the former Gladys who had divorced her husband of twenty years and declared that she was a lesbian. (Marcus and Gina had replied, "We already knew that, didn't we?" proving once again that the declarer is always the last to know.) To complete the metamorphosis, Gladys changed her name, so now, everyone calls the former Gladys "Twilight." It's listed in the phone book that way. She was on the northern lights phone tree: for five dollars, the night park rangers near Helena call every time the northern lights appear.

That's what she called about, aurora borealis. Marcus roused everyone, started throwing open doors, "Get up get up, it's your lucky night" and before I could even think about it I was fumbling with my clothes, hurrying to dress warmly, nervous that something was going to happen in heaven without us. We rushed outside.

"There!" shouted Marcus, and we turned fast around in circles in the dark yard. Ducks quacked twice. I thought I saw a finger of light beckon and disappear. Silence. Cool, sweet summer night scented with raspberry bushes. Marcus rubbed his beard and said, "They faded back behind the hill," which was a mountain it would take an hour to climb but in Montana that's still a hill.

Gina, sleepy and skeptical, waved good-bye and stayed home as the three of us piled into the jeep to chase lights like ghosts, across the

Canyon Ferry Dam toward Helena. Every sight transformed somehow into some special thing we just had to see: the green reflection of dashboard lights in the car windows, cigarettes glowing bright orange in the dark, the moon on Canyon Ferry Lake. I thought I saw light. I pointed and cried out and we drove faster to get to someplace where we could stop to see. The glow turned from green to orange, obscured by the hills and extremely faint, as if I were seeing the air as particles. The colored air was falling apart like sand, some grains orange, some green, some dark, all circulating in front of me, and I was describing all this out loud in detail, its motion and consistency and then Marcus cut me off: "Just let us know if you see something."

I don't know. I didn't then. What were we seeing? We were staring out our windows saying, "Mmm," because it was vast and dark and beautiful, even without the aurora borealis; now and then someone said, "There!" and so we kept driving, thinking the really beautiful thing was just around the next bend. Then we saw, on the northern horizon, not spindly streaks but bright bursts and flashes, explosions of light: orange, yellow, white. "Oh my," cried Madeleine. "Wow wow wow!" I said.

Marcus said, "Looks like we found 'em!"

We parked the jeep at Devil's Elbow, a long empty field with a parking lot for hikers, and our jaws fell and we stared. Marcus watched the horizon, and Madeleine climbed the chain fence around the parking area and sat on it for the show. We were witnessing not just the northern lights, but the most spectacular cosmic light show anyone who ever lived had ever seen, and poor Gina was missing it, and Marcus said, "Well, that's her choice, that's how you miss things." We leaned against a chain fence necks bent, yawning, scratching, watching, and there! On the horizon, it happened again: an orange burst and trail and glow silhouetting the mountains.

We could have stayed and watched that show forever. It went on and on, but after half an hour we were tired, and Marcus had work in the morning, and so, reluctantly, with the sky still exploding, we hopped off the fence and got back in the beautiful jeep with its orange dashboard lights that were still just a little beautiful in their own way, if you thought about it, and we drove back up around Canyon Ferry Lake home, watching the orange glow as long as we could see it, then still watching the empty sky until we were back in sweet-smelling York full of joy. Just when I'd seen it all, heaven said, "Wait, there's more." Ducks quack hello. The universe is delightful.

When morning came, we woke early with very little sleep and thick heads and bright smiles still aglow from what we'd seen together the night before. Had that orange sky been a dream we were now trying to recall? Madeleine and I were drinking coffee and I was thinking about the glory of heaven when Marcus came back from his walk to the Friendly York Bar, which is also a newsstand and grocery store. He had a morning newspaper, and he slapped it on the table and poked at a big black headline on the front page above a tremendous photograph of a flaming structure: "EXPLOSIONS CHAR FOREST. Fuel plant blows, fire raging."

"Here are your lights, ladies," Marcus said. We sipped coffee and read silently about what that beautiful sight last night must have been: "I was ready for Armageddon . . . the rumble could have been a bomb, could have been anything . . ." "I woke up, and I could tell something was coming, something real bad. It seemed like it was the end of the world. And I didn't stop to think, I just ran."

Where ya headed?" Marcus asked. It was time to leave. We had stayed four nights, and now we were drinking coffee and looking at the map, taking in the vast expanse of Montana and all its remote corners and all those waiting possibilities. We were trying to decide the best route back toward Livingston, then Bozeman, where eventually Madeleine had to catch a plane, which did not seem possible; there could be no going back. Could there be?

Marcus pointed at the map that was spread out on the kitchen table, then he put his finger on Emigrant Peak, turned the map toward me and said, "Used to be a town called Basin down there, the whole place pretty much run by women, a whole town settled by lesbians but I'm not sure if they're still there. They used to run the auto repair shop and the post office and the fire engine, everything I guess, until some born-again Christian preacher got all the neighbors scared. I don't know what it's like there anymore, might be interesting to check it out."

I nodded my head, staring at the map, acting like a little town run by lesbians was the most obvious tourist site west of the Mississippi and he probably sent all his guests there. And I wondered what that would be like: a town run by lesbians. Lesbians behind cash registers. Lesbians at the bakery. Lesbian mechanics in jumpsuits leaning down to smile into your car: "Fill 'er up?"

Madeleine said we were going to visit the Emigrant ghost town. Did he know how to find it?

"This Basin place is on the way," Marcus told her. "Really sad what fear can do. I heard it was a great place, like a lesbian utopia for awhile, someone even wrote a book about it."

She examined the lines of the roads. "I don't think we'll have time. There's nothing there now anyhow. What about the ghost town?"

Marcus stood stiff beside her and stared down, tapping the table and not speaking, and then after a few seconds he finally turned the map back around and traced a route to the ghost town with his forefinger and said, "Here, this road goes to Emigrant," and Madeleine looked on, and I walked away. I wandered off to the car by myself, and waited.

After a while Marcus came outside and stood with me and appeared to wrestle with discretion before he said, "I just wanted to say, it's okay to wonder about things. You know, eventually it all works out. Really." He scratched his beard. His sunglasses were back but it didn't matter because he wasn't really looking at me. "You'll see," he said. "Everything will all get easier, and then watch out, you'll be just like the rest of us."

He laughed, and I looked at him and smiled as if I knew just what he meant by that. It troubled me that everyone seemed to know just exactly how desperate I was. Marcus looked out, quiet. I pretended to be someone with nothing to hide.

"Well," he said, "whatever happens, you know you're loved." He hugged me. And as he did, he said, "Welcome to the family."

And I thought, "What family? The family? Was this it? My initiation? Had I just joined a cult? Was that the secret? And why is it nobody ever knows what anyone else is talking about?" Marcus hugged me, and in his hug I felt a joy of belonging. To something. Whatever it was. It didn't matter.

Marcus grinned at me and then he walked back to the house. He and Madeleine came outside shortly, carrying the last of our bags, her laughing a little and kicking a rock in the driveway as they talked, then walked over, and Madeleine actually put her arm around my shoulders and we said good-bye to Marcus and I felt so proud of that arm around me because I knew she loved me, I just knew, and suddenly I belonged. Marcus the wise man made it so. And at last we got into the car and waved and pulled away, her turn at the wheel, my feet on the dashboard.

I looked at Canyon Ferry Lake as it appeared before us on the road toward Helena, and as it passed out of sight, I felt an ache, like fear: time had tried to reassert itself. Why were we leaving? And what if I never saw that lake again? How would I ever describe it? I would not be able to; whatever I might say later wouldn't matter, because even the memory would change, become a lifeless thing; in all the years to come, remembering Marcus waving to us from the driveway as we turned onto the road, leaving, I would see him as I knew him and as he was then, but never would be again, after he and

Gina moved away from York, and then started fighting, and then finally got their divorce. This was it, the best life there was, and yet even this was not everlasting. One day there would be no reason to go back to the Friendly York Bar. Time was passing and it was slipping away and I wanted it all to just stay; I wanted to stay.

"What's the matter?" Madeleine said, and she shook my knee.

"Nothing," I told her.

I closed my eyes, and as she drove she stroked my hair and it was just right, just exactly right. "We'll come back, don't worry. We'll see them again. You know," she told me, "you don't ever really leave the people you love, once you love them."

She said, "We can go to Basin if you want. We can swing through Helena and head south and maybe find some place there to eat lunch, and we can find a campground near by and sleep in the tent. But we probably don't have time for both Basin and Emigrant." I told her that it didn't really matter to me what we did.

We found the old mining ghost town of Emigrant two miles up a rut road full of potholes. It spread out before us after we drove my car in the treachery between a sharp drop-off and the mud face of a cliff. There was nothing in Emigrant but disappointment, and yet it was somehow marvelous, a still life and sublime: falling down wooden buildings that we pelted with weightless curiosity, like tossing stones. Why would people just leave things this way? The big dance hall, the stores, the saloon. Why?

"What happened?" I shouted, and it rolled down the hill like a coin into a fountain. Soon, thunder answered from the green distance, way out over the mountains, and that frightened us, all alone out there at the end of a bad dirt road with a storm coming; yet the ruin was unmoved. I imagined spending life in such a lost cause as this one was, like Rapelje but more so, and lifeless. Emigrant was just a place where wonder had led us, but never kept anyone for long.

Back in the time that seemed the last solid minute before everything in my own young life changed, before the end of the Cold War, before a long recession and the Persian Gulf War, before prosperity returned and changed the world again, and again, before another Persian Gulf War, back when the new millennium had not arrived and Jerry Garcia had not died, when my friendship with Madeleine was new and was all that mattered, and she made wishes out loud that always sounded like plans, and I believed in them, back then, it felt like we had started out all over, together, and everything was ahead of us, and it could have turned out to be the marvelous life I had been promised and had wanted to keep, forever. But then the days wound down and insisted this was just vacation, after all. We drove away, heading for Bozeman, then Livingston, and finally we reached the last night of our stay. How could this trip just be over? It was like we were dying.

Had I found what I had quit my job and gone west for? No. Had the secret of the universe been revealed to me? No. Had I had a religious experience? Had I been offered large doses of mind altering drugs? Had I found lasting love? Was Madeleine staying to wander on with me? No. No. No. No. Nothing so dramatic had happened or was going to, apparently, because she was leaving.

We suddenly found ourselves rushing through the last of an itinerary like a scavenger hunt, seeking precious moments to take home. We planned our final night: we would stay in Livingston so that Madeleine could photograph the neon lights in that old railroad town. We were quiet in the car on the way there. And I started thinking that promises mean nothing and talk is just talk. In the end, the only way anything ever happens, the only way to change the world, is to do something and hope for the best.

And so I had to do something. It was time. And there she was, just waiting. I stared out the car window.

"Madeleine," I said. "Don't leave tomorrow."

"Ha!" she said. "I wish I could stay."

"Stay."

"Got work Monday."

And that ended the conversation. Could I imagine saying the words? "Madeleine, just stay with me here because I love you. Let's do this." No. I had come to a wall, one of those moments where destiny is made, when I would either act or live with my failure to act and regret it. And I would keep living and reliving this moment through countless lifetimes until I got it right. An initiation, after all.

She chewed her fingernail, watching the road. And I kept thinking, looking for the answer. That night, before she was gone, I had to act. I would need to be brave, but, it would be okay because I wouldn't speak, I'd just do it. I knew it was the only answer. We hurled forward through the sage brush and grass and I told Madeleine: "The answer is love."

"Love is always the answer," she agreed. "Love is the great commandment."

"I knew you'd say that," I said. "People should be allowed to love anyone any way they want."

She said, "Love is free."

"But romance is expensive."

Her top lip curled over her teeth and her crooked eyes rolled behind sunglasses. We pushed on to the end of our journey in Livingston, Montana.

Livingston was a hard town with blocks of hotels and bars lit with red and yellow and green neon, so that as the sun set over the rail yards and the pale day receded, the town ignited slowly with a textured light, glowing robust in stripes and bands and giant cocktail glasses. The Mint. The Ritz. The Murray.

The lobby of the Murray Hotel was hung with stuffed buffalo heads and the elevator was operated by a hotel manager who pulled the gate closed and inched back a great white throttle. We took a room on the fourth floor with a view of the neon Murray sign and, across the street, the railroad station. Freight cars came and left listlessly all through the night, pushing down the track, slow and heavy. Across the hall from our room a door stood slightly ajar. I walked up to the crack and saw a man lying flat out and fully dressed, boots on, asleep on his bed; he might have been dead, it seemed, but I stared for a while and then I heard snoring.

The light bulbs in the hallway and in the rooms were bare, like in stripped down tenements or Depression farms. Bare bulbs here looked to me not like poverty, but toughness; no frills. This was a cowboy flophouse, not a sissy hotel. The rugs had cigarette holes. One of our bedspreads did, too. The Murray had been standing for the whole of that century; it's air had been breathed in and out by so many who had passed through with fates unknown. And I can't speak for Madeleine, who liked her hotel rooms, as her rivers and most things, pristine, but for me the Murray was perfect. It was a bit dangerous. When I saw it again years later, the Murray would be changed; the California people would come and put art galleries in the hard town and the Murray would brighten up, add lampshades, even add a four-star restaurant in the gilded lobby. But on that day in 1989, things were different, they were raw, they were the way I thought they should be because they were the way I felt. This place said I dare you. Jump in, do something. Find out what life really is.

We ate beef dinners at some neon-signed place with checkered table cloths, crying babies, and cowboys drinking at the bar. Then we drank some more in the cocktail lounge beneath the hotel. We were relaxing and getting on fine. There were only a few hours remaining. We would go upstairs soon, and I would act and find my answer.

Then, sitting at the bar beneath the Murray, Madeleine fixed her eyes on one of only two other people besides us in the place. It was

Libby, the guy who played keyboard in Paradise, the band we'd seen up at the Blue Goose. That felt like years ago.

"Is that you, Libby?"

He was hunched over a glass, rubbing a hand through his beard, and he lifted his head and squinted his eyes. "Hey, I think I know you," he said, coy, like teasing a sister. Of course he knew her. Everyone did.

"Libby!" she said. "This is too cool!"

Libby's head bobbed.

She got up and said "Come on" over her shoulder to me and dashed to the other side of the bar. She climbed up onto the stool next to his; I hoisted myself up on a stool, too. She was talking fast now with her back toward me, like she'd found her long lost friend, and I said, "I didn't realize you two were old pals," but they looked at me sort of odd, and Madeleine said, "Well, you remember. We met Libby at the Blue Goose." I said, "Oh."

Libby was drinking vodka straight up and soon we were, too, and playing Billie Holiday on the jukebox and playing quarters in our vodka glasses and getting the kind of drunk that makes everything go double and eventually blank. It was not a sloppy drunk, just one whose joyful feeling began slowly to rise into the head, numbing, and then moved on to a spinning feeling, the sort in which it helps to hold on to the bar until the room settles down and you can find the confidence to light your weaving cigarette. We held on to the bar; we lay ourselves half down on the bar, laughing, then we lay half on each other, and on any steady thing.

Madeleine's multiplying smile, in the white light of a glass wall stacked like ice behind the bar, was the vortex in the dizzy room; her teeth sparkled in otherwise darkness. She had a great dirty laugh. She twirled her long hair, and the silent bartender poured refills. How unreal it seemed. There were no windows. We were not loud, I think; we were not animated, or gushing; we were just huddled at the bar without much to say and hanging on and laughing over nothing.

Libby chuckled under his beard and stared at his vodka as if avoiding Madeleine's eyes. I thought, "Are they flirting?" The room stood still for a second. I tried to speak, to ask what was going on, but my sentences rolled out in mumbles, and then I just laughed, never mind. I remembered: Madeleine loves me. More than ten, less than one hundred. I never finished the thought.

It seemed like the kind of bar that would never close or kick us out, and hours passed. Maybe *this* was how we'd spend our lives. Eventually Madeleine and I just drifted off and left Libby without any farewells that I remember, him still grinning through his beard over a glass of clear liquid, arms folded on the bar, as if he had always sat and would always just sit there, and she and I were delivered again into our lives, to a hotel room filled and refilled over years with all the others who had also come and had to leave, to never return, to disappear, or perhaps even to die seeking life out in the wild plains beyond.

Upstairs in our room, Madeleine stripped off all her clothes. Without stopping or seeming to be distracted from that goal in any way, she got into her bed. She picked up the phone and asked the desk for a 7 a.m. wake-up call and then laid back, closed her eyes and sighed. I was standing there, looking around the spinning room. I decided to sit in the chair at the foot of her bed.

And then she started talking about how perfect it had all been, our trip, how perfect, and how happy she was. The red-orange glow of "Murray" shone through the window. It had been an adventure to remember all our lives. Magic at every turn. "Such a good feeling, good feeling," she slurred, "to just lie here in my bed at the Murray Hotel and bask in it. I'm basking. See me bask."

I sat in the leather chair and watched her as she lay there, a talking silhouette against the cracked plaster and the yellow drapes the color of old cigarette smoke. My tongue was fuzzy, thirsty. I tried briefly to talk myself out of whatever I was about to do. If I sat very still, this would already be one of the best moments of my life, the end of a long trip with miracles and friends everywhere. I could have just left it at that. But then, the Montana Madeleine had shown me would end. I wanted to keep this and I had reached my last chance. I looked at her, as she waited for sleep with a smile on her face, in Livingston, Montana, of all places on earth. And I imagined I saw in her being as it huddled beneath the covers on her bed everything that was good in the world, all my hoped-for happiness, a whole world where the only thing still missing was me. I had to do something now.

I said, "Can I get in bed and bask, too?"

"Sure," she said. "Go to bed."

"No, I mean, can I get in that bed with you?"

It took some time. She had to process that request. Then she said, simply, "No."

Fire. My neck and face were swallowed in fire. No? She said no? How could she say no? I hadn't thought of this. I thought I had figured out the answer. Had she misunderstood? Oh my god, why had I not just kept my mouth shut and crawled in?

"Just to lie there, that's all."

"No."

The room was very hot, and it was larger than it first seemed. Madeleine was far away on the other side of this chasm across which, to be heard, I might have to scream. I tried mightily to not speak too loud, to not scream.

"I just want to lie down. That's all."

The leather seat creaked beneath me.

"You won't let me do it," she said. "Will you."

"Do what?"

"You aren't going to just let me bask."

"No, go ahead," I whispered. "Bask."

Silence. And then in a moment I said, "I'm going for a walk." She didn't answer.

The chair sighed as I left it and I felt for the door. I left the room and fumbled down the stairs. I walked: out into the empty streets of Livingston, past the neon and crowded bars, along the empty train tracks that led out to a vast and real nowhere. After maybe half a mile, I slowed. My careful steps on the cracked sidewalks said, oh, sure, if I can't climb in bed with my friend Madeleine then my second choice would obviously be to wander the streets drunk and alone. It was two in the morning. I couldn't walk straight lines; I knew that I wasn't safe, but it still seemed safer than to be near Madeleine, who had rejected me and must surely hate me and would hate me forever now. Fuck. I'd ruined it. What an asshole. Who the fuck tries to get in bed with her friend? No, wait. Who the fuck asks first? Coward. I had made the same mistake with lamb eyes, hadn't I? Strike two.

Bad as things were, it seemed to me it would be too melodramatic to sleep in a doorway. Where else could I go? I could walk a while but eventually I would have to go back to the room where in the morning Madeleine would not speak to me, and who knows how bad it would feel. In the silence I expected, I would have to consider the fact that I had been wrong. Love is not the answer and she was not wishing for what I wished for and I was alone once again on the spinning earth. How did one survive mistakes of this kind? One didn't. No, one died.

I circled back around a row of parked motorcycles and headed back to the Murray Hotel.

I thought, "What, am I just going to drink and fight until I die, like my cousin Bill in Red Lodge? I'm tired."

I flopped down on a chair beneath a moose head in the Murray Hotel. Janis Joplin sang faintly through tinny speakers. No one was there but me, and dead Janis, and I fell uncomfortably to sleep in that spot for a while.

Madeleine left in the morning, rushing for the plane, both of us still a little drunk when we woke up and started packing in a frenzy. We drove right to the airport, fuzzy headed and raw eyed, listening to the Montana State University radio station that she loved, one last glimpse of it before returning to the life she had made instead of the life or the lives she could have had here. The highway cut through dry fields dotted with houses and billboards. Marianne Faithful was singing "Say It in Broken English" as the road curved to the airport parking lot. The airport was small, spread out in the open away from interfering mountains. Inside, the terminal was sterile and echoed with announcements, its look, sound, and smell alarmingly like any other airport, anywhere, as if the fantasy of the world outside ended at the door, and there we were now in the neutral place between places. Madeleine checked in, and we found her gate, and then before she picked up her duffle bag for the last time she said, "I don't need to hug you, I'm going to see you again," but then just like every other friend she had parted with on our journey I got my hug, the woman at the end of the line.

Madeleine said, "You stay on the road as long as you can, don't rush. This is your adventure, right? Just stay until the money runs out."

"Yeah, I'll do that." Whatever. I swallowed hard, feeling sick to my stomach. I began to wonder just when, exactly, the money would run out. Did I have money? Did I remember where I'd left my checkbook? Did I have any kind of plan, now that my real plan had turned out to be completely stupid?

"Alright, well, have fun," she said, and then she hoisted her backpack up on her shoulder, passed the woman checking boarding passes, waved back once as she crossed the tarmac. Then she was gone.

Watching the plane rise up behind clouds full of planes bound for other places, I thought about how much I would like right then to have a great, big, tall glass of water. I didn't want to just drink it. I wanted to dive into it. I wanted to be the water. But when I looked at the metal water fountain the thought of taking any liquid in made me feel nauseous. My chest grew tight, particularly at the thought of vodka, and then at the thought of where I might have misplaced my checkbook and where I should go try to eat breakfast, and then at any thought about what I was going to do next. I wandered to the car and then drove back up to Bozeman.

The sidewalks in Bozeman were moving with young people in brightly colored outdoor gear, sunglasses, sporty sandals, women with ponytails, men with beards, all walking with their faces toward store fronts, all looking for the strong cup of coffee and sporting gear they would need before dispersing into the wild and onto their own adventures, their clean and wholesome adventures, probably not adventures involving cults and drugs and sleeping with their friends, just sterile and sane good times where none of them did anything too crazy or stupid, like I did, because none of them wanted things they could not name or that they weren't supposed to want to begin with. I didn't know what my own adventure was going to be now, or how I was going to survive it alone. Where did I think I would go? How had I not considered this? Did I think somehow that I was going to drift around Montana acid-den style, onto the welcoming couches of strangers or people I barely knew, as if their lives were all open to an odd young bum of a woman who just wanted to float through the world for a while, seeking something, as if that were okay, as if whatever they had they would share to aid my search, as if such yearning and wandering was acceptable behavior outside of one psychotic, delusional moment in a past decade, which amounted to just about ten minutes in the larger life of our national consciousness? Was I poised to leech my way into the settled worlds of people who would never dream of drifting aimlessly back to my house to find a spot on my couch because they knew better and they were too busy being responsible to wander anyway, and they wouldn't stoop to becoming grubbing waifs who wanted to share my food and couch until their money ran out, until the drugs wore off, or longer?

Yes, that is exactly what I had in mind.

I didn't know how to do it. With Madeleine there, things had just happened. On my own I had no idea what to do next. I stopped for eggs at the Cowboy Cafe, and after staring at but not eating them I walked off and drove out of town and kept going. I decided to go camping, real camping, at last; it was cheap; it was easy, and if I pitched my tent, I could take a nap.

I pitched my tent at the Kampgrounds of America lot outside of Bozeman, the one with hot sulfur pools to soak in. The camping lot at the KOA was parked nearly full with trailers, but I found an open spot among a row of small tents. Kids at the campground were playing games that involved a great deal of running around objects like campers and trees and tents and me. I sat at the picnic table near my tent and slowly, carefully tried to write a poem while I drank a bottle of water and ate plain, dry crackers.

My tent site was behind a row of large camping vans. When the KOA parents in one of those vans started feeding their kids Lucky Charms at the picnic table and the kids wouldn't stop running around and the mother fired a barrage of foul language, I decided I'd better leave for a while. I started walking. Across the paved road beyond the KOA was a farm house with a black-and-tan dog tied to a stake at the back door, barking, yearning toward me, choking himself and growling foam. A split rail fence ringed the yard, and a lone chestnut horse ran up to it to get a better look at me. Someone somewhere on this trip told me that horses get lonely unless they move in herds or at least in pairs, and I could see that this particular lone horse was feeling out of sorts. I stopped to say hello. The horse just stood there. I resumed walking. He followed, then he sneezed. Horse sneezes are long, violent, flatulent events, possibly because horse noses are so long. I stopped and looked at him and he stopped and looked too. I walked on and he followed me. Down at the corner of the farm not far away was a wider road, busy, lined with houses and cars parked in drives, kids riding around on bicycles. The horse sneezed several times more behind me, and a car honked at me as I stepped into the intersection. I jumped back, grabbed my head, still thirsty as if I would always be thirsty, and confused, and lost for the rest of my life. People were trying to get on with their daily routines. The late-night shift was coming home from work in Bozeman. The kids on bikes were skidding in the gravel around me, seeing who could make the longest marks, and stopping on their bikes and looking at me. The horse was sneezing and sneezing. A military transport plane floated large above us, like a pregnant dragonfly.

I couldn't take it. I ran as fast as I could back to my tent and started tearing it down. I had to go somewhere peaceful to feel the full force of my abandonment.

Two hours later, I was at a state forest on the edge of the Beartooth Mountains near Fishtail, near where my cousin Bill had lived with his horse for a few months. Bill had followed deer trails to find ponds of fresh water and caught fish for dinner, and now and then had gone into Cooke City for a beer or a shower, and that's how he figured things out and put his life together, and I decided I would do that, too.

In a deserted state campground at the foot of a mountain, I parked my car and pitched my tent. It was quiet there; it was peace at last. Now what? Peace is harder, sometimes, and maybe that's why there is so little of it. I had nothing to do, all alone, and wasn't thinking clearly enough to be able to go through the motions of a happy traveler, to just sit back and relax, read a book, make myself camping snacks, do things I might enjoy. I didn't even know what I might enjoy, given this chance to do whatever I wanted.

I decided to climb up a wall of rocks, thinking maybe at the top I'd find a clear view. The rocks were steep, like a cliff, and climbing them took concentration. I pressed on, climbing quickly. It was already well after noon, and trees obscured the sunlight. The view on top of that rocky mountain looking into the state forest would surely be spectacular, wild rolling woods and mountains and waterfalls, and no houses at the bottom, or highways, just the sweet earth. I expected to see the true unspoiled world there, almost close enough to touch, and maybe I would have; maybe I would have found great grand nirvana or some cosmic orgasm or the face of God right there in front of me, if it just hadn't been for the terror.

I began to see monsters. Hairy, toothy, hungry beasts promulgated in the wilderness as the sun set and shadows grew. Every crevice in that rocky slope turned out to be riddled with them; every shadow was another lair of wild, bloodthirsty creatures. Maybe. Mountain lions, mostly, that's what I thought. Mountain lions who eat little ducks and could leap on top of your head and chew you up like a duck before you knew what hit you; or maybe there would be a bear, a grizzly bear, eight feet tall with clawed flesh-ripping paws the size of my face, a grizzly bear could be watching me that very moment waiting to chew me into bloody pulp. Oh, Jesus. Snakes? Snakes?

I quickly ran right back down that mean mountain just one step ahead of the lengthening shadows. Rocks jarred loose beneath my feet. In the safety of my campsite below, with the day fading and nowhere safe to go, I thought, "Now what should I do?" Should I have crackers for dinner? I wandered to the cooler. Should I make a campfire? I wandered to the fire pit. And I thought, "I just want to be alone, that's all."

That's when I started crying.

Why was I always alone? And why was I always afraid? And why was I always making decisions that led me to places I couldn't handle, like Livingston, or these mountains, or to life in general? Where was Madeleine, and oh god, where are you, and where am I, and who will lead me out of this wilderness? I cried in shouts and convulsions, and my mind wandered among all the new friends I had left behind; they had such good lives, and such warm souls, and I wanted to go back to them, but I couldn't; they weren't mine now that Madeleine was gone; I grabbed my heaving sides. I had no one, no one in the world at all.

The cry was going very well. Tears streamed and I thought of things like rain and thunder, and death in the woods. I cried so hard that I stumbled around the campsite, blind, weak, finally falling to my knees by a log laid out like an altar in the clearing near my tent. With my elbows on the log, I looked to the sky above the mountains, and said: "Why, God?" out loud. "Why has it turned out this way? Why am I so awful? Why am I alone?"

And after I had cried for a while longer and listened to an owl in a nearby tree, sun setting slowly, it entered my mind that I was not alone, as long as I was with Jesus.

"No, not Jesus!" I screeched, and then I cried even harder. I became overwhelmed with the fear of having a born again Christian experience. I had come to Montana primed for a transforming experience and this looked like my last chance to let one rip but, of all the changes I welcomed for myself, I just could not tolerate that one. Not that: an uncle on my mother's side was born again and it was impossible to talk to him now, unless you wanted to convert. There in the meadow wet with tears, had I come to the ruined moment in which I might be touched by the Lord and be born again? And from now on watch Billy Graham preaching on TV Sunday mornings, and like it? Would I then drop out of the unsaved world, spend my life on the road driving into small towns like Basin, Montana, with my Bible, and my finger pointed, telling everyone to repent or be damned?

Women had lived happily in a creative, loving community in Basin until a preacher came and drove all the poor lesbians away. Oh, the poor lesbians; I cried harder.

I was crying with such force by now that I fell over; I had just renounced Jesus and I was just plain damned. I said, "God, don't show me something as frightening as Jesus, or mountain lions, or grizzly bears, or cults; just send me a friend, a harmless friend, something to keep me company until I'm okay, something like a bunny. A big, fluffy bunny, with no sharp teeth. That's all. I think I could handle a bunny if you sent me a bunny, God."

I lay in the grass until I was utterly emptied of tears. On my back, I stared up to the tops of the mountains. I wanted so badly to go there, if only I hadn't been scared. I was tired. I decided that I should make a fire and calm down with simple, real, activity. Then I could go to sleep and forget this day. I could start fresh in the morning, just like a newspaper.

I hopped up and started down the dirt road to pick up some firewood. As I walked around the bend in the road I stopped short: there, about twenty feet in front of me, was a rabbit. A big, fat rabbit. It was orange. The rabbit was not a cartoon. It was real, and it sat there twitching its nose and looking sideways at me. We watched each other shocked and frozen for about two minutes. Then we both turned and ran away very fast.

I arrived panting at my campsite and crawled directly into my tent. In this shelter I was determined to sleep the deep sleep of the wretched and just end this awful day. In that tent in the mountains, waiting to drift away, I lay still as the world grew dark, as dark as any darkness I had ever seen. And only then, on my back in the blackness all alone, did I realize with slow-welling dread that I had left myself completely exposed to ax murderers.

And that's when I heard the scratching.

I tried not to move. On the nylon top of the tent I heard scratching and understood that the scratch was too light, and too deliberate, to be a woods creature. Such scratching could only come from something much more devious, with much more muscular control. The human animal. I heard the scratch again.

An ax murderer! He'd probably been itching for days to find an idiot camped out alone like this. Me, of course. He had watched me at a distance and waited, probably. He watched me blubbering and weak and he waited until I was prone, and now, he was going to kill me. I knew how it would happen: I would be assaulted first, then slowly killed. Little scratches, little scratches on the tent, just to let me know he was there. Probably he wanted me to poke through the tent flap to look for him, then whack, ax on my head. Holy Jesus God. I would not look outside. This was a test of wills: I tried to hold my breath in absolute silence and become invisible as that demon stood outside, scratching the tent to say, "I'm here, I'm here and I'll kill you when I'm good and ready, little girl, not one moment sooner, ha ha ha ha ha."

I lay as still as I could for hours while the ax murderer bided his time, hovering. The scratching sometimes stopped, then started again. Stop and start, all night, as I lay sweating and stiff and terrified.

After many hours spent staring at the dome of the tent the dark receded, just enough to reveal faint forms around me. I searched for some shadow, some sign of my assailant, who would surely attack now, in the spreading dawn. I scanned over webbing and seams and my tent dome. I stared at zippers and flaps, looking for the horror; I scanned the length of my sleeping bag, until at last I saw it. There it was, rubbing on the thin blue wall of my tent as I breathed. My elbow. I breathed, and the elbow moved, and its contact with the tent produced a tiny scratching sound. Every shallow breath drawn in panic caused another little scratch from my elbow. Every small scratch convinced me that I was in danger, and sunk me deeper into hell until the dawn came, and I saw that this tormenting noise was just me, and had been just me, all along.

Next came laughter. Peels of it, and then a manic giggle.

That was it. That was all there was to it. No one was out there sending me messages of any kind. The whole world of hope and doom lived simply in my mind and died there too. I laughed and said this out loud, it was so basic, so obvious: "The only thing I am afraid of is myself." I laughed some more. I had done nothing so foolish, or so wrong, that somebody had come to kill me for it. I knew it then: that what I feared so terribly was just me and had been only me all along, forever, for always. And if I carried that fear in me it would make me insane. It nearly had, already.

I dropped fast into sleep then against the hard earth. I thought of my Montana cousin sleeping like that once, alone, for months in the mountains; maybe it wasn't so hard, after the first night. You learn to live with things. He survived, and I would also survive.

In the daylight when I woke again, the campsite seemed to have regained its innocence. The whole episode, my whole life even, in that moment, seemed to be nothing more than a dream, vaguely remembered. I packed up my tent and my gear and started planning. I would begin with breakfast somewhere and then, who knew? I had a world full of possibility, with a car, some money, and no commitments. Maybe I could camp out for a month or two just like Bill had, or I could take a job on the road; I could have tried to find my checkbook, which I discovered much later had been hiding in the cracks of the car seat, and I could have wandered south to Mexico, or I could have started making beeswax candles and selling them out of my own yurt. But then, the wind blew. Really, what did I want? My best friend was back in New Jersey already. It was never really Montana that I wanted, not really. I just wanted to be with my friend Madeleine and to be happy. Did I really need Montana for that?

This is how it is for women like me: We think we want amazing things. Is that how love feels? We wonder. Is that what lies waiting for me, somewhere? Something amazing? But hard as we chase it, the notion slips away, and slips away, until the world is finally nothing more than what it is, and there we are in it. It's disappointing sometimes and screwed up and full of broken promises and death and bullshit and sooner or later, you have to accept that. You never really want to. But if you're going to have the life you imagine, you have to stop running from what hurts and make something better. I didn't think this, exactly, but as I drove away alone I understood something I was going to forget: there was really nothing to find out there. I sought magic, but even when magic stared up at me from the eyes of an orange bunny in the middle of the road, it didn't really mean a thing. It was just magic, just like sky is sky, and all that is just is. None of it matters more or less than anything. All that really matters is to get yourself home, somehow.

So I wouldn't wander around crashing on strange couches and trying to Find America or anything else anymore because what I was searching for was not hidden in those places. I decided, instead, to point myself east, to New Jersey. And there, I could begin again, from the beginning.

Go! Go! GO! It makes no difference where just so you go! go! go!
Remember at the first opportunity go!

from the diary of Jeannette Rankin,
Montana congresswoman, at age nineteen

In pictures, my grandfather stands in a suit next to men in bib overalls with Scandinavian names like Pieter and Sven, men with bushy mustaches and dirt in their nails who grew mountains of potatoes.

These photographs were taken in Montana. William was in his forties and his head was mostly bald, and he looked very much like my father had looked at the same age, in New Jersey. My grandfather was unlike the farmers who moved west; he was unlike the cowboys before them, rough and alone. His gray hat is tipped back, his vest is buttoned; he stands outside by the potato mound with his knuckles planted on his hips and he looks like he's working, but not in the dirt. Dust gets into his shoes. Sweat rings his collar. Farmers beside him wear baggy overalls.

Somehow, he did not belong there. With hindsight and photographs, his improbability is clear; it just was not the right thing for him, this scheme in dry land. Perhaps he might have tried California, instead, and developed real estate. But there was Montana, the ubiquitous fantastic idea taunting from posters and advertisements, the dream that refused to release his imagination, and so the dream he pursued.

Why didn't he content himself with the life he had? You don't just quit good jobs; you don't just pick up and leave with no assurances. Back in sturdy, settled Racine, Wisconsin, a bump on the shore of Lake Michigan, lots of people seemed to think it was enough to stay in place, their eyes turned west only as far as the next family farm. The fertile land there was already thriving. Around the Case factory, rows of homes rose, pale stone and lumber, built with livery stables in the dirt alleys behind, all of this, the bland washed-out gray, white, yellow-brown of the Midwest, predictable and enduring. Today the working class neighborhoods of Racine are dwarfed by the monster of Case Machinery, the tractor-selling giant, the firm where William might have become an officer, and a very rich man, had he stayed.

But in America in 1912, the future was big and fat as fresh cigars clamped in the square teeth of bloated old industrialists. Think of the Morgans and Rockefellers and Carnegies, the fortunes they made. William read about them in the newspapers. The bankers were the engine of the country's prosperity, making fabulous deals; selling tractors in Wisconsin was not how men conquered the world. Was it?

Case salesmen put flat feet up on the desks in their offices and did their certain jobs and at the end of the day dreamed of lakes up north where fish grow big as men's arms, and fat, with teeth like razors. William was mild and serious and not active outdoors; he was dapper beneath Scandinavian flips of thinning blond hair, humming marching band melodies, squinting through his wire glasses at numbers in books. All those farmers who bought Case dozers and tractors were pelted endlessly with messages from the railroads, trying to lure them from the safety of their Wisconsin farms to the bold frontier, the West, where the land was unbroken and fortunes lay buried in the unturned soil. William looked out the Case windows toward the silky heartland and squinted hard to see farther. Could his life be waiting way out there?

He folded his newspaper, tucked it under his arm.

"Goodnight, Mr. Case."

"Goodnight, William."

"Goodnight, Bill."

"Goodnight."

He was not yet thirty years old. He had a bald spot threatening the back of his head. It was the beginning of the twentieth century.

He went home to Florence, checking his watch against the church bells at five. He had never been west beyond Iowa, but one night he came home and said, "I've been thinking about Montana."

"MontANa," cried Florence, "Oh, William. Let's go, let's go." I hear this like an aria: Let's GO, let's GO.

And I think of what I know about them, of all the small clues my father left me, and it seems to me that it's not entirely William I have had to understand, in order to know this story; William, leader of his home, decision maker. No. What made me think this? History says it was a man's world, those early days of moving across the continent: all violence and ambition. At times it was a place for slandered, manly women, mining camp molls, Calamity Janes mocked or glorified in memory; they stare at us from posters of Bar Gals, or the Whores of Montana Calendar (which I bought in Bozeman for my dad and saved for Christmas). We witness in pictures the drawn faces of women who survived there the only way they could, and stood stiff for the camera in long, layered skirts beneath which rumors were started. History writes of women who suffered and died in the West: in childbirth, in the backs of wagons on the trail, taken as teenage brides, brought west like property, held hostage by husbands to nonnegotiable dreams and passions and wedding rings that were eventually stolen by bandits; the West was a place where women felt homesick, we're told; but their money was gone and the horses were dead and there wasn't any way to get home. History tells the trauma of their going, of their hard lives and how bravely they endured them, how simply they accepted their unique and often terrible fate.

But then, consider Florence. She was a small plump woman with big blue eyes, her laugh was loud and contagious, or so her friends say, and so her face tells us as it laughs out of line in the teeming rows of her Minnesota family. There they all stood, so black and white and motionless, draped in their enormous skirts and billowing hats, all the men in bland, untailored clothes. And there she was, smiling, the ball of light, the impish daughter, sister, soon-to-be wife who preferred checks over cash because she could write checks as big as she wanted, and how could anyone be poor, with enough blank checks around? Florence, newly wed, bought Persian rugs and floral china and clothes her husband could not afford, nor could he find the heart to take them away, because it was this spark that he had courted, this life, written on the face of a woman to whom he had brought bright, exotic flowers even out of season and then took for long rides in his new autocar. He wanted to be near her, because she was different. If Florence could have only one coat, she once said, it would have to be red, and that could only have meant that there were many coats, and many colors, in her closet really. Florence, from her huge family, made sure she never got lost in a crowd. She wore red coats, she had black hair, she held your eyes in her blue eyes like sky. She taught herself to play the piano, and she sang, she always sang, sometimes she wouldn't speak because she had to save her voice for singing; it is said that she sang at the opening of every public function in Rapelje, Montana: weddings, parties, funerals.

"Let's GO, let's GO."

He followed her.

Railroad exhibits all around the Midwest advertised land in Montana, causing the soul to stir: the last of the Wild West, the free West, fields running to mountains, boundless, like she was.

"You'll start your own bank," she said. "There'll be more wheat growing in Montana than anywhere, even Minnesota, and there'll be farmers with more money than you can keep in your vault, Mr. Banker. We'll have plenty of checks. We can build a house with flowers all around it, and a front porch that looks out over the prairie full of tall grass and meadow larks. It will be our own house built just as we like it, with big clean bedrooms and a stone fireplace, the most elegant fireplace in town for the most important businessman."

William quit his job. They packed up their home and shipped it all to Billings. Florence made food to eat in the car, and as they drove she sang; there was no other music as they passed buttes and craters and the big flat earth, west to Montana. But Florence sang as they drove, loud happy songs, her hat whipping as the wind blew through the car windows.

I think maybe William left everything he knew and moved his family to Montana because Florence said let's go, and he followed. He would have believed whatever she said, because he loved her. So they made a life in Rapelje, and they stayed longer in that place than almost anyone else did. But it didn't last. In 1950, they died four months apart: Florence first, then William; he followed her in this world, and then, I think, he followed her out.

It took four weeks to get back to New Jersey. I needed to wander just enough to make myself a convincing road warrior, in case anyone at home might wonder. I felt lonely and aimless, but I wanted to be able to say I'd had adventures and not that I'd just given up. Why not take in the sights? I left the campsite in the Beartooth still feeling hungover and tired. I would be tired for days and days, but there was plenty of time to recover. I pointed myself right back out toward the flat eastern part of Montana, right straight toward the road that lead east to Rapelje. All around the land was dry and thirsty and aching but no one could ever make it more than that.

I kept going. I stopped for a good-old grilled cheese sandwich in Sturgis, South Dakota. Madeleine and I had stopped there on the way out, while Sturgis was in the middle of Bike Week and it was all hogs and halter-topped women and tattooed arms pumping off the enormous shoulders of big, hairy men. I thought I saw my brother in the rearview mirror, always near me in Sturgis; it was a biker paradise and he would have loved it, but he was not there because he'd dropped dead on the kitchen floor of our childhood home while cooking a grilled cheese sandwich.

Now, eating a grilled cheese sandwich of my own, Bike Week was gone like a mirage and everything was empty. The place was still, all the beer cans and leather scraps swept up, all the banners put away. I sat in a booth in a cafe where a sign in the window said, "welcome back students."

September. I spent a night in a place of no consequence in central South Dakota, a little farther east, in a motel with the sounds of roadside sex pressing up against the walls. It was nicer outside: I sat in the painted aluminum rocking chair next to my motel room door; I watched over the parking lot and fields to where porch lights switched on, signals from other people's lives. I was lonely and being lonely scared me but I just sat there and felt it because that is how it really was to be there: lonely, without direction, without anything insisting I should be something more, or better, and there was peace in that.

Through the Midwest, the wide dry spaces were erased just as the mountains before them had been. Late corn sprung from the fields all around, closing the horizon and narrowing the world.

I called her, and the next day called again, and each time I left a message at the tone: Hello, hello, I'm calling from Cow's Breath, Ohio, and I'm driving east just as fast as I can. I'm heading home, Madeleine, there's nothing left to do here.

As New Jersey grew nearer and more cars shared the road, I understood better that I had been to a place truly different: a place of less, of light, where plain earth and sky dominate. Now I was returning, and I didn't know what home would feel like. Autumn was coming. I rolled down my windows and sang, loud, "We've all, come, to look for A-mare-i-cah . . ." and packs of cigarettes, days of no showers, stopping in odd places night after night until I was accustomed to the strangeness; anything could grow familiar over time, like cottages in a pine wood with a distant hum of motors on a lake or some lost western town, abandoned, but still there because where else would it go, and what else would it do, but be there; or some place like a Motel 6 in Youngstown, Ohio, some sterile any-place, with wrappers on the toilets and cable TV.

When I hit Pennsylvania I couldn't stop anymore, I just kept rushing home. Across the Delaware River at last, up the eight wide lanes of busy Route 80. I was finished. I had made it back to the beginning. I sped into Morristown, the Colonial hub: Washington slept there, now young couples with combined incomes twenty times the size of mine sleep there too, in huge mortgaged homes, and that night, after eight weeks gone, I would also sleep there.

I arrived at my shared duplex, the one with yellow aluminum siding on a near-noiseless cul-de-sac, on a late September afternoon, past commuters streaming home from the train station on sidewalks lined by leaf piles. Summer had been gone a long time there. No one was wearing sandals or had sand in their hair. And no one was in my house when I called through the door.

I stood for a moment on the cluttered porch of the big dented aluminum house, which looked changed because I was. It seemed older when I saw it now, and dumpier, its decay more vivid: porch paint chipping harder, bushes overgrown and slowly dying. Or was it always so?

"Hello?" I called as I entered. But no one answered.

My cat saw me coming through the door and he ran upstairs. My mail was in a cardboard box by the phone. Madeleine hadn't answered my calls; I found no messages. I spoke again to her machine: "Hey, I'm home. Gimme a call." Then I stood there, trying to remember where I came from.

What's with Madeleine? I wondered. Maybe she was away again. Maybe some horrible news had been uncovered and she was busy taking pictures of that. I carried my bags in. I took a walk. I phoned my parents: "Well hello," my father said. "What did you think of Rapelje?"

"Dad, it was wild."

"See the old house?"

"Burned down, Dad."

"Burned down?" he said. "Wasn't worth the trip then."

"Not worth the trip? Oh, it was worth it, Dad," I said. "It was really wild there."

After about ten days, when my skin had faded back to its ordinary paste and everyone in the house had stopped acting surprised to see me as we crossed on the stairs, Madeleine called. She said, "Hi. When did you get in?"

"Last week. I left messages. Remember?"

"Was it last week already?"

"Yes."

"Well, hey," she said. "Things have been crazy at work. Actually, Joe retired, and I'm still looking for a new job." I could hear her doing something, slinging jugs of chemicals around in her dark room. She was back behind the round darkroom door that I had watched her spin into so many times back when I used to work there, too. I wasn't there anymore. I wasn't really anywhere.

"Aren't you curious about my journey?"

"Sure. That's a long drive you had, isn't it?"

"About as long as the way out. Have you been avoiding me?"

"Avoiding you? What makes you think I'm avoiding you?"

"Like, maybe that you haven't visited or called."

She said, "And you think this has something to do with you? I have been busy."

Quiet. Was it possible that Madeleine spent whole days not thinking about me? Why did she sound like she hadn't been there, before, with me in Montana?

"Hey," I said, "I just thought you should know how the trip turned out. That's all."

"Yeah, you're home so soon. What happened to your adventure?"

"Well," I said, and I thought of the motels in South Dakota and Minnesota, and the pool game I shot with some guy in the North-woods who was just let out on parole and wouldn't tell me his name or his crime, and how yellow, yellow was the flat state of Indiana. "Well, there was nothing to do, really. I drove a lot. I took some pictures. You'll see."

But it was a long time before she saw.

Autumn was dull, not what I'd expected; the whole long fall was spent without much point to it, home from what might have been the rest of my life on the road or in some new extraordinary place where I could just send for my cat and settle down. That's what I was supposed to do apparently, but I didn't, and now, I didn't know at all what the rest of my life would be. It would require money. It would need some kind of a point. There seemed to be no point in living there, jobless. What if there never was a point again? I couldn't take that. I would have to work, and I knew of no place to find work from my position as an unemployed road warrior, except maybe, at the *Herald and News,* which I had quit in triumph only months ago. But now I realized that I'd have to have a job and at least over there I knew who to call.

"Say, Walter," I said on the phone. "Things are going great in my personal journey, but I wouldn't want to stay completely unplugged for too long, you know?"

"What's on your mind, cosmo?"

"I need a job."

With his sympathy, which he apparently did have for young journalists but really no one else, I started working part-time on the newspaper's copy desk; I didn't want to work more than three nights a week, at first. I was back but I was changed, after all, and part of me was in some faraway place, leaving about half of me available to work part time. I didn't want to go back, but I began to feel afraid, and that was not a bold and beautiful Montana feeling, it was a camped-out-all-alone feeling. I could hear myself breathing.

So I worked, hung around, and played cards with my house-mates; we played poker and bet pennies so that it never really mattered if you lost or won. Every now and then, I shut myself in my attic room and tried to compose something, to write stories, usually stories about young people who didn't fit in. The young misfits didn't even know how misfitted they were, that was what I thought made them so lovely. I'd work on my characters for a while, fine tune and fine tune until I'd get bored with their hopelessness and end up writing letters to Madeleine. She was still so far away. Six weeks home and I had not seen her.

In a letter, I could explain to her what I had learned in the mountains, about how I had nothing to fear but myself, and about how there was no point in wandering, without your best friend. She was my best friend, and I loved her, and it was all going to be okay; we could be friends again and we could be together.

That's what's nice about being women: we can love each other, and it's okay. That's what Madeleine told me, remember? I had learned. But the only way to prove it to her seemed to be to stay away. Or write a letter.

She wouldn't want a letter if it wasn't funny. Keep it light. I tore up the false starts, rip rip rip. I was trying too hard. I had to try to look like I wasn't trying. Copy over the good parts of that one, add some better stuff, and then . . . Rip. I went out for donuts and coffee and brought them upstairs. Crumpled pages. Dear Madeleine, could it be the poison air of New Jersey, could it be that what's beautiful has choked on . . . Rip rip rip. Madeleine, tree nymph, beautiful bright soul, it is so pointless and empty here in my life without . . .

Rip. The pursuit of this message to Madeleine began to give a sick structure to my fantastically boring days. It was my new project.

It couldn't be a love letter. She was just my friend. But if that were the case, then I shouldn't need to write to her at all, we'd just go for coffee. Okay.

"Hello, Madeleine," I said in a detached and sophisticated voice on the phone, having called her at work where she had to pick up, because if the phone rang and you didn't pick it up you could get fired. "Madeleine," I said, very casual and cool, "would you like to meet for coffee?"

"Can it wait? I've been working overtime. I'm tired."

"Oh come off it you're ALWAYS busy I'm so goddamn sick of this." (Oops.)

"Hey," she said softly. "What is your problem?"

Her rebuke was spoken intensely; it was not the way you'd speak to just anyone. It was quarrelsome and I analyzed it closely. She rejected me as if I were someone who, secretly, she really wanted to see. Right?

Late October. Colors on the trees, and birds crowding the branches, ready to leave. It began getting so cold that I couldn't even sit out on the old car seat on the front porch at night, drinking beer. Winter coming; everything sinking, and me giving up hope that I'd ever be happy again, and then, she came. She called and said she was going to be nearby that day, a Saturday, and would like to stop over, if that would be okay. I said, "Stop over, great," casually like she was just any old drop-in company, but then my heart started pounding. Where were my pictures? Where were my presents and things? I gathered up all the stuff I had to show her and then I scooped up all the newspapers and magazines strewn about the house and threw them out, a mad gesture toward cleaning, and I tried on a few different sets of clothes—is it too cold for shorts? Of course, don't wear shorts—and I waited. I looked at the photos and remembered: we had sailed on Canyon Ferry Lake and it was perfect, perfect, ah and how could all that joy be gone now? It wasn't gone; she had it.

She came in the late afternoon, climbed the steps fast and I was there before she could ring the bell, holding the heavy storm door open and letting it go with a rattling slam. She was smiling and I smiled and she kissed my cheek and gripped my arms, and looked at me, and I looked at her and then at my feet and smiled. Then she kissed Jonathan. She went inside and kissed my housemate Lou the exact same way, and then she even kissed Kathy. Kathy was shy; no one ever kissed Kathy. Madeleine kissed Kathy, then asked Lou how business was going. He told her. Then she and I sat in the front room with the sliding pocket doors pulled shut and we looked at pictures: her laughing on a horse, me holding a baby trout.

In about an hour she had to go. I was going to tell her something, maybe like "I'm sorry," but everything happened so fast.

"Come again some time, maybe . . ."

"Alright. We'll do something, soon."

She was gone.

I didn't want to stalk her, but I didn't feel forgiven.

In November, I drove out to Newark, to her house on Kinney Street. She would have to see me then, if I just showed up. I had not been to the Ironbound since early in the summer; the grim streets had not changed but they were new again to me and I missed them. I missed the tar shingles and graffiti, looping and jutting about like it had something to say but you could never understand it. I missed her. I knocked on the back door and stood there, beneath the clothes line and gray wooden steps that climbed the back of the house. All was still. There was no life in the blue house or gray yard or any-where. I stood feeling then as if I had done something terribly wrong by coming, afraid she would think I had followed her home, that I had circled the house and looked in her windows, and she would wonder how many other times I had done it and she would say, "Get off my property. What are you doing here? Get out." And I would say, "But, but . . . I'm sorry." And it would be too late. Insufferable pain. Perhaps she had seen me already.

I knocked, but no one came. Not Mike, not anyone. I stood, heart pounding, but the house stayed silent. I went away.

I walked back to my car, so ashamed still for having scared her away forever, apparently, and so embarrassed on top of that for hunting her down like a maniac. But I had to. I thought, "If only she would talk to me. God, then I'd never have to talk to her again."

I began going to bars in the afternoons with a neighbor from the aluminum duplex, he talked a lot about the years he spent addicted to heroin, back when he lived at home in the same town that I came from but in an enormous mansion; his family was really loaded. My neighbor had stringy blond hair and wire glasses. He was just some guy. And he wondered, what did it matter if one more rich kid wasted his life? It was evolution: waste comes to those whose ancestors reach the top of the food chain. What was left for him to do?

"It's destructive, their success," he said. "It fucks us up."

We drank Budweiser. Sometimes we skipped the bars and just sat in our coats on the front porch and drank and watched the cars turn around in the cul-de-sac.

Sometimes I would lay on my bed, just thinking, with my cat by my shoulder sniffing my cheek. The cat stretched and said to me: all you have to do, to be happy, is abandon your desires.

I didn't listen. I thought: all I really want, is to live with the people I love, like a family. I want us to live well and care for each other, so that we never have to be lost and alone. And maybe if we're lucky, we could raise children and teach the children to love the world and help each other. That's all. Not much different, really, from what anyone wants. Not much different, even, from what my grandparents did. We could fill our home with music, like Florence playing

163

her piano in the parlor, where thick crimson drapes and gold cords framed her view of dry prairie grass and stubborn sky. I just wanted a life, it's all I'd ever wanted, and just then I thought I'd even give in and take the only life that seemed to work for anyone: maybe I could marry someone. Maybe Lou, or my drug-addict neighbor. Just someone. We could just start with that and try to build something, because all those other ideas I once had, all that romance and obsession, it was all crazy and had left me unhappy. So maybe I could marry Lou and then it would be safe again to be with Madeleine.

I lay on the bed in listless afternoons and stroked the cat, and stared out the window, and I wondered if I'd ever see Madeleine again. Sometimes I thought of all the things that are better shared, like eating, and walking, and coming home from work and getting up for work again. I thought about how lying in bed on a Sunday afternoon in late autumn, as birds and voices echoed up from the outside cool and hollow, how that was the perfect place and time to be wrapped in thin sheets with a lover. A lover. Would I ever have a lover? Someone to hold in the covers while the world continued, unaware, someone who lays down with you, and turns, and puts a bare arm across your waist and pulls you round until you touch, and kisses you, and kisses you again. And this time the kiss does not let go for a long time. And the cat jumps down from the window and runs, and slowly the covers sweep away. And in that place and time with that person, you are loved and content and connected, and fear is forgotten, and pain is forgotten, until at last only one small ache remains.

That's what I thought about. But I was just dreaming.

Christmas came. Fuck Christmas. I didn't care about Christmas and didn't plan to care. Little dancing elves, people lying to their kids about Santa and I did not want to go home for another god-awful turkey dinner. Hadn't I been through enough hell?

And then Madeleine called. She left a message on the house answering machine. It was her: maybe I had been mistaken, maybe she was never really gone from my life and I just overreacted. I played the message twice. It was her.

Madeleine said she was having a Christmas party, a tree-trimming party for all her friends to come celebrate her new and long-sought much better job with a big New York news agency, and she invited me to come and said I should bring Lou. She said, "The more the merrier. Bring ornaments, too, homemade ones only. Don't spend money. We're trimming my tree."

Lou and I, excited and nervous, had only a week's notice for the party. Lou's main ambition was still to lay every woman alive, and he had failed with me so far, but hey, what about my cute friend Madeleine? I could see him reasoning: why would she invite him to her party if she didn't want sex? I knew the road he was on; it was a long one. We had much at stake and much, suddenly, to hope for, even if it all lived in died in our heads.

All of which meant that we had to make the best possible ornaments for Madeleine's tree, to secure top positions in her esteem. Mine had to be better than his, and he was working really hard. We spent a night cutting and filing and painting hunks of wood to turn them into great things Madeleine would love. We spoke as we labored.

"She just got a great job, that's why the party," I said.

"She's a great girl. Why hasn't she been coming around these days, anyway? I miss her."

"Me too," I said, sanding wood. "She's really busy, you know, she's really been working hard and I think she's going places."

Lou's ornament was a wood block carved into the shape of a camera. It had fine details, like a lens cap and the little button you press to take a picture. It held great potential to be the best ornament. He held it up. It was good. Mine was better: a mahogany peace sign that I sanded smooth as ivory. Simple, elegant.

Lou and I drove down to Newark together in his pickup truck. When we arrived at Madeleine's she gave us both quick hugs and said, "Come in! Come in!" then floated into the crowd behind her, and Lou and I made our way through people jammed against the kitchen walls, packed into the hall, milling in the living room. We found the tree and hung our ornaments side by side, front and center, beaming out practically screaming "We love her! We love her!" and we smiled stupidly with admiration for our work and each other and eggnog floated by and I was then cornered by a man named Bob, who wore a long black coat and a beret and was a writer of fiction, and he described his unfinished novel to me in full detail and then came up for air and handed me his phone number on a card four hours later, when the party ended, and I left with Lou, with Madeleine graciously calling goodnight behind us as we walked out her back door, back to the car, back up the back roads to Morristown, both of us silent all the way.

I didn't hear from Madeleine for weeks after that. It would be hard to talk anyway. She had a new job off in a world I'd never seen. Was it possible to lose someone you had loved for lifetimes?

By February, bills mounting, I had to go back to work full-time, five days a week from four until midnight. Going back to my awful job full-time was a matter of survival. It was what a young woman did to get by, in New Jersey, where there were no elk to shoot: there were only lousy full-time jobs at crummy newspapers where bosses yell a lot.

"Scum scum scum, so you want a job, huh? Well . . ."

Walter the editor, beady-eyed, his face shades of gray like he'd been dead for nine hours, trotting around the office with his stiff war-ruined knees, took pity on me. Except for when he was yelling, he always slurred his words. It was unwise to ask him to repeat what he muttered; it was better to listen hard. And fortunately it wasn't often difficult to guess what he said: "I hate flowers, I hate donuts, I hate I hate," whatever he'd see. He was supposed to be joking. I wrote headlines for him, and he let me work on the editorial page when he was short-handed; he hated the edits I wrote, too.

Meanwhile, the news was very bad as spring neared, and it got worse quickly. A recession was coming. My first recession, or at least, the first I'd noticed. There is nothing quite like that first recession. It feels like the complete and irreversible disintegration of all we know and love and economic ruin never looks quite so close at hand again, after you've seen it all fall apart once, and then recover. I had not lived long enough to know that it would all come back—money would come back, anyhow, and things that made people happy. It always did come back, eventually, and always did go away again, too. All I could see just then was how everything was gone. That year, it began to look as if civilization had reached its end, the world was over: crime was up and taxes were up and Madeleine and I were barely speaking.

Well, to hell with her. I started going out after work, late at night, with an editor named Fred, who was pigeon toed and overweight and never could get a decent haircut. He wore a patchy beard over round red cheeks that rose up puffy to hide all but a slit of his eyes. He wore gold-rimmed glasses. He liked to twist bits of paper up into tiny little balls and flick them. He was always nervous. Fred and I sometimes drove to New York after work in search of the young, hip, and wild life; we found a blues bar in Greenwich Village one night, forty or fifty blocks south of where Madeleine was working at that very moment. My friend Madeleine loves the blues, I told Fred. I started rocking my shoulders and clapping my hands and shouting out, "Yeah. Play it. Yeah," every so often.

"This is one hot band," I said. "Madeleine would love them."

"Yeah, they're really great," Fred answered, smiling so hard his gums showed. He was in the big city now, revved up, his pale hands flopping down rapidly on the table as he tried to also love the blues, and he loosened his tie, and he shouted "Aw-right" and the beer flowed. And I thought, "Maybe I could start over. Maybe I could put my world back together with Fred as the glue, maybe I could fix things." My mother's father was also named Fred. Destiny?

The Irving Louis Latin band slipped into a Jimi Hendrix tune, and Mr. Latin sang: "When I'm sad, she comes to me, with a thousand smiles she gives to me free," and I was sad, and hearing that someone out there had a thousand smiles to give to some other sad person touched me; I wanted someone to come to me, and then I hurt deeper than the pouring beer could reach; I began to cry, and Fred saw me, and he looked alarmed and then sorry, his red mouth making an "Oh" shape at the center of his hairy cheeks. He stroked my arm; he seemed as if he would like to touch the deep hurt for me, so right then I decided: I'll let him. I'm going to have affairs and feel good, and wild women know there is always someone else to love. Raise hell, that's the way it's gonna be now, uh huh. Lovers galore and deep mystery and I am going to stop wishing and dreaming and damn it I am going to start living my life.

Yeah: after the blues bar closed I went home with Fred to his little apartment in a brick apartment complex in Little Ferry, New Jersey, and marched into the bedroom where I got quickly naked, so bold that I turned myself on, oh come get me, just like I'd invented free love—free!—and he ran over and spread a clean sheet on his futon mattress on the floor, oh this is so groovy this bachelor pad with no furniture it's so free and wild: I knelt there on that mattress in the dark bare room, swaying, one hand stroking at my pubic hair and a silver pendant hanging between my breasts; white sheets crumpled under me, come on baby, let me see it, yeah, let me see, and he got naked too as I called him, Freddy, let's do it, Freddy. Kneel in front of me, so I can hold my hands out and touch that pale, pale body, long touches, ooh. I felt his rubber hands move over me, frantic, searching for nipples or other things fast like twisting bits of paper what's happening, what's happening, and unprotected, my legs opened up to scream "put that thing in here, mister, put that in me now," chests bumping, hips bumping, rump bumping hard onto the mattress I grabbed his bad-cut hair and when he squeezed bunches of me up I arched and yelled come on, come on, and then at last, at long last, he stopped me. Umph. He pushed himself up and kneeled before me, ran a twitching hand through his hair. I waited. Then he apologized. He told me it must be the beer, and that he was sorry.

"You mean," I said, "is it . . ."

"No," he said. "It's just . . . not going to happen."

"Oh." I sat up. "Is it . . . is it me?"

"Oh, no," he said, "it's not you." We sat there and saw the sad truth between us, the sad little truth upon his large thighs. And we never tried that again.

"You want a coffee?"

"Uhm, no."

"Hey. Are you still sad?"

"Oh gosh, no. No, don't worry about me."

I stopped going out with Fred and pulled an old card out of my wallet and called Bob. We went to a diner and ordered burgers. Bob wore a goatee and a beret and he chewed with his mouth open, eyes pointed up at the tin ceiling deep in thought. Even though I had met him only once before, at Madeleine's party, on this day when he finished chewing that hamburger Bob asked me if I wanted to go to Czechoslovakia.

"You'd have a great time."

"I don't know, Bob, it seems a little far."

"But you like adventures," he said, "don't you?"

"I like some adventures."

"What, Czechoslovakia's not good enough for you?"

"It's not that it's not good enough."

"Alright, then just come for two weeks. You don't have to come for the whole four weeks."

"Bob, I barely know you."

"But," he said, "I think about you all the time."

It seemed too bad, somehow, that everyone was crazy, and everyone wanted the same thing but not from each other, and that there was not a chance in hell that I would go to Czechoslovakia with this man. He seemed to be offering everything I wanted.

"Come on, please? Why won't you go to Eastern Europe with me?"

"I don't want to."

"But, we could be so great together. I . . . I . . . think you're beautiful."

It was terrifying. I had to stop returning his calls; even though I did like adventures, even though I did like Europe, even though I wanted to be wild, no one else was wild, no one else could have fun and then just let go; life-altering mistakes lay around me like quicksand. Those who mate successfully learn very young to cut their losses and move on. One desperate, lonely night, for example, I called the frog. He wisely said he did not remember me. The frog would no doubt be successfully married within the year.

Bob, on the other hand, left me long messages on the answering machine; his phone messages were artful and passionate and full of longing. He made love to the answering machine and I thought, "If someone ever loves him back they will make everyone blush." I didn't answer any of his calls so Bob sent me letters, letters he had struggled over, maybe for hours alone in his room, writing, taking breaks for coffee, then writing, to me, some more.

I saved his letters. I thought: "God, why can't I just love him?" If just one of us could have turned around on this long chain of lovesick people with their eyes turned in other directions, we'd have started a revolution.

"There's something wrong," I said at work, standing in the parking lot where the copy desk staff smoked cigarettes in exile from the healthy world. I made polite conversation with Fred. Tension had sullied the rising spring, so that even slightly warmer weather offered no joy, and longer days meant only longer twilight. A cop shot a black kid in the back in Teaneck, and the town rioted for two days. Everyone I knew seemed distressed. No one could say why. Maybe it's just how life was and always would be and I had begun, weakly, to accept it.

In the parking lot I said, "Isn't anyone happy?"

Fred said, "That's a recession for ya." And indeed, the "downturn" was huge. The 1990 economy was souring. The first George Bush had been elected expressly to keep all the greedy fortunes safe but even he was failing; everything was failing. But all this malaise had to be about more than that; I couldn't get up some mornings, and no one really seemed surprised because most people I knew couldn't get up, either.

"It's probably my fault," another editor, Brenda, said as she held her cigarette philosophically and scratched her chin. "When I was six years old I got a bad haircut one day in November and the next day, President Kennedy was shot. All the bad things have always been because of me."

But it couldn't have been Brenda. Her theory fit my world view but there was an important adjustment: I was at the epicenter. The problem had to be me, everything was good until I ruined it, like a missile buried in a silo deep in blissful vacant Montana, armed, hiding. Kaboom.

And if I needed any more convincing, I sat at my desk at work and read this in the *New York Times:* "THOUSANDS PLAN LIFE BELOW, AFTER DOOMSDAY."

It was a story out of Livingston, Montana. March 14, 1990. Elizabeth Clare Prophet, leader of the Church Universal and Triumphant, issued a warning. The ascended masters had told her that the end was coming, the nuclear holocaust. People were streaming to the compound by the thousands to go live in the bomb shelter. The time had come. The tension was building. Guru Ma said it may have seemed like the danger was gone, with the Berlin Wall dismantled and the Cold War over just a short time before, but in fact, that happiness merely signaled that the real danger was nearing and it would catch us off guard.

I put my face in my hands. So it was true, if you believed the guru: the bright future we had all once imagined would never be what we'd hoped for, because there was no future. And then, depressing as that was, I began to feel relieved. I no longer had to mourn the total loss of everything I had once believed in because, fortunately, we'd all die soon. There was no future for us; there was nothing. Maybe there wasn't even a Montana; that was just a made up place.

Months passed. I was still alive. Another Jersey summer came to swallow up our air, leaving nothing much besides heavy particles for poor lungs to live on. Must be global warming, we figured, smoking our cigarettes outside. It was already almost a year ago that I was in the better air of Montana with my greatest pal, breathing free, and now she had a great job in Manhattan and was too busy with that to spend any time with me.

"Yeah, I know," Fred said. "You told me."

"You'd like her," I said.

"I met her, remember? I met her when Photo Phil quit last March and she was at the party."

"Oh, that's right, it's just sort of funny because I haven't seen her since then and she used to be my best friend."

"Yeah, I know," Fred said.

"Well, I never get to see her anymore and I just feel sick about it. I don't even know if I should call her anymore."

"Let me ask you something," Fred said, looking over his shoulder and then leaning in. "You've been saying the same thing since, what, since January. Why are you so obsessed with her?"

"I don't know, Fred." I took a long drag off my cigarette and blew smoke up like a Paterson chimney. "I don't know."

"You seem to have very strong feelings."

"I do. That's true."

"Why do you care so much about her?"

"I think it's because . . ."

"You can tell me."

"I think," and I looked at the traffic out beyond the parking lot. "Oh, what does it matter, I'm practically dead anyhow, I guess I could tell you the truth. If I told you the truth about everything it couldn't kill me any more than I'm already dead, could it?"

"What the hell are you talking about?"

"Well, this is going to seem really weird, you're going to get all freaky about it but it's just the truth. You really want to know?" I was going to tell him.

"Of course."

"If you promise, I mean promise, that you won't tell anyone else . . ."

"You can trust me." Fred's feet started tapping and he stared down at me; his beard was wiggling.

"Because if I trust you and . . ."

"You can trust me."

"Well, I've never told anyone, and . . ."

"Tell me."

"Wait," I said. "Wait. I can't trust you, are you kidding? Who's the biggest gossip in the newsroom?"

"Hey, woah, I don't gossip."

"Then how do I know that Ron only has one testicle, because Rose slept with him, and she told you, and you told me? How else would I know that?"

"Well, I can tell you things, I can trust you so I can tell you but I don't tell other people."

"Fred, you tell everybody everything."

"I do not."

"Well what about, you know, you know . . ."

"I never told about, you know, you know . . ."

"Oh no?"

"I didn't. I swear."

"Then why has Walter looked at me funny ever since we did that?"

"He always looks funny."

"No, this is a different funny, like he's going to vomit on me or something, like he's picturing me naked. He never yells at me anymore, he just looks at me like I'm sitting there naked."

"Oh, and that's my fault? I'm doing that?"

"Oh Jesus, I can't fucking believe this. You know, I'm really better than this. I'm so much better than all this, I really should be someplace else very far away from here."

"Yeah, no kidding, who shouldn't be."

"Forget it."

"Forget what? Don't forget it. What the hell is wrong?"

"Nothing is wrong."

"What did you want to tell me?"

"Nothing."

"Oh, come on, tell me. You know, it might make you feel better."

"I doubt it. I really doubt it."

"Things that seem big are really never so big when you hear them out loud. Just talk it out. Let it go. Whatever it is. What is it?"

"God, I just wish it weren't such a big deal."

"I bet it's not."

"I mean, I can't say it. Why don't you guess."

"Come on, that's silly. Just tell me."

"Well, alright, but," I said, "I don't know how to say it. That's the thing, it just won't come out. Like, alright. Let me ask you. If you could have anyone in the newsroom, who would it be? God, I'm starting to sweat, this is so unbelievable, it's so hard."

"How hard could it be? Come on."

"Just tell me. If you could have anyone. Who?"

"Have? You mean, have? Well, you know, there's always, you, I mean, I'd try again with you if that's what you're trying to . . ."

"No, no. Come on, really. Who? Maybe, like, how about Gina?"

"Gina?"

"Yeah, you know. She's cute, right?"

"Well, yeah. Right."

"Cuz, you know, I really think she's cute. You see what I'm saying? I really think she's hot."

"Hey. Hey. What are you getting at?"

"Just like you, you know? I think that myself, that she's, you know, hot, she's got something about her, and well, I'm not really as different from you as you think, about these things, I mean, do you know what I'm saying?"

"Yeah, I think so, but you're wrong about me. I don't like Gina. She's into witchcraft, spooky stuff. She reads vampire books. I don't want to get mixed up in that. Hey, you shouldn't be all upset just because you think I like Gina, because that's just wrong."

"No, Fred. No, Fred, that's not what I'm saying. Listen."

"I wouldn't date a witch. You know? I'm not interested in witches. I care about you, though, if that's what's got you . . ."

"No, listen to me, that's not what it is. I'm trying to tell you that I think I am, I think that I could be a . . . I am a . . . Aw, shit," I said. "Why should I tell this to you?"

Fred's fingers worked over the butt of his cigarette. His eyes darted back and forth between my eyes, searching as fast as the twitch in his cigarette hand. What Fred was looking for had fled. I rubbed my face and looked at the empty building across the street and felt despair, in a poor city that seemed robbed forever by despair, that's where I was, and no one could help me.

"Okay, Fred. I am trying to tell you that I have been tricked by a witch. I've been tricked by a witch just like Gina but not Gina. That's all. No biggie."

"Now, come on, the only reason that I, you know, that I couldn't that night, I had all that beer, that's all it was."

"Listen to me, stupid, okay? Listen: This is not about you. Not at all. I think Madeleine has done something to my brain. Like, didn't do something to it, just like, brainwashed me or something."

I wanted him to know that I was living with a problem, even if I would not tell him what it was. I just wanted someone to know how I felt. I felt panicked, like I was dying, like everything around me was dying and no one could save anything. I felt this way all the time, and yet, nothing ever actually died; it was like a terrible flu I could not shake and no one could diagnose effectively. If I told anyone how much I loved Madeleine, and how she had rejected me, I thought the revelation would only add to my problems. But no one can help you with a broken heart if they don't know that it's broken. I had been trying as best I could for months to pretend that nothing ever happened, nothing had been broken and nothing had changed, but that wasn't working for me, either.

"Okay, listen, this is it, I'm just going to say it: I think that once she was maybe recruiting me for a cult, and, I guess I just haven't gotten over that."

"Recruiting you for a cult?"

"Yeah. Madeleine was trying to get me like, hooked, I guess, but it didn't work, and now we don't talk. God, don't ever tell anybody this or I'll totally kill you but like, think about it, I quit my job and took my money and followed her to Montana and I would have done anything, probably, cuz I thought I was so happy, I would have lived in a bomb shelter full of people who think they're some special family, you know? I believed all kinds of crap when I was with Madeleine but I was wrong about it and I've been trying to get my shit back together ever since then."

"A cult? A cult? Jesus, that's serious."

"Well, no, not that serious, she's not really in a cult, and I'm not either, so I was just, you know, wrong. That's all. Never mind."

"Oh man, that's nothing to mess with," Fred said, inhaling hard and running an unsteady hand through his insane hair. "Once they're in they're always in, don't let anyone fool you. She's definitely fucking with you if she was in a cult."

He scanned the traffic lights that ringed the Herald and News, as if looking for assistance, maybe for a cop, and finally he turned to looked at me, sternly. He put a hand on my shoulder and squeezed it. "Hey. Maybe you should get some help or something."

"No, I'm alright, Jesus."

"Seriously. I'm worried about you."

"I'm okay."

"They recruit, you know. Don't ever trust those people."

"I said I'm okay."

"Are you sure?"

"I'm okay," I said. I took a last drag and dropped the cigarette butt, ground it into the black pavement long after it broke apart. I put my hand across my mouth and rubbed.

"Hey, Fred. Forget what I said about the cult. I'm just confused a little. You know? I think I did something that made Madeleine drop me, or something."

"Drop you? Why would she drop you?"

"I don't know."

"You think she dropped you?"

"Well, she's gone."

"She's not gone. She's where she's always been. Hey. Maybe it's better this way. Ever think of that?"

"Better? Ha. Why is this better?"

"Because of the cult."

"I said forget the cult."

"Okay. Are you okay?"

"I'm okay."

"You're sure?"

"I'm sure."

"Okay." Fred watched me steadily from underneath his heavy lone eyebrow and twitched at his cigarette. "I still don't get what's bugging you."

"Me neither."

"What do you think's the matter?"

"I'm lonely, that's all."

"I got news for you," he said. "Everybody's lonely."

After that, when people looked at me strangely in the newsroom, I couldn't be sure what they were thinking. They could have been observing my usual panic attacks, and my efforts to hide them, which involved holding my head in my hands and gasping for air; or they might have been looking at me for signs of whatever Fred had probably told them about the cult; or they might still have been reenacting in their minds whatever they must all have heard about me and Fred and that night on the futon mattress. Whatever they were thinking, they all had the same sort of sideways look of muted horror. Except Gina. Gina developed a habit, as she crossed the newsroom, of stopping at my desk and smiling, then walking away. I was shaking all the time. Something had to happen.

Then Madeleine called. She said she'd been playing darts with some guys from my office at a bar. She said they talked about me.

"Oh, no."

"Nice guy, that Fred. We had a very interesting conversation."

"Oh, that shithead Fred. Oh god, what did he tell you?"

"Nothing bad or anything. Don't worry."

The potential nightmarish scenarios, the betrayals, the embarrassments, leaped up in my mind like shooting gallery bunnies, leaping up and leaping up and mocking and taunting, all very fast, in the space of an instant on the phone.

"He just said you have been a little lonely lately," said Madeleine.

"Yeah," I muttered, "yeah, a little lonely."

All I could think to say were ugly words like nimrod and asshole. I wanted to tell her that whatever Fred said, he had lied, but I wasn't sure what lies he'd told her, if they were some of mine, or his, and being confused, I had trouble speaking.

Then she said, "I'm sorry."

"You're—what?"

"I'm sorry that Fred hurt your feelings. It stinks, getting hurt."

She seemed downright excited about that. Like we were all off the hook. "Hey, come on. Nothing to worry about," Madeleine said. "They're all jerks. They're boys. You're going to get over it."

Then she said, "You know, I've been meaning to call you. Mike is moving out of my apartment. It's going to leave me with kind of a problem." It would leave a bedroom open in a place where no one wanted to go.

"Really?" I said. What would she do?

"I don't know," she said. "I kind of like it here. It's home, you know?" I did know.

I said I missed spending time there. I said I missed her.

"Well," she said. "I miss you too."

We dropped the conversation about the apartment. Moments later she asked me if I wanted to go with her up to the Catskills, a little road trip to go visit her friend John.

"To get your mind off that boy," she said.

"My mind isn't on that boy," I answered.

"John's house is haunted," she said. "You will love the haunted house."

"I am a haunted house."

"I know."

We were both working strange hours. She worked the overnight shift at her new job, the "lobster trick," all alone in the office from midnight till eight in the morning, and I worked four until midnight, and it was hard to find a way to make our days coincide but she said, let's go up for the Fourth of July, and that seemed like fun: a holiday together. We hadn't spent a holiday together since Earth Day, 1989. So I packed a bag and drove tenuously out of the suburbs to Newark, remembering old roads. I pulled through the gate across the driveway and honked. There was Madeleine: she bounded out her kitchen door with a backpack, tossed her hair back, dropped the pack to the ground, and bent to fix her boot lace. She looked up and squinted in the sun like she had not seen daylight in too long, and then she looked at me and smiled. I was happy to see her but when I did, I didn't feel like smiling. I didn't feel anything, really, because I had become so hopelessly sad that when I saw her all the feelings just sort of canceled out and I was neutral. She looked different: Her hair had grown very long, past her shoulders. Her arms and legs in shorts and a T-shirt were pale; she glowed.

She opened the car door and said, "Hey, I have missed you, where have you been?"

"Where have I been? Where have YOU been?"

She threw her backpack into the back seat and flopped in beside me, and she looked at me and started tee-heeing through closed teeth in a big smile. I don't think I smiled back; I think I stared, like seeing a ghost, and she poked my rib and she said, "Let's go!"

I looked in the mirror and saw my own eyes and backed out. We hit the road.

John and Paula's house had a potted bare tree in the living room with little white lights strung around it, standing in a plate glass window. From the driveway I could see the tree, as if the woods continued up to the wall and then inside the house, strange and fascinating, and as I was staring at it John popped into my view and frightened me. "Hey, where ya been? We missed ya," he said, and we hugged. John was a small man who always seemed a little bigger than he was because he was pumped up with energy. He couldn't sit still. There was too much to do, too much going on, and damn damn damn the universe was so abundant it was crazy. His eyes were dark and close together, intense, and his brown hair was slowly receding. Sometimes he wore a beard, but you never knew what to expect. I'd met John back before Madeleine and I left for Montana. His house up in the Catskills was her favorite place to go when she wanted to escape Newark. It was like taking a vacation. I went with her a few times and John had started to feel like my ex-boyfriend, too; we were all just one big family, and his wife Paula was so busy taking care of crazy John and their baby, she didn't seem to mind her husband's ex-lover and her young blond friend hanging around sometimes, but maybe she was faking.

"Wait till you see what we're having for dinner," John said. He'd been fishing at a lake nearby, hadn't been tossing his worm in more than ten minutes when he got a magnificent incredible tug and he reeled in a fish the size of his forearm. He shouted to heaven, he felt so blessed; then he killed that thing right there on the mosquito-swarming shores of Lake 13. It was the most spirited intelligent fish he'd ever caught, and it was delivered to us just especially by the god-force for this weekend of joy among friends who love each other.

Madeleine was just then producing the trout from a bag in the re-frigerator. It did not look so intelligent, gutted, with dull eyes seeing nothing from the sides of its head. This beast, this sea monster found deep, deep, in a lake, not a river, was a brown trout, and I'd never seen a trout so big, even in Montana. Especially in Montana. John, smallish, wiry, with dark and perhaps always dilated eyes, and extraordinary energy and a "come-on, tell-me-a-secret" grin, caught the greatest fish ever, landed that fish so clean that it hadn't even eaten the worm.

"What lake did you say?" asked Madeleine.

He said, "Lake 13."

"On worms?" She looked at him and shook her head. He looked back and said "I know I know forget about it."

"What?" I asked.

"No live bait allowed on Lake 13," she said, holding the monster. "This guy never knew what hit him."

We looked at the fish that was caught on the illegal worm, long dead by now, too late to go back, too late to do better. Should we like this fish, or not? I looked across it's pale gray snout hard into the eyes of the struggle at the center of my life: if this moment was so perfect, then how come it was still not right?

"Oh well," John said. Mistakes happen, especially when John encounters nature. "I'm human," he shouted, and snatched the fish from Madeleine's hand.

Paula shuffled into the room. She had crazy frizzy hair and her eyes were big and wide and she had an alarming way of talking with her face looming too close to mine: "It's still a fish, right?" she said, eyes wide and head tilted two inches away from me. "It's dinner."

The warm day was easy, as if my life was still related to Made-leine's and all the people in it, and this had never been in doubt and did not need saying. John seemed to think we should all live up there with him, or that we did, really, and just had to go away to other places from time to time. He had told me I could visit any time, that I was family, and now I thought I really knew what that meant and I liked it; I liked it that Madeleine alone could not expel me from the family, but what I really wanted was for John to tell her that she had to keep me. I was still in shock to be there, to be with Madeleine again at all, and so I was very quiet. I spent most of my time sitting on the deck, staring at the Catskill Mountains. Madeleine brought the illegal trout out to a table on the deck where John filleted it on a broad sheet of the *Albany Times Union*. He wrapped the fish head in coverage of a July Fourth parade. I started to clean up but Madeleine said, "Nah, forget it, I got this. You and John just sit here and stay out of trouble." She balled up the scaley paper.

John said, "You know, you two have been married in a past life. I can see it."

I arched my eyebrows and pretended to be surprised. Madeleine carried the fish and garbage inside. John said to me, "Nothing personal, you know, but you were probably the man."

"Do you think so, John?" I inquired casually.

"Sure, sure, just look at how she pushes you around. But hey, there's nothing wrong with a little reincarnated sex change. I've been a woman a few thousand times before, absolutely, in my previous lifetimes. I'm a man now of course, no doubt about that." He raised his eyebrows in Groucho Marx fashion. We lit cigarettes. We put our feet up and stared at the Catskill Mountains across a garden of budding zucchini.

"Women, men, it changes all the time from life to life. We can take any form we want to on this planet," John said. "Didn't Maddy ever tell you this?"

"No," I said, "not really."

"Well," John said, "she knows. She's very well educated in the cosmic order. I think she went to college for it. Most people can't deal with the truth. Most people, if I told them what I just told you about me being a woman once, they'd just think I was a homo or something. They can't see it."

He said, "You've been everything and you could be anything still. You could change, you could zap right out of this whole illusion if you decided to and the only reason you can't is because you don't believe it."

John worked on oil tankers, like Madeleine's roommate, Mike, and he chased ships to ports up and down the Hudson River to inspect the cargo in their deep hulls. He would tell anyone who'd listen that the oil barons were evil bastards who had enslaved him, and all the rest of us, only most of us didn't see it. He had answers; he claimed truth so that the burden fell to me to disprove him. I rarely bothered.

"Now, see this," he stuck his cigarette in his mouth and held his hands up and examined them, "these bodies of ours are just toys but we got too attached to them, and now we can't remember how to get out again. If you want, you can leave your body. You can leave your whole world, any time. Easy."

I inhaled. "How?" I exhaled slowly.

"You don't believe that you can do anything, so you can't. But just bear in mind, you could. If you believed, then you could."

John's daughter Krista ran out the door and yelled at the top of her little two-year-old lungs, "Daddy, Mommy says come inside! Now!"

"Me, I'm too attached to the world, to my family, and work. I've forgotten the secret. We're all born knowing, but I forgot. I'm such a moron for it. Every day I think what a moron I am that I forgot everything I knew about being a beautiful energy form darting through the universe. But here I am, it's my karma."

"Daddy, come inside now," Krista stomped her foot.

"Krista, Daddy's talking," John hollered, and Krista ran inside shrieking.

John had two main obsessions for deep conversation: evil run amok on the planet earth and the forgotten cosmic powers by which we could escape this rampant evil. I listened and waited, but no actual procedures were ever revealed for harnessing these powers, only conviction. In a way, he came as close as anyone ever had to describing how I felt: trapped and disillusioned. It was like he said, I was a beam of light, unable to escape myself. He had explanations, which I craved. But in other ways, John scared me. I could not handle all the plots to enslave the world and I wanted to say he was nuts but the thing is, it all seemed true.

"There are forces," he was saying, "they're acting all the time. They could take over, and there's your social security number on everything and your bank card gets shut off and you've got no cash, nowhere to run, nowhere to hide, and any minute on a whim, bam, we're all fucked. It could happen like that." He clapped once. "It will."

"So what do we do about it?" I said. "I mean, I vote."

"You vote? Ha!" he said. "Get a gun! Jesus, get a gun!"

Madeleine stepped out and said, "Come on, you two, there's fish to eat."

"Maddy, come here. How come you never told her any of this?"

"Any of what?"

"About how humans are trapped here, and all that other important stuff."

"Because she knows." Madeleine walked over and scissored her fingers onto my cigarette, took the last drag before dropping it and crushing it out. "Let's eat," she said, and we followed her.

We filled the table with fish and salad and coleslaw and corn on the cob; meals at John and Paula's were frenzied with fast eating, loud talking, the passing of salt and bowls and much reaching across the table, all of which would quiet down for about five seconds as John, Paula, and Krista blessed everybody's food by wiggling their fingers over the table and saying together, "Oooohmmm." There we were: a family. After the eating began, John said, "The absolutely wildest thing that ever happened to me, have I ever told you? On the beach down in South Jersey, it was the year after Madeleine left me for Montana. I was about twenty. Oh, wild—hey, Krista, stop putting your hands in the food—it was night, maybe 3 a.m. and we were on the beach and I was looking at the stars, just lying there looking up at those lights and then they started pulling me, like this."

John looked up blank and slack-jawed and rose slowly out of his chair as if he were irresistibly drawn to the pewter chandelier with fake candles. Paula said, "Krista, put that salt shaker down," and Krista dropped her corn on the floor.

"I was flying," he said. "There was nothing to stop me from just rising up into the stars and flying through them. I could have materialized on any other planet in any other form because I'm just particles, get it? I'm just a lot of pieces of the same stuff everything else is and I can be anything, I can be this table if I want, see? I knew I could go anywhere, do anything. I KNEW this."

Madeleine stabbed at her salad and said, "How much acid did you take?"

Paula looked up and locked her wide unblinking eyes on me and said, "Remember when that guy Art Linkletter's daughter was on acid and jumped off a roof cuz she thought she could fly?"

"Mommy, who's Art Linkiter? Who's Art Linkiter, Mommy?"

"Yeah but that's different," John said, biting into his corn.

I said, "Buffy from *Family Affair,* she died on acid, right?"

"Yeah," said Paula, "that's right."

John said, "Alright, but listen: I know this is true. It doesn't matter, I know, it's the truth, that's all. You can fly, but you've forgotten how. Right, Maddy?"

"That's right," she said, stabbing her salad.

"Okay," John announced. "I've said enough."

John gave me a few books to take home: *The Hollow Earth, Masks of the Illuminati,* and *None Dare Call It Conspiracy.*

We spent the night, her on a guest bed, me camped out on the couch beneath the bare tree in the haunted living room. No spirits bothered us but our own, me thinking about past lives and John thinking who knows what and Paula putting up with it and none of us could really read Madeleine. As we drove back to New Jersey, I asked what she thought of all the things John said.

We decided he liked to scare himself because he was getting bored in his marriage. "Ya know, a little terror," Madeleine said. "Kind of reminds you what it's like to fall in love. Keeps things spicy."

I closed my eyes.

There was John in my memory: waving out the window good-bye, stuck in his good life. He raised his arm to wave at us like he was testing a wing, and then he dropped it. I understood that I loved him (though it was not "that kind of love") because he, like me, was desperate for something, and maybe it is the same for all of us.

Madeleine and I arrived back in Newark on Monday at noon, and I dropped her off, and as I did it occurred to me that we might not see each other again. We had no common days off. We worked strange hours. There would be no time to spend together. As she took her bag out of the back of my car, I said goodbye and left it at that. Even seeing her now, I didn't expect anything to be different than it had been for the past year. So much time had passed that it seemed to me I'd really lost her; we could never be so close again. What I felt, after that short trip to see John, was that I'd finally been forgiven.

Then she phoned me at work. "Hey," her voice sang in my ear. It was nearing August, those sweaty days when everything normal dries up or runs out and leaves a vacuum of weirdness.

She said, "I gotta kick Mike outa here. He's getting kind of crazy on me. I wish I could do it now but I'm never going to find another roommate."

"Oh," I said. "That's a problem."

"Yeah."

I said, "Maybe I should move to Newark."

She said, "Really? Do you think you might?"

I said I'd think about it.

When we hung up, I went outside to stand with the gang around the back door smoking. They were talking about the recession and how it sends crime rates way up. "Recession comes and people start popping each other like flies. All hell breaks loose," Fred said.

"Like the savings and loan thing?" said Brenda.

"Oh, those thieving banker scum bastards," someone shrieked.

"Now, that's bad," Fred said. "But it's just the beginning of something really awful."

I stared gloomily at traffic for a while, then I dropped my cigarette and slipped back inside.

At my desk, I looked up at the TV screen hanging above the newsroom and saw file footage of a priest who was charged with molesting young runaway boys at his famous New York charity organization. The image flew past, along with a rapid succession of talking faces; the city editor rifled through channels by remote control and finally settled on cartoons. From the meeting room, I heard Walter growl, "That goddamn lousy son of a bitch." It was 6:30 and in five hours I'd be leaving to go home, to the house I shared with strangers.

But I can go anywhere. My soul of light knows how to leave this world, if I can just remember. "I'm just a mass of particles," I thought.

I decided that I would move to Newark with Madeleine.

"Newark?" Lou said simply when he heard the news. He helped me pack boxes into the rented van, clearing out the prized attic room for himself. I said, "You didn't think I'd stay in Morristown forever, right? I got places to go."

"Okay," he said, and he waved as I left.

"Newark?" Fred said. "Woah, that is serious. I hope you know what you're doing." He reminded me that Madeleine was, after all, the person I had recently suspected of recruiting me for a cult.

I asked Fred to please forget that I had ever said anything about the cult. But he would never forget it because it was too good. "Well, you are sort of following her," he said and I told him he had it wrong. I was a cosmic light ray landing here and there and Newark was like the frontier; it was a new planet to explore out in the universe of my life and I could go there, I could do anything.

I told my mother and father I had a new address. They said, "Newark? Newark? Why would you do that?" How could I explain?

Newark has been called the most dangerous city in the world. Cops shoot people, ten, twenty times a year there, depending; the streets are wide and bare, and back then almost no one lived in the place who didn't have to. In the Ironbound section, shingled houses form a neighborhood of tight rows, tiled and barred, where once men stood on rooftops with shotguns to keep race riots away. In 1967, the Ironbound survived while the rest of Newark burned down; it had not given up its life. I liked it. It was strange. It was not what was expected for me. And Madeleine was there.

First thing I did when I moved in, I hung a hammock underneath the wooden staircase that climbed the back of the house. Before I unpacked, before I did anything, I hung that hammock above the black top. I lay there in the half-enclosed square outside the kitchen door where a row of garbage cans stood in a faint stench of rot, with bitter undertones of urine. Raised voices from neighboring kitchens echoed overhead in languages I didn't comprehend. I looked up and considered the variety of shingles on roofs, the aluminum siding and tar-papered walls, the crisscrossed clotheslines and telephone wires, the abundance of falling apart or unfinished stuff.

Who but me could understand why I had gone there? I stared at the clutter above me, out of reach, and I thought: "I have exactly what I have always wanted. Finally. No one else needs to understand."

Moving day was August 1. The newspapers reported that this was also the day Iraqi soldiers invaded Kuwait, provoking a war that was apparently very important but very few of us understood much about. Was it a coincidence? There I was offloading boxes as soldiers trampled borders, gouged out eyes, shot people, spilled oil into the Persian Gulf. It was dreadful. I filled the small back bedroom of my new apartment with boxes of my cherished things. I traversed the yellow kitchen door in Newark without knocking, because I had my own key now.

The metal gate between the sidewalk and our drive creaked when it swung open; that's how I'd know when Madeleine or the Sanchezes upstairs came home. Headlights grazed the front window when cars turned in the drive, then the chain-link gate creaked as it closed. Where the chain links met the garage, frail red roses spread wild on a vine. After we moved away, a teenage girl was shot dead on that drive, shot running away from a jealous boy. She died in the spot where I used to park my car, I'm told.

When I moved in, we decided to redecorate. We thought we'd like to make our place a home. But, what did that mean? Food cooking all the time and babies growing into happy children and paying the bills and planning vacation? A place with cool pictures on the walls and shelves full of stuff easily broken by children? A space shared by consent? Could Madeleine and I have a home just by living in that place, together? I felt nervous about it. I wasn't sure what to do. How could we make a home together and still just be roommates? I had tried to learn not to want what I could not have but now I had what I wanted, didn't I? This place seemed almost like what I'd dreamed, or anyhow, close enough. We could hang curtains, she said. We could fix the cracked glass. Madeleine dragged an old screen door out of the basement, and I fixed it up and hung it outside the kitchen door. Why was every door in Newark solid metal? Why not have a screen door like on the front porches in the Great Plains? What kept people from good lives? They simply lacked imagination. We could make a home together, right there in Newark, if that's what we really wanted to do; we didn't need to be in Montana to live happily together.

I bought a big rack that, when you drop a stack of newspapers in it, wraps the stack in twine and makes recycling easy. We loved to recycle. Everything that dies gets a new life, even bottles and cans have something like karma. It was very gratifying.

Upstairs the Sanchez family mostly left us alone, happy to know we'd pay rent on time but sad for other things less predictable. Mr. Sanchez was out of work with some kind of complex brain condition that made him unable to remember technical things, but he could still drive a car. Grandpa Sanchez, who turned ninety that year, had lost big parts of the function of his own brain to age, and his body was failing too, and sometimes when he couldn't make it up the zigzag back stairs in time he would urinate outside, near our kitchen door, back by our recycling bucket. Then he'd zip his fly and shuffle away, out onto the sidewalk in front of the house where he stood in his slippers, watching. An old woman in a periwinkle housedress, brittle as a bird, marched up and down our block every day, jabbing the asphalt with a long fat walking stick that kept her marching like a metronome as kids tossed balls above her head and cars whizzed by. Her eyes fixed forward as if those laps would take her somewhere, or keep her strong for the day she would be liberated, as if this was not where she belonged, and one day someone was coming to get her. Every day, twenty laps, maybe more, she kept walking. Grandpa, hands clutching the chain fence for balance, watched her. And sometimes I did, too.

Madeleine and I had an arrangement. When I left work each night around eleven, I'd drive home in time to take her down the street to the 11:42 Manhattan-bound train so that she could begin her overnight shift; at 8:27 the next morning, a train would bring her back again. Public transportation couldn't take me to my job in Passaic, so I had to drive my gas-sucking car but at least I could help Madeleine safely uphold our commitment to mass transit.

"Don't forget to lock the doors," Madeleine would say, knowing that I would anyway, and then she'd jump out of the car and scramble past the junkies at Penn Station. She would arrive at work after midnight, very nearly alone on the thirty-fourth floor of an office tower, transmitting news photos to the world by computer.

Fifteen minutes and a world away up the highway, my mother had driven my father to the commuter train almost every day for twenty-five years, through a lawn-covered suburb in the daylight, where it was safe to walk, even after dark, but she drove him, anyway. They charged out the door each day after breakfast, started up the car, wiped off the snow in winter. She'd honk from the driveway until he appeared in his dark suit, his briefcase full of the morning's newspapers. My mother would drive fast for six blocks, getting my father to the station with seconds to spare. And so each day was started, and each night he would come home, in a cycle that continued even to that day, when I had moved to Newark to live with Madeleine, and we began rituals and cycles of our own, much like theirs. Only different.

In Newark, the sidewalk and the people on it were just an arm's length away from the room where I slept, alone, in a twin bed on a loft platform I built from a kit. I'd hear sirens in the streets, more sirens than I'd ever noticed when I'd been to Newark before; they were there every night, not just on Saturday, and the siren-like crying of babies, too, drifting out through open windows to the double-parked streets. Vandals scrawled obscenities on the one way signs. A ruddy man in a black windbreaker and blue jeans stood on our corner, every day, watching up the block and down, and the neighbor lady pointed with her chin. "You no mind him. Never," she said.

Madeleine called me at home. We lived together but still hardly saw each other because of the strange hours we worked, so she called. She'd had her big new important job for eight months now. She worked all night until at least eight in the morning, double shifts until after noon some days. She struggled to stay up all night, lonely in her empty office. She'd come home and lie on her bed unable to sleep in the daylight. She bought a mask to cover her eyes. She drew the blinds, shut out the sun, created a perpetual darkness to dwell in, but it wasn't helping: she was exhausted. She called me and talked about vacation. "I gotta get out of this rut," she said.

She called at three in the morning, when she was at work, bored, and I'd answer the portable telephone I'd brought up into my narrow loft bed. I kept the phone at my pillow in case someone tried to get in through a window at night when I was alone, or, in case it rang while I slept high above the floor and it was Madeleine.

"I'd like to get out to Montana every year if I can," she said. I heard her keyboard click. I heard television news droning. My bedroom smelled like cigarettes and licorice. I rubbed my eyes. If all hell broke lose, she'd always counted on Montana.

"Oh Montana," I sighed. "That's terrific. Wish I had some vacation coming."

In half sleep it came back to me that life shouldn't be left to live on vacation. Life, I could remember, was something waiting inside like a warm and wide open place without long lines and I was still and always on my journey, the one that had started on the road to Montana and Montana was still out there, wild and beautiful. Everything I knew was all still there, somewhere. But it was late and I was tired.

"You wouldn't really go to Montana without me, would you," I yawned.

"Well. Maybe you will come too."

"Nah, I don't think so. No vacation time, you know?" When she hung up, I lay on my side and stared at the streetlight shining on the floor.

Madeleine called while I was in the orange kitchen, washing dishes. "They're sending more troops to the Gulf. A hundred thousand," she said.

"What's this?"

She said, "Looks like war."

"War?"

"Yup. War. Look," she said, "it's happening."

"But, why?" I wanted to know. It didn't feel like there should be war. The world didn't seem to be in any urgent trouble, just the usual depressing malaise.

"It's the Middle East," she said. "Anything can happen."

What happened next was unlike anything we'd ever really seen; ever since Vietnam, the country had been sort of reluctant to actually send ground forces anywhere. Now this huge force was amassing in some desert. It was so strange: of all the promises that had been made and broken in our country since I'd known it, it did seem that everyone agreed that there'd be no more big wars. Vietnam had been too much. Now even that promise seemed doomed; we had no idea what sort of quagmire might be coming but we feared it. Half a million U.S. troops. One last piece of faith I might have had in the life around me, that we were done with war, was being extinguished.

It happened so fast: people just disappeared when they called up the National Guard. All the invisible forces unknown to me: they were everywhere, they'd been there all along, just waiting. Bank tellers, teachers, journalists, all of these ordinary people were privately training for war, on weekends, all these years. Guys down the street pulled on uniforms and left. Like they were all in a cult and there had been a summoning to the shelter. And if everyone was apparently in on it, why had I not received any training? Why had I no plans to don a uniform or participate in the coming Apocalypse? People disappeared, plucked as if by giant invisible hands out of their homes, out of their offices, even out of traffic jams, shuffling off numb into a war where we saw their bewildered faces turn up again on TV: soldiers in camouflage kissing kids goodbye, boarding one of Marcus's planes, next seen patrolling the desert, ten thousand miles away. People had no idea how long they would stay there. War meant marching up roads and diving into ditches when tanks came and staying away for years, didn't it? Or cataclysmic explosions and the earth cracking, time ending, the bomb. Madeleine just kept pressing her lips together tight and arching her eyebrows and throwing up her hands—see? I told you—because she had known for so long now that this was coming. This is what had always been coming: doom. Yet somehow I still clung to the idea of the peace-and-love days coming back, and staying.

Simple lives, daily routine, even the weird world of Newark tore away like tissue, exposing the underside of everything ignored everywhere, until it was too late. Look, there are unbelievable powers: love and hate, greed, desire. We think we control them and yet they make us do strange and perilous things. We ignore what we are afraid of, but that doesn't make the invisible forces just simply go away. Invisible forces cause wars, cause people to act strangely, cause all of us to do great or awful things.

Face it: we had known since August that something could go wrong, but we hoped that if we ignored the trouble it would go away. Death bristled, heartache waited just outside my door and I wished vainly to go on in silence, holding off the coming pain forever, but there are forces much stronger than me at work in this world.

At the office, the local rotation of chaos continued, day after day, in the slug lines for stories in our newspaper: Rob, shoot, stab. Burn, rob, kill. Decapitate, embezzle, steal, slay. We sat and watched helpless, almost felt like it was all our own fault, because we had to put this stuff in the paper, and we had contributed to the pain with three layoffs in the newsroom. Soldiers hugged their kids good-bye, and Madeleine grew strangely unwilling to buy curtains with me. The crisis grew and it grew clear that damned fall that the only route forward was through it.

"Wish I had an eighteen year old, wish I had an eighteen year old," Walter trotted stiff-kneed laps around the newsroom. "I'd send him."

One autumn afternoon I was watching TV, and the sharp woman on News Four New York told me about poison gas. I contemplated the horror of poison gas. Whose bright idea was that? Why did we even have to think about it? Against a beige studio set, the anchorwoman timed a Marine zipping into a chemical war jumpsuit, with a hood like a space-age knight. Then the anchor pulled on her own gas mask and asked, "Now, will this work for nerve gas or does that soak through your skin?" She tapped her pencil on the arm of her chair in the bland studio.

It was surreal. In my apartment with the windows open a crack, I could hear the old woman smack her stick on the asphalt, marching up and down the street. I worked nights and stayed inside all day, suddenly frightened of Newark. How had I ever felt safe? I remember thinking, we're going to die here. There's no way to undo these mistakes. This is the end, and there is not one thing, not one thing, I can do about it.

The deadline was set: January 15. Iraq must pull back entirely or face war against the international peace forces. Iraq said that, if attacked, it would blast Israel. It was presumed that Israel would respond; Israel had the bomb, and I figured they'd use it, and then Iraq's friends in Moscow would fire back, and we'd fire back, and so on, and so on, until the final missile blast. January 15: Armageddon was coming.

Panic ripples: I closed my eyes. Finding a local fallout shelter had been early on our list of things to do, but we had not done it.

John called for Madeleine when she wasn't home and so I tried to tell him: "It's awful, and no one seems to care, no one seems to realize what's happening and you were right about everything, John. There are evil forces in the world."

John said, "Yeah, true, but this Iraq stuff is nothing."

Nothing? How could this be nothing?

He said the twelve aligned families who run this planet with their unimaginable wealth had simply sounded the call to save their oil, and the armies of the world came running. "This is nothing," John said. "Wait and see."

But I could think of nothing else. It wasn't even war that scared me by now; it was the presence of the invisible power that could cause war and made peace so elusive. "So much going on, all repressed," I muttered to Madeleine in a late-night phone call. ("Suppressed," someone at work corrected me, but I kept slipping.) I said, "Journalists are censored. They know things they can't tell anyone, it's just insane." She had her own concerns: "The photographers can't go anywhere alone," she complained. "They need to be alone, you know. They can't have tag-alongs. That's just the way it works."

When I woke up in the mornings, sometimes I'd find Madeleine already home, watching television with a glazed look. Her skin grew more purely pale. Her hair had grown quite long in the past year and she sometimes twirled it absently with a finger. Her body had not adjusted to the overnight shift, and she'd begun to give up; she ate when she couldn't bear to lie awake in bed anymore. Comfort foods: smoked oysters on crackers and sandwiches filled with German meats. She put on weight. She parked herself on our couch on insomniac mornings and watched CNN and then the Richard Simmons diet and exercise show. I'd walk into the room silently and sit next to her and try to watch him, a curly haired freak with a high-pitched and too happy voice, dashing around hugging large weeping women. She needed a comfort that she would not take from me, I knew that, but, Richard Simmons?

"Richard understands," Madeleine would say, staring ahead. The morning light in the living room was flat, and Madeleine was a ball that longed to sleep, burdened by her inside-out life in ways that I could see but didn't really understand, because she never told me. I sat there and I wanted to hold her till she fell asleep or somehow fill the place that smoked oysters and Richard Simmons and a big city job had failed to reach; I wanted our world to be as good as we imagined, and for our life there to be enough. But instead, the tension was growing.

The deadline approached. Another bland Christmas and the new year arrived: 1991, an uncomfortably symmetrical number. At the UN in January 1991 we went to rail against destiny, and endings, and powerlessness and pain. I cried at the UN protest because I was sure something awful lay ahead and worse than that, I was beginning to realize how little it mattered what any of us thought of this, or anything. It wouldn't make a difference. Madeleine went to the UN with a sign that read, "Love your mother" above a blue and green earth. My sign just said, "Love."

People laughed when they saw our protest signs.

"Cowards!" they said. "Morons!"

"What do you think this is, Vietnam?"

But of course it wasn't Vietnam. It was worse: it was what could happen despite Vietnam.

"Peace now!" I shouted, and shook my sign, which a policeman took away because it was stapled to a yard stick.

He said, "Sticks can be used as weapons."

I said, "Why would I need a weapon at a peace rally?"

And then, the protest got bloody. Police batons came out. I was there and I saw it but it never made the news, nothing made the news, the news was repressed. Madeleine and I watched frightened angry Americans sit down in the streets around the UN, refusing to be pushed any further. They were trampled. Crowd control let no one near the platform to hear the speakers, if there even were speakers; I couldn't see them or hear them in the chaos. Cops on horses sneered down, just doing their jobs, and swiped at us with clubs, penned us with barricades, divided us. People rose up and were crushed. Chants filtered ominous above the din, and there was drumming, and I couldn't hear what anyone was saying, and I was losing Madeleine.

Madeleine: the establishment, armed and on horseback, made a wedge between us. I saw her face, I saw her hair. I tried to stay near her. Police cars with whirling circus lights blocked the streets, riot patrols moved closer, claustrophobia descended on the square. People screamed. Nerves were so taut, we might have erupted right then into a crushing stampede and just died in that horrible place, in a horrible moment, if we had reacted with fear. Madeleine turned back once, and I briefly found her eyes, brown-green, serene; she saw me, too. And then I watched her slip further back into the roiling pent up crowd. And I lost her.

I have a clipping from the *New York Times,* about war, and women, and Montana:

AMERICA ENTERS THE
GREAT WAR
REPRESENTATIVES VOTE 373 TO
50 TO OPPOSE PRUSSIAN MILI-
TARISM; MISS RANKIN SOBS 'NO'
Miss Rankin of Montana, the only woman
member of Congress, sat through the first

roll call with bowed head, failing to answer to her name, twice called by the clerk.

On the second roll call, she rose and said in a sobbing voice, "I want to stand by my country, but I cannot vote for war."

For a moment then she remained standing, supporting herself against a desk as cries of "vote! vote!" came from several parts of the house, she sank back in her seat without voting audibly. She was recorded in the negative.

New York Times, April 6, 1917

My father told me: war is to men as childbirth is to women. It's a rite of passage, he said. We were in his kitchen, making coffee, and he spoke as if he had pretty much enjoyed World War II.

"Dad!" I protested, "How can you even suggest that?"

He told me: "War was part of manhood. We didn't question it. There wasn't really any choice about it."

The only really awful thing that could happen to a young man in his day was to be left behind. My father was not left behind. He was at a basketball game at Billings High School when the news of Pearl Harbor arrived. My father left dry, land-locked Montana for the Navy. My father isn't sure where he was when he heard that the war was over; probably in the mess hall on his ship, he thinks. The loud-speaker might have said, "A large new bomb has been dropped on Hiroshima." At first, it seemed to mean the invasion of Japan had begun, and the dread was overwhelming: countless lives would be lost, it would be terrible. It was several days before he learned more: that there would be no need for invasion.

"What really gets me is when people say it was so awful we dropped the bomb," he told me. "GODDAMN IT. Iwo Jima,

Guadalcanal, in 1945 we still believed we were invading Japan. I sure didn't want to invade Japan."

"I know you didn't, Dad. And I'm glad you didn't."

We looked at each other and nodded our heads.

But how could I understand? I didn't, really. I thought, "The world is insane." And I imagined this: Sitting in the yard in the morning before work. It's a clear day, a fine day for flying. There's tension; there's a war, because there's always a war, somewhere, and neighbors, sons, friends are gone. It's in the headlines, even in the newspaper you are reading today, but nothing, not even a siren, warns you of the danger just above your head. You sip your tea. One single bomb tumbles through the air. When it is close enough, without your even looking up, a percussion awakes, bawling, and your whole being blows apart just as you swallow the tea. All of it, lips and tongue and blood and hot tea, it all hits the ground together.

When World War II came, my father left Montana. Really, but for a short time, he never went back.

On the eve of the deadline in 1991, Congress prepared to vote on whether or not to wage war on Iraq, Madeleine worked a double overnight shift, and I read Nostradamus.

"When a fish pond that was a meadow shall be mowed," Nostradamus said, "Sagittarius being in the ascendant; Plague, famine, death by the military hand. The century approaches renewal."

I pondered this beneath a sky too bright with city lights to see any ascending constellations or any stars at all. On the hide-a-bed in our living room, where I slept in front of the war news on TV, orange street light streamed in distorted through slatted blinds and splayed across the ceiling. Car alarms wailed, clouds closed in, and planes flew low to land in Newark. At 4 a.m. sirens, at 5 a.m. hail, at 6 a.m. lonely and staring at the ceiling, planes landing, world ending, I cried. Everything I wanted for the world seemed finally, fully impossible and wrong. I felt impossible and wrong.

I picked Madeleine up at the train after the war started; she had worked a long double shift, she was tired, and she had been thinking of Montana. She was almost in a daze. She showed me a picture that had moved across the wire: a mountain view from somewhere. It looked like Montana in winter, a snow-packed hush so far away that maybe no one—no friend, no parent, no lover, no soldier, no IRS lawyer, no nuclear bomb—no pain, no harm would ever find you there, if you didn't want to be found, and you could just be there and be happy. I gazed starry at the photo. It looked so remote and strange. Somewhere out there, Madeleine's friends were making fires in their wood stoves and watching the northern lights.

She said, "It's better there."

At home, she dug out her bags of tea from the Missoula herb store. We drank a pot called Midnight in Missoula, petals floating in it like potpourri. "Let me pour you a cup," she said. She was suspiciously kind, like after a terrible shock when, finally devastated, all the fight just drains out of you. She sat beside me on the couch and smiled, dreamy, and crossed her legs beneath her. She poked me with her teaspoon. "Want to know something?" she said. She told me she had reached a decision that day. When she looked at me her eyes were very clear and, I noticed, she was smiling.

"I've decided I'm going to Montana. To stay," she said, voice as soothing as herbs and warm water. She looked at her tea. That's where she wanted to spend the rest of her life, she said: in Montana, in the wild, fresh air.

"I'm almost thirty," she said. "It's about time I figured out how to live." It was obvious this was the answer; it was the only place she had ever felt truly happy, like her real self, not just someone stuck in her skin. It was the only place she had ever loved. Even if it would be really hard to do, she knew then that it was worth the pain that going there, and staying, might cause. "I'm moving to Montana. It's just right for me, you know? This is my life we're talking here."

I thought of nothing. I could remember nothing. I made myself a blank slate and listened to her. She said, "Yeah. I figure I'll take photos and sell them. Freelance. And you know," she poked my ribs with her teaspoon. "I was thinking." She wrinkled her nose a little and laughed behind her teeth, cheeheethee, and she said, "I thought maybe you could go, too."

I tried not to. But I thought: "Montana, Montana! I'm saved!"

Oh! Montana is an unpicked flower, the ache in my heart the size of the deepest canyon and my longing echoes there, hangs in the air like a cloud in the big sky, drifting wind stretched toward an end of the earth I cannot see, an end I cannot even see! I long for this place, where I can be who I am, where I can be whoever I want to be, where I can be free. Of course I would go. Let's go! Let's go! Our life together isn't over, it's just beginning and we're saved.

"I'd love to go," I said simply. "But what will we do there?"

"Well," she said.

Did it matter what we planned to do? Montana, at least, was still a free country, etched with winding roads, cattle grates, rolling grass foothills spread out like giant sleeping dogs. In Montana you could get by selling things you made, like jam or candles, or by doing odd jobs; if you had to, you could even live in a tent until you had a better place to go.

"I'm thinking we could be a freelance team," she said. She had thought about it all night, and she had a plan: We would go to Montana. We would pack our belongings, pack our cars, take our notebooks and her cameras and just go do what we do in a good place, together.

"We should wait until summer, save some money," she said.

We would tell Mrs. Sanchez with plenty of notice that we planned to cancel our lease in July. "Rent's due," she would yell in her monthly manner, leaning to peer through her slatted back stairs. I would reach up to pay her between the steps of that Coney Island roller coaster staircase. "Rent's due, ladies. How are you?" she would say, and on February 1, 1991, I would reply: "We're moving to Montana," and hand her a check for five hundred dollars.

"Oh, you girls," Mrs. Sanchez would answer. "Why would two nice girls do that?"

But it wouldn't matter what she said; we knew. We had decided, as if it were the plan we'd both had all along and now we were both finally ready. It was natural, it was right. And it was obvious: we couldn't stay here. Grandpa Sanchez had grown too tired to make it down the back stairs most days, and the old woman with the walking stick had simply disappeared. Mrs. Sanchez told me what happened; she shook her head, what a shame. The old woman was walking in the street and got hit by a car. "Hit by a car?" I gasped. How awful. Two broken legs, that's where all her marching got her, and that wasn't where she meant to go at all. That was it: we had to go to Montana. If we didn't, we'd die. Mrs. Sanchez said she wished they could just move away and leave all the sorrow of this place behind them. And I thought: "You can do it. You can leave this world any time you want. All you have to do is remember how, Mrs. Sanchez. Even you can go."

Of course, it is not easy. First you have to decide, which is a large enough accomplishment all by itself. Then, the odds are still against you. I took books down from the big bookshelf in our living room, books about Montana that Madeleine had, and I took out books from the library about the West. I bought *The Tao of Pooh,* anything that would help us learn how to go. Emigrants who kept journals of their western journeys recommended these provisions to survive on the trail: one prairie schooner, drawn by six oxen and/or horses (which would probably be shot when the grass dried up and disappeared and the beasts were bound to starve anyhow); a gun, of course, because among other things you'd need a gun to shoot the oxen and horses when the time came, along with any other creature that stood in the way of your progress; bedding; good leather shoes; ten pounds of coffee (could this really be enough?), five pounds of sugar, dried beef jerky, flour, canned goods. The kids. A dog.

Pioneers slogged across the continent, wet, tired, dirty, dying of small pox and influenza; losing their possessions to bandits, rivers, fires; losing their beef jerky and horses to starving wolves or grizzly bears; losing their children as they jumped off the backs of moving prairie schooners and were crushed beneath the wooden wheels; leaving everything behind when the horses died and the prairie schooner became useless. Men lost wives; women lost husbands, were left to the mercy of others on the ride who buried bodies in shallow graves, fought bloody with natives witnessing the whole domestic shift as invasion. Little or nothing marks most of the dead pioneers' graves, swallowed by a wilderness they could not resist.

It wasn't much easier for those who survived. They went hungry, they froze. They were homesick. They missed their pleasant towns, their families, their former lives. They talked about going back but mostly they couldn't: too dangerous, too expensive, too late. They farmed feral land, they suffered natural disasters, they confronted other pioneers run amok in the unrestrained freedom of a preborn country. But was it really any better to have been left behind? Being left behind: that was the worst thing.

It was while I was preparing to move to Montana that I learned what gaiters are and so I bought some; Madeleine already had hers. I bought lined all-weather boots that I could wear with the gaiters in the chest-high snow. To go to Montana, we would need things, and collecting these things made us feel closer to going. A collapsible fishing pole. Power tools. I didn't want to wait to buy them; it was easier to shop for supplies in the East, where there was too much of everything, including shopping malls. In Montana life was different.

There was no Ben and Jerry's ice cream in Montana then, wasn't even a McDonald's in Bozeman, and there was certainly nothing like the mall in Short Hills, with its Saks, and Barney's, and its giant crystal fountain. The Short Hills mall is a shopping temple, where people park monstrous four-wheel-drive vehicles on the parking deck and buy gold watches with compasses on them at the sporting goods store. There is a mall in Bozeman with a hot pretzel stand. What really made the Bozeman mall alluring when I saw it were the stuffed grizzly bear and elk in the hall.

We would need to shop in the crystal ball mall to get ready for Montana. We would need to order from catalogs. Madeleine, a master planner, let me in on a secret: anything could be done if you had a good list. A good list is the difference between strategies and pipe-dreams. And so we made lists, copiously, of all the things we would need:

Wool socks, thermal underwear, heavy coats.

Sub-zero grade sleeping bags.

Two really good flashlights.

Then Madeleine said we would really need new cars. She had it worked out: I would need a truck to take us into treacherous places, off roads and into the mountains; she'd need a car with good gas mileage to drive us back and forth across that long state. And so she bought a Honda and I bought a big Ford truck with a six-cylinder engine and four-wheel-drive. I drove it home, a rougher, stronger me steering through the smaller cars to which I was no longer beholden to yield, bullying back home to Newark's narrow potholed streets in the enormous truck I had to have, even if I couldn't afford it.

But it wouldn't be enough. Madeleine thought one of us would need to learn how to fly. To go on remote stories, she said. It would help on deadline. What if we had to drop off film? It would also help to see Montana from its fabulous sky.

"Learn to fly? Seriously?"

"Seriously," she said. Montana is the fourth largest state in the country. It contains huge wilderness areas that you can't even get to in a car. We'll be writing on deadline. We'll want to fly.

She was right; this wasn't crazy. Why, I could look up in the sky over Newark any time, right then even, and see that busy people were flying themselves places in small planes all the time. Flying is possible; I swear, anyone can fly if they just try. Why had it taken me so long to see that all I needed was a license?

Madeleine was exhausted from working the all-night shift every day, and I still hated my job, but now Montana was back in our grasp. She'd get home at 8 a.m. and we'd continue planning. "Maybe we should work some contacts out West, see if anyone will ever buy any of our stories," I might say, and she'd say, "That's a good idea, I'll call my friend and," then she'd stop; suddenly her eyes felt heavy as if her insomnia might go away; if she laid down immediately, maybe then at long last she could get six to eight hours of sleep uninter-rupted and feel at last rested and alive, like she remembered feeling once, back before she was successful and had to work in the middle of the night, back when she was a mere photographer for a tiny paper that was about to die. When a wave of sleep urge rose in her, Madeleine would drop everything and leave quickly; she'd stop talk-ing, leave her briefcase and camera bag and shoes on the kitchen floor, off with her socks, off with her blouse, off with a sandwich in her hand and a trail of discarded things leading to her bedroom, chasing dreams down the hall to disappear behind her door. Slam.

Maybe it was all just a dream, something we spoke of in som-nambulant fog. But we kept busy with it, stockpiling supplies in the corner of the living room. In preparation to move, I took on car pay-ments, I spent the savings that came from living cheaply in Newark, and when that was not enough I used my Mastercard. I had to. We needed snowshoes.

We came up with a list of story ideas for magazines, some to start immediately, for practice, to make sure we could do it when it came time to live that way. Then Madeleine called an editor named Isabel who'd just moved to Denver; we needed to prime the market for the flood of journalism we intended to unleash on the world. "We'll be freelancers in Montana," she explained to Isabel. "Doing features, like on the rodeo, and forest rangers." Isabel said, "Great. We could use you. Say, can you girls fly?"

We'd have to move to Montana in two trips. We'd drive out in a caravan, her little car and my growling Ford, then I'd fly back east to bring the rest of our stuff in a rented truck. How big a truck would we need? Think: Mountain bikes. Swiss army knives. Jumper cables and flares. Rain gear. Batteries. Accessories for the new cars: grill guard, speaker upgrade, trailer hitch. Cash.

We definitely needed at least ten thousand dollars each to take with us, maybe a little more, to cover a year's rent and car payments. It was not as easy to get the money as it was to get the cars, which salesmen were eager for us to have. Money was going to take a long time. So we devised a financial plan: I would get a better job.

Madeleine called Isabel in Denver again, because Isabel had once been an editor at the big newspaper in Newark, and she might be able to get me in. Isabel said, "You bet, let's try."

I thought there wasn't any point in starting a new job only to leave it, but I did need more money to move west. The *Star-Ledger* was the biggest newspaper in the state, a well-read daily making buckets of money, and if I got a job at the big paper, it wouldn't be too long before I had a bucket of money of my own.

"I don't know," I told Madeleine. "That's the kind of place people go to stay. Why would I go there to leave?"

She said, "What do they pay?"

And it was decided: I got a big newspaper job, more than doubling my salary. It seemed like they'd made a mistake, just giving me money like that. I left the *Herald and News* and its petty paycheck behind, but this time I got a little drunken party, because I had not left to go find myself; I had left, instead, for another job, and that was something journalists liked to celebrate. But leaving was nothing; in my mind, I had never really been back at the *Herald and News* at all, I'd just stopped by in the middle of my long journey which had, delightfully, finally, resumed. At the drunken party Fred worried for me; slate-gray Walter looked blank like he'd forgotten my name. Everyone else was just drunk. I left early and nobody noticed. A week later I began my new job and started bringing home checks big enough to pay for all the things I'd need to move on.

We were going to Montana. We'd buy a house on the fringe of town with a deck and a hot tub under the shooting stars. She would cook meals from our garden. I'd do tai chi in the yard.

Two-way radios. File cabinets. Police scanner. Snowcaps. Sunflowers. Logs burning on the fire. A box of pins with colored heads. Montana.

One night she had a dream: that we would need a copying machine. Mornings in Montana, I would read the papers from all over the state, and she would clip stories I had marked to save, copy them on our copy machine, and file them. The dream was a sign; we put "copying machine" on the list in ink.

Modem, portable computer, flannel sheets. Shotgun.

In Paradise Valley Velma and Joel had built a home out of stuff that they'd found. Floor boards. Dried flowers. Pieces of colored glass. We found old windows in a dumpster. We stored them in the basement, to come along with us later, to use in our own house, in Montana. People knew what to make of things there: floor boards, door knobs, or even whole doors. We hunted, and we saved: all of these were things we would need out West, when we found a place, some better place, to put all our pieces back together.

In April, the time came to tell my mother and father I was leaving. My mother was making a big dinner for my visit, and I helped her in the kitchen. We would have a roast and potatoes and some kind of vegetable boiled until it was certainly dead. I made a salad, though the weather had not been very good for lettuce and what was in the refrigerator had gone brown. Meals in our house often seemed to reflect this take on life: do your best, be creative, but in the end, make do. We put biscuits in the oven and when there was nothing left to do she leaned back against the counter facing me.

My mother was standing underneath the kitchen clock, in the place where, while making himself a grilled cheese sandwich one morning three years before, my brother had died of a heart attack. And that was the end of his life. She found him there, in the kitchen, as she came home with bags of groceries; she'd had to step over him to put the groceries away. That's what the neighbors told me she was doing when the ambulance came: stepping over the three-hundred-pound corpse of her son, trying to keep things in order.

I never saw my brother after he died. I don't remember the last time I saw him. I have imagined him sprawled on the linoleum in his mustard-colored terrycloth bathrobe. I have often stood in the kitchen and wondered about it. My mother had said his life was lost long before he died; maybe that's why it wasn't so hard to step around him. Frozen yogurt was melting in a grocery bag, and that man on the floor was already ruined.

How would you know if your life was ruined? Could it really be? Did the news come in a horrible revelation, or jar you from a deep sleep like the roar of an unmuffled Harley? Or did it lay itself out just as unremarkable as lettuce in a crisper turned brown?

I wished my brother had not stayed here. I wished that he had gone to Sturgis, South Dakota, or some other place; I wished that he had found a place where he could have lived his life any way he wanted. I could think of so many places where he could have lived, where Steve the big loud crass boy with strong teeth and a strange wide goodness in him could have existed very well, even been loved, just exactly as he was. He could have been loved, but not here. Instead, he stayed in New Jersey and he died. It was a sad thing to see happen to anyone.

I looked up at the clock above my mother's head. "Ma," I said, "the biscuits are done." I left the room.

I'm not exactly sure how my new job's salary corresponded to the lines in my father's little ledger. No doubt he had penciled it in, because both he and my mother were pleased to hear about my job at the *Star-Ledger*—finally, a newspaper they had heard of. I was going to have to break it to them that I intended to leave, which would surely destroy the family statistics because my father would have never just left a good job. And here I was, doing it twice. Maybe he would have to tear out my page. In those days, he was busy planning his retirement, which he decided would begin that summer. He was sixty-five years old, and in neat lines on a yellow legal pad he had calculated that, considering the average male life expectancy (was he really average?), the end was as close as eight years away; thus he had only about three thousand more days, and each passing day reduced the percentage of his life remaining.

He showed these calculations to me, the detail of them, the logic with which he could reason out any problem. He pointed out that he had lived 88 percent of an average male life, and each year of the 12 percent left was about 12 percent of the time remaining. The business of current events, the world of newspapers, things that would be useless in a day didn't seem important to him anymore, in light of his findings. And that's how he decided to retire.

And maybe that's why he appeared for dinner in his bolo tie that day, as if he were having a past life regression right before our eyes, now that his life in newspapers was finished. Now his mind turned back to Montana. This was especially helpful to me because I had just had a proposal accepted for my first magazine article—a story about Rapelje for *Montana Magazine.* Now I had to write this thing, and I didn't really know what to say; there was not really very much to say about Rapelje, Montana. So I would have to ask my father to tell me all he could about life back there. Then I would tell him that Madeleine and I were going. On the screen porch overlooking his backyard, waiting for the roast beef with his bolo cinched up to his second chin, my father smiled at me.

Unfortunately, in the suburbs of New Jersey the sound of airplanes flying low to land at Newark Airport had grown too loud and too frequent over the years, making it hard for me to hear my father talking on the screen porch. In the sky behind his head, planes took people away, thousands of them in bins, like conveyor belts, and every so often one flew so loud that he had to stop talking. Disruptions upset my father; they might cause him to withdraw, even at the moment of revelation when, in the silence between planes, he came close to telling me what happened to Rapelje. I coaxed him, seeking answers.

"Why didn't Rapelje last, Dad?"

He looked off, thinking, but then he lost his opening.

"Florence was BEAU-tiful, and she SANG," my mother said, stepping onto the porch. My father shut his eyes tight, as if a plane had flown right through the room and he was fighting to stay focused. My mother had her own opinion of Montana, and of Florence and Bill, the in-laws she had never met but had imagined. She adored a good romance, and she had her own version of the mystery of Montana: its haunted, million-year silence stirred by melodies Florence provided, her singing sustaining her in the hard life of a late-coming pioneer. My mother did not have to meet Florence to know she was a lovely, charismatic woman, the type you would find in a perfect picture of the West; my mother revealed for me this portrait in all its detail, the spinet, the blue eyes, the red coat, all she could recall before remembering that something on the stove right there in Short Hills might be burning. She ran away.

My father smiled nervously and showed his teeth, which were bridged faintly with gold. This need for dental work before he was even twenty-five, my mother claims, was the result of my father's one rebellion: as a boy he was made to drink sweet milk from a cow and since leaving home he had refused to drink any milk at all. It is my mother's theory that his teeth were ruined as a result of this stubbornness.

"What happened to Rapelje, Dad?" I asked again. "Why didn't it work out? How can you just lose a whole town?"

He said, "It happened to many towns back then."

"But Dad, Rapelje was the hub of the spur line. It had four grain elevators, it was really something, you know? It wasn't supposed to just turn into dust."

He smiled at me, for knowing the importance of these details: four grain elevators, boy, this was one busy little town. My father said, "They should have known." Then from the kitchen came my mother's voice, and he threw his hands up and said, "Aw, shit."

"What do you want to drink with dinner?" she shouted as she neared to take our orders.

"Milk please," I yelled back, as is the custom.

"Water," growled my father. When the shouting subsided, my father said again: "They should have known. The first thing I would have thought of is water. How can farmers make it in dry land? They must have seen, there wasn't any water."

He squinted thoughtfully, irritated by this long ago lack of foresight, and trying to remember things. Then my father told me Rapelje was, in railroad terms, a "jerk water" town. The trains pulled up at the end of the line and railway men refilled the steam engines from a water tank, with one jerk of a chain. Then the engines pulled the trains away. There was enough water for that, at least.

I asked my father if he knew why his parents went to Rapelje, with its uncertain future. Weren't they afraid that something awful could happen? That they would die? My mother has told me that they were pioneers, as if that word might explain everything; as if they were born that way and there was no sense in trying to fight it. That evening, bringing dinner to the table, she said it again, "They started a town." She nearly whispered; the courage of such a venture is too incredible to say plainly. Our own lives do not contain such chances.

My father, however, said it was not like that; Rapelje was a business deal, and that's just how things get done. A business deal: I pictured the empty sidewalks. My mother left the room. The explanation is dull and she didn't like it, and I didn't understand it, that day, and it seems at times as if the logic does not even satisfy my dad, Mr. Logic: I have seen his blue eyes moisten, on the kind of days when he takes out his "Danny Boy" CD and hums along. On Danny Boy days, he breaks down, and once, on such a day, he revealed the truth as he saw it, then; the secret of the whole crazy family: his parents had gypsy souls. "Gypsies," he whispered, smiling weakly, too weary to even show his teeth. Could that explain it?

But this was a different sort of day, and my father in his bolo tie moved his newspaper from his lap to the floor, stood up, and started singing the University of Montana fight song. I listened smiling dumbly and bobbing my head. Then the phone rang. The dog barked wildly and my mother dashed onto the porch with the steaming roast on a platter, set it down and dashed away to catch the phone. The dog stopped barking and stood up on a chair to lick the roast but I screamed in time to stop her. My father searched the walls as if he could find the real source of this chaos and smash it like a fly, as if finding the real source would matter, as if the chaos would ever be finally found, and destroyed.

My mother returned carrying heaping bowls of food and said it was Madeleine. She had told her I'd call back after dinner.

I said, "Madeleine and I are leaving in July, for Montana."

My father said, "Hey, that's great, honey. You're a real Montana kid. How long will you be gone?"

"We're going to live there."

He looked at the food and laughed lightly. It was just a little laugh to keep him from speaking as he thought of some safe reply. We waited stiff in our corners. My mother passed the broccoli and said, "Why would you do that? You don't just leave a new job," she said. It wasn't a question. Cautiously, my father said, "Why would you want to move to Montana?"

I held my breath: because New Jersey is sucking the life out of me. Because I have a gypsy soul. Because it is the free place, the good place, and I am young and I believe and don't you get it? Montana is where my life is.

Wait: it's a business deal. I told him: "We're going to be freelancers, Dad, freelance journalism, you know."

"Well, if you want to be a journalist," my mother said, "I don't know where you'll find any stories out there."

I listened to forks hit Corningware with the rhythm of steam engines. On that day on the screen porch, with the lawnmowers humming and the dinner disappearing and the planes from the airport flying up and away, I didn't know what stories there might be for me to find; I didn't know yet about the Montana Militia or the Montana Freemen or the Unabomber. I was not even aware, as we ate dinner in New Jersey, that thousands of dissatisfied Americans right then were moving to Montana; more people were picking up and moving there, then, than to any other state in the nation, and that hadn't ever happened before, even when the government was giving land away. So, what did that say? But what seemed a reasonable thing for others to do seems to be a different matter altogether when it comes to your own daughter. When it's your own daughter heading in such a direction, some might think, it's bad or wrong or dangerous. Or, if you're my parents, going to Montana was just another idea in a long line of my crazy ideas that probably need not be taken too seriously. It would pass, too. But what a shame, to leave a really good job.

My parents ate in silence, which I took to mean that they did not believe that I would really go. And that was more insulting than actually arguing with me about it, so I just let 'em have it.

I said, "I thought you'd be happy, Dad. I thought of all people you would understand. You know Montana is different, you know what it's like to go two thousand miles away from home. New Jersey may be right for you, sure, but it's not me, okay? It's not me. And I'm leaving."

My father winced, and ate his meat. I said, "I'm leaving," and for a while no one said a thing. Then, when he was sure I had finished talking, my father broke the silence without looking up from his plate. "Nobody ever said you had to stay," he told me, and kept eating.

John came into our kitchen wild-eyed, wired from working all night on the docks in Newark Bay, striding in through the back door and bouncing from the counter, where he leaned briefly, to the table, where he sifted through our mail as if it were his own, and then he hunted through our apartment for an ashtray. A Marlboro hung from his lips and made him squint over heat rising from the ash. Permanent lines were developing at the sides of his eyes from years of grimacing over cigarettes.

"You wanna hear something wild, listen to this," he told me, and launched into a story about a fantastic meteor he'd seen streak across the sky the night before, glorious from where he clutched a ladder and measured the acrid cargo of an oil tanker.

"We were looking into the tanks from the top of the ladder, PITCH black night, when a meteor sails through the sky, sparkling out a trail so close I could reach up and, BLOOP, touch it. It was heading for Boston." His cigarette stroked the air. "Unbelievable."

I said, "Wow, so it wasn't a missile, was it?"

"Nah," he said, dousing his butt in the kitchen sink and flipping it into the garbage. The Gulf War was over, and John had been right: it was nothing, just an environmental catastrophe. Oil dumped in the gulf, flaming oil wells spewing thick toxic clouds, oil well fire-fighters out risking their lives to cap off the gushing fortunes of the oil lords.

"So it was beautiful?" I said, picturing the meteor.

"Outrageous. Wake Madeleine. No, I'll do it." He started for the hall.

"I'm up," we heard a voice behind her door. Madeleine stumbled out of her bedroom to the kitchen in her blue flannel pajamas with her sleep mask pushed up on her forehead. It was ten in the morning and she'd been home an hour and, apparently, couldn't sleep again.

"Maddy, get your scissors, please pleaseplplplleeeeez."

"No haircuts," she croaked into the refrigerator, where she looked for something and then gave up.

"Aw, come on," said John. And she sighed. "Alright."

Then she said, "How are you?" and reached out an arm with which to hug John. They met like under water, suddenly slow, it seemed, and wading through something thick and invisible until they met and embraced. I blinked. Her smile over his shoulder was serene. Not even her smile. Someone else. It was like something had come over her. Oh my god, they are still lovers, I thought, I can't believe I didn't see that until just now, how had I always failed to see everything important? And I was mad. Then John and Madeleine let each other go and the vision faded and the room resumed its usual dimensions, their faces looked as they had always looked. Just friends. Silly me.

John sat on a kitchen chair and Madeleine draped a bath towel over his shoulders and pushed up her pajama sleeves. His knees bounced. "Quit bouncing," she said, "or I go back to bed."

An Indigo Girls song came on the radio in the kitchen and we were all slipping into a pleasant spring trance. Madeleine leaned and bent to get a better look at her objective, like the way she rotated and adjusted herself when she was taking photographs. She touched John's hair intimately, as if the task of cutting it gave an unusual permission to stroke one's friends in an otherwise prohibited way. This was curious to watch, this act of tender grooming; Madeleine could be so sensuous, and her touch brought friends to connection with her. She never cut my hair, though.

"Me next?" I asked her. She looked up from John's scalp and took a few steps over to me. She ran her hand through my hair four or five times, lifting and letting hair fall. "No. Too complex." That was all she said.

John was beginning to go bald in the pattern of a medieval monk. Madeleine clipped along the bald spot with concentration. Bald spots in men I knew disturbed me because they foretold of all our decay. He stared out the screen door where he could not see the telling span of scalp, only the blessedly mild spring day.

"What are you doing this summer?" he asked. "You two could spend a week up with Paula and me, get out of the city for a while." I liked that he spoke of us as a pair.

"We won't be here," Madeleine said.

"Where you going?"

"Montana."

"What? Oh, come on, are you still on that?"

"You know that's our plan, John."

"All right. So you'll go to Montana. How long you staying? A week? A month."

Madeleine clipped steadily. "John, you know we're moving to Montana," she said, squinting down at hair held up on her comb.

"Come ahhhn," John said. "You're not gonna go. Why would you want to leave your friends? Your friends love you."

"Well," Madeleine told him, "believe what you want." She clipped a while without talking and then put her scissors down and lifted the towel off his shoulders. John jumped up from the chair. Madeleine dumped the hair out the back door onto the pavement, then came inside and took the towel up the two steps from our kitchen to the bathroom and closed the door behind her.

John ran a hand over his shorn head and lit a cigarette and then noticed our list on the refrigerator. He studied it. Thermos, tire chains, canning jars. Shotgun.

He said, "Shotgun? What kind of shotgun?"

I said, "It says shotgun?"

And he said, "Yeah. Shotgun." He put his finger on it. "So, what kind?" he said again.

I said, "There's more than one?"

"There's all kinds. What do you want it for? Hunting?"

"Hunting? No. I don't think so."

"Why not?" said John, and he cocked his head, and he sized me up with squinted eyes. He'd been trying to bag a deer for years. He spent many mornings motionless with a rifle in the woods behind his house, covered in deer hormones and camouflage and still no luck. Deer left fresh pellets on his drive every day to mock him.

John tossed me a Marlboro. I sat on the counter and said, "I don't know why Madeleine put guns on our list. I don't like guns."

"Wait. You're not one of those gun control nuts, are you?"

"Well, actually, I just. . . ."

"Wake UP!" he said. "Let me tell you, every one of us has a duty to protect ourselves, and yes: with guns. That's the way this country was designed. You're smart, don't you study history?"

"Well, I read that . . ."

He said, "Madeleine's a great shot. Didn't she ever tell you?"

"She never said exactly that, no."

"Yeah, I had a gun when we lived here, you probably should have one now."

"Why?"

"It's Newark, man." Hadn't men stood on the rooftops of this very neighborhood, holding their shotguns to keep riots away?

"I thought you Deadheads were more like hippie types," I told John, who had for a long time been a Deadhead but whose fondness for paranoia had exposed him to the powerful influence of far-right philosophies. It was a strange mix. "You're supposed to reach out to your neighbors, right? Peace and freedom, right? Not like some redneck."

"Hey, groovy chick over there, hello, a gun is the original liberator. Man. Try living in a tent in the middle of nowhere with no gun. Lookit," he poked the list. "Shotgun. Somebody knows."

Madeleine emerged from the bathroom and said, "Good night," as she took a magazine from the table and started down the hall.

"Wait," I said. "Are we getting a shotgun?"

She said, "Well, I don't know, we can talk about it." She marched back to her bedroom and slammed the door.

John had jumped over to the radio and was messing with the dial. I watched him, thinking about guns, and about John and Madeleine shooting targets in the basement, like she once told me they had done, and I wondered why nothing strange like that happened anymore, or if it did but just not around me. John always told me stuff that Madeleine failed to mention.

"John," I said. "What happened with you and Madeleine?"

"What happened? You mean, when? What, what happened?"

"Like, back when you lived here. Why did you guys break up."

"Oh that was her fault," he said. He found a new radio station and, satisfied, he hopped over to the window to look out through the blinds. "She dumped me. When she went to college."

220

"You mean, when she was in Bozeman?"

"Yeah," John said. He laughed a fast conspiring kind of laugh as if he had misbehaved somehow and that had cost him his life with this woman. He looked naughty, thinking of what had happened ten years before: he embarked on this story with his signature vigor, straining at low volume like it was news of an alien sighting, something too strange for anyone to believe, only this thing had definitely happened to him. It was not theoretical, it was not something he perceived while he was sitting on a beach tripping on acid, it was not some dubious fact he found in an underground book but something like a nuclear bomb that had actually gone off in his own life and laid the groundwork for understanding all future devastation.

"I followed her to Montana like a chump but she had another boyfriend already. Boom, like that, she's gone less than a month and she dumps me. Didn't even want to see me. I drove all the way across the country with my head in the clouds, just a silly male of the species chasing after the woman he loved and then, bam, like that, I'm out and some other dude's in. And I had no place to go, all the way out there in Montana. She kicked me out."

"No," I whispered. But how could this surprise me? Had I thought that endings happened any other way? "What did you do?"

"What did I do?" he said. "What would you do?"

"I didn't kick you out," Madeleine called from behind her door.

"Then why did I sleep outside?" he yelled back.

A pause. A muffled dirty laugh. "You like camping."

John rolled his eyes and leaned in to me a little so that the rest of this talk would be private: "I figured what the hell, I'm out there, might as well hang around. So I went camping," he said. "I stayed in the mountains for about a week. And I'll tell you, that's about how long it takes to get the last song out of your head from all those days driving and listening to the radio. A week of lyrics in there going over and over. But finally, my mind was blank and I was walking around—you can go pretty far in a week—and I realized I had gotten completely lost in the woods, I was way the hell out there and I didn't have anything like Ay Shot Guhn." Here he cleared his throat and stared down his nose at me with crooked eyes and wiggling eyebrows. "And there were bears out there, and bad things trying to eat me, and I was about to get scared. Okay, I was scared, I was totally lost and I started to panic, and I said, Oh god, oh god, what now?" Eyes pleading with the ceiling, face pinched up in mock distress. "It was the end of me, I figured. Dead. And then, this crow landed on the tree above me, I swear, this crow showed up and made this noise." Here he made a "caw, caw" sound, imitating the crow extremely well. "And I decided I was supposed to follow it, so I did, and in about an hour I was back at my truck. That is a true story."

I said, "Wow."

"No kidding."

"I once went camping alone in Montana. Did I ever tell you that? Then I started to pray and I . . ."

"You did what?" John turned to leap across the kitchen in a single bound, and he clutched the radio, where a Grateful Dead tune had just perked up like a gift from the clear spring nowhere and John cranked up the volume and that changed everything. "Girls don't camp alone," he yelled, and raised his fists in featless triumph as the guitars chirped loudly behind him.

It was "Bertha." And with the volume so high on a song so loved, it was only seconds before the door to Madeleine's bedroom burst open and she bounced out and started hopping across the kitchen in her flannel pajamas, waving her hands above her hair. "Bertha" on the radio. The melody created a storm in the kitchen and swept those two into a sort of tribal dance around the table. From the counter I watched John shake his knees like a skeleton dancing the Charleston. And Madeleine was a butterfly flitting about his head. Out they dashed through the screen door into the world, chasing each other back in time, chasing themselves back into the kitchen again shaking their arms and legs crazy. It was beautiful: it was springtime in Newark, which is not like anywhere, and we were not just friends but karmic soul friends, baby, and for an ecstatic moment I believed that, and I sat there, and I watched.

> When we pause and consider that of its 35,000,000 available tillable acres only 4,000,000 have been put under plow, it seems no extravagance to say that, when Montana becomes peopled even as densely as Minnesota, it will be the premier agriculture state of the union.

That's what the posters that the railroads plastered up once said.

My grandparents were in Rapelje, Montana, for the big boom of 1917, when hundreds of farmers planted their first crop of wheat and up came a fantastic harvest. They filled their four grain elevators; they made undreamed of profits in a market that was up through the roof, inflated by the First World War.

It was supposed to go on that way, pulling profit from the dirt and building a dream right there, out of nothing. Hard work, prosperity, the American dream and what could stop it? Nothing could stop it, except the unforeseen.

Grasshoppers came. The summer of 1918: A rain of locusts descended on the Montana grass like a swift and violent plague. Thousands upon thousands of insects beating wings swarmed the green shoots of new wheat and flattened every planted acre of Stillwater County. Men, women, and children rushed outside swinging towels above their heads, barefoot in the dirt, chasing clouds of thumb-sized predators away. The catastrophe was half over before anyone understood what was happening. Just an hour or two, and the fields were bare, and the grasshoppers gone. Rapelje stood in shock, in ruins; in the months ahead only the pessimists survived, and how many pessimists were there in the land of promise? Everyone had put their profits back into the land. Just a few had tucked away stores of grain from the past year's harvest to replant, not fearful but wise to expect this unexpected pain and now their farms were the only ones left to try again.

The next year grain fell back from the inflated wartime prices and there was not so much money to be made on what little was produced. In one season, so many dreams already were lost, and William, the banker, soon began the vile business of foreclosing on all the failing farms.

It was 1919: less than two years since he'd arrived and already there was nothing where something had been. And there was William and everyone else who had come, all dumbstruck in the middle of it, stubbing toes on wheat stalks and rocks. Who had warned them of the possibility of failure? What railroad poster had ever shown it? Now, there was nothing to do but keep starting over, if they could; many had no way to get home, or no home left to get back to.

In 1919, the war at least had ended. There was hope in that; the soldiers who had survived poison gas and bullets came home, with souvenirs and stories to tell and lives to rebuild. All this and the germs of Spanish flu, also, clinging to them. Rapelje, so small and new, had lost no one to the war but still, Rapelje got the flu. It came: a hot, tight grip around the throat falling down into the lungs with a sudden breathlessness. In the church across the dirt alley from Florence and William's home, scores of stricken lay on boards, panting, lined up in rows in quarantine, unable to bear the sudden pneumonia, fever, dysentery, sweats, and so, dying. Florence sent food to stricken families, and prayed, and the neighbors came to cry with her when more and yet more died, so many died, about a thousand people lived in that town then and half of them feared they were dying. Perhaps a hundred of them did, in a week's time or two, just gone.

A story survived to be passed down through our family: a woman ran to Florence, hysterical, because her husband had died on his board in the sick hall and she wanted him in clean clothes when the undertakers came. His clothes were soiled and there was no time for the woman to return to the farm for fresh things. My grandmother folded a pair of her own husband's trousers and a fresh white shirt and brought them into the room in the church where the dead man lay. The women tugged wool trousers up one lifeless leg and then the other, buttoned a neat shirt across a still-warm body, and sent the man to his grave.

To die, to be buried in the clean trousers of a strange man in a strange place, lured to it with hope and earnest vision and some belief that life is fair, somewhere, in a glorious land of free lots, where you can do something, actually do something yourself from your own imagination because it is not a cramped and desperate place like Racine, Newark, any place left behind: to die there, caught in the act of wanting something better and then finding it worse, seemed to me an incomprehensible sorrow, when I first learned of it and first recognized the pallor of utter futility. All this struggle, all the desire and necessity that puts one up to it: life promises so much but owes nothing to anyone. It is not enough to dream or wish dearly. It is not enough even to try hard, sometimes; some certain endings are unforeseen, and even these heartaches are lost quickly in the plains, in the parched, empty world that absorbs all vain crying.

The funerals ended. Florence sang at all of them, spent days not speaking to save her voice for singing. Faint yellow and dust and gray consumed the spare landscape, and humans resigned themselves to this lesser fate, this survival. In Rapelje, the stubborn and

225

committed held firm, and waited for their luck to change, and held on to their mortgaged farms for as long as there was something, anything they could do.

"Listen here, Bill, you've got to give me just a little more time," the pressured farmers said. At the mercantile, at the hotel, they cornered him or maybe they were cornered by him: "Just a little more time," they said. "This is the only chance I've got, don't you see?"

"I'll do what I can," William said. He tried to be fair, but he was a businessman, too, and these economics grew disappointment, and he came to see how a good man can be reviled.

And then came fire. After the wheat prices crashed and the farmers went belly up, after the locusts and the flu, all that enterprise in Rapelje—two lumber yards, two hotels, pool halls and pharmacies and doctors and bars—followed. In one night in 1921, flames flattened most of downtown Rapelje. Not the whole nineteen blocks square, not the whole map of a carefully zoned western town; that vision had yet to be completed, so it could not burn down. But the tall, center blocks of commerce that had briefly thrived were singed away. There wasn't any water; the nearest fire engine was thirty miles south. Once the flames started, all anyone could do was stand outside and watch Rapelje burn down red hot beneath gaping heaven. Later, in the soot-dark daylight, there was work to be done, cinders to pick through, relief goods to haul off the train, and all those big insurance claims to be filed in Columbus.

How could they not have known? There wasn't any water.

Drought came. Drought just existed, and every few years there was maybe some rain. William Soderlind rallied his neighbors into the streets, summer after summer, called them together in front of his bank, and led them in prayers for rain.

"Dear heavenly father, we're a small town, hard working," William reasoned, making even God a believer: "We could do such good here, we've got the equipment, an excellent location. We only ask for a little rain." Summer into fall, the lake in Stillwater County was just a puddle in a crater. Crops withered; cows died.

William wrote long letters to philanthropists and industrialists and waited for them to write back. He reasoned that it would be a wise kind of charity to help poor families start again on a Montana farm. I've seen a copy of a letter he sent to George Eastman, founder of Eastman Kodak, in which he said: "Wouldn't you like to sponsor some farmers in Rapelje? We're a growing town in the heart of Montana, a place where a family can start at the beginning and make a good life . . ."

As far as I know, Mr. Eastman, in his den above Rochester, New York, never answered this faint cry across a vast continent, if he heard it at all. How feeble it must have sounded there, in his commodious heart of power.

Then, my grandfather ran for the state assembly in Stillwater County in the 1920s, to wage his battle for survival in the capital. But he lost the election. People say he never quite got over that. He used to corner farmers: "Harry, goddamn it, after all I've done for you, I bet you didn't even vote for me. Did you?"

He'd try to get them to confess, and he never quit the hard work of calling Rapelje together, planning, vowing to keep starting over and over until they found the right way.

And nothing happened. Nothing stirred. Rapelje went on, awesome land of grit and sage, godforsaken. William's hair fell out. His belly broadened and his gait slowed down. He smiled less, grew deep lines across his forehead. The gold cover of his vest-pocket watch wore thin beneath an agonizing thumb and forefinger.

Any number of events could have finally proved too much. Giving up could have been a decision made while foreclosing on the farms of people he, personally, had recruited to come settle: tractors auctioned off, livestock going to the highest bidder. The women were leaving, if they could, or the men were walking all the way to

Billings to find work and send money back to families in the cold; long winters kept coming with nothing to stop the viper wind from lashing disintegrating homes. And Depression? What Depression? The economy was always dead there. Perhaps the backers of his bank insisted he pull out: a business deal, over.

I'm not sure when he decided to go, what he knew as the final moment, but I did find an article in the *Rapelje Advocate* from 1936: a bandit known as Red left a note for William Soderlind telling him to bring thousands of dollars to a designated meeting place or, upon failing, he would find his whole family dead. So William led the sheriff to the meeting site, some place just outside Reedpoint, and the man called Red was arrested.

Maybe that was really nothing to him, a small brush with violence in a dangerous world, but still, shortly after receiving that threat, even before the tangible improvement of electric power had arrived in their spot at the end of the spur rail line, William quit. It was over. He walked away from the false-fronted bank for the last time, across the wooden sidewalk that led nowhere; Florence pulled shut their kitchen door and did not bother to lock it. The old Ford waiting on its gravel patch beside the house was pointed south, toward Columbus, where they would stay for one year while William tried to rally in a small bank; they would return, finally, to Billings where he would find decent work as the treasurer of a large corporation, a place a little like Case Machinery in Racine, Wisconsin, but nothing at all like the small bank and the small town he'd known, lit with oil lamps and an imagined bright future. As it dimmed into memory, he would not look back with any sentiment; it was not his way, and Florence would not cry, even when the neighbors who loved her came to bid their weepy good-byes. She would plant a rose bush in Billings. He would build her a lily pond in their yard; they would never again want for water. The family packed what they could and sent for the rest; they piled in the Ford and left as easy as they'd come: William and Florence, and Paul, Shirley, and Jay, and nine-year-old Sterling Eugene, pressed up against the rear window of the car, watching the dust rise and fall as their wheels spun out of Rapelje, forever.

I arrive at my new job on the third floor of the Star-Ledger building in Newark at 4 p.m. At 4:15 I walk down to the second floor for coffee and delicately portage a full styrofoam cup back to my seat. After that I wait for something to do, sitting quietly at the "rim." The rim is a horseshoe-shaped table ringed with editors who stare at computer terminals. In the center of the horse shoe sits the copy desk chief, known as the "slot man." Rim editors read stories and write headlines whenever the slot man doles work into their computer queues. Until that happens, rim rats wait.

An hour passes. I read a book. I grow sleepy. I look around.

"Welcome, new kid," a man grunts over my shoulder and I swivel sharply round to greet him. He is chinless, and his mouth works in the gel of his face as he introduces himself by his nickname, which sounds for an instant like "I'm Dead," but turns out to be Whitebread. He speaks in a monotone. He has a photo album from the vacation he has just returned from, two weeks in the wilderness kayaking among the killer whales, with seven other over-forty singles who relish travel and adventure. He sets the album in front of me and says to bring it back when I'm done looking.

I stare into space and picture Montana, buttes and coolies and thin air. In the distance in the newsroom a telephone rings ceaselessly; someone behind a distant partition laughs out loud. Someone I don't see jars my arm. Hey there, new kid. Let's look alive. Heh heh heh. I make a fair sum of money doing this and my parents are proud. I have attained some level of success.

At work when I have nothing to do, which is often, I slip back to a corner of the newsroom where I can use a telephone to conduct further research on the rise and fall of Rapelje. This is my real work, my life raft, as I languish in a very good job I took only for a while, I swear. The editor of *Montana Magazine* bought my idea to write a story on Rapelje for an unusual reason. She told me that her parents had actually met each other in Rapelje. Back in the 1920s, when they were very young, they had both been teachers at the Rapelje school. "That makes us like cousins," the editor declared, and she said she would love an article on that place, and that she would buy Madeleine's photos to go with it. This first success as freelance writers seemed profoundly symbolic to us; our ideas on black bears in New Jersey and Hudson River pollution and a few other things had gone nowhere, but with Montana we had a sort of cosmic good fortune.

Nonetheless, the article was not going well. I had never attempted to write a magazine article before. I didn't know what to say. Even with research, I couldn't quite figure out the point of Rapelje, some kind of theme that would pull things together beyond just a dry timeline. I found some newspaper articles about big events in the town over the years: one story in the *Billings Gazette* marked the anniversary of a big fire that swallowed up most of the place in 1921; in 1982, the *New York Times* reported the closing of the Northern Pacific's spur rail line, which seemed at last to seal Rapelje's fate. If there was no railroad, well, there was no Rapelje. But I needed more than this to write about.

After work I spread notes out on the kitchen table, random thoughts about my grandparents and things I knew had happened to their town, and tried to put the lives and the facts all together. I smoked cigarettes and struggled along, getting nowhere. My own photographs of Rapelje showed only emptiness, and Madeleine and me standing in it, amid a rich world we imagined was once there. Now Madeleine and I were planning our own future in Montana and it would not be a sad story like the one I was writing. I was saving money. We had a plan. I didn't exactly know how my grandparents had managed to do the brave and crazy thing they had done but Madeleine and I, we'd made sure we were ready for anything, we'd bought stuff, we were going out to make a life and we were so prepared, nothing could beat us back down. My grandparents' dream failed. Failed. How could that happen? Had they thought of it that way? I crumpled pages and started over.

There was a rhythm to our lives in this planning time. To know we were leaving made us feel half gone already and that felt good; it was a giddy time, like the start of a romance that you know is heading for big love. I planned, and shopped, and worked on my article; Madeleine got busy saying good-bye. Her all-night work shift, her insomnia, seemed not to worry her so much; they were suddenly just temporary. All the pointlessness, the hard work and double shifts and sleepless days in front of Richard Simmons or news about our first Iraq war, all that stuff stopped feeling so bad. I wrote about Montana, and she talked about it all the time: she started calling long-lost friends, people I didn't know, to tell them she was moving. "It's good to hear your voice," I'd hear her say; and "yeah, that's right, Montana. I'm going back." Just about every morning, after coming home from work, she would call someone. Later, she'd wander through the apartment, maybe tell me something new she had thought of like how my truck would be more useful if it had a plow. Then she'd make another phone call. She was excited.

You could tell: she appeared at the door to catch the train for work wearing shorter dresses, made of lighter cloth and brighter colors, with flowers on them. She wore lipstick in shades of various flowers, and she looked relieved. Montana was getting closer. In her short, flowered, happy-looking dresses she started going out, for fun, for a series of good-bye events, good-bye drinks, good-bye concerts, good-bye drinks at bars where there was dancing. That made her even happier. She started going once or twice a week to a big old barnlike bar that always had live music; she loved live music. She went with the old friends she had been saying good-bye to and started meeting new ones to eventually say good-bye to as well. All this fun made her even more tired at work but, hell, she'd been exhausted for a year and it couldn't get worse, and anyhow, by the end of July she'd be in Montana.

Montana, Montana: we were so close, now.

Buds swelled on the trees and her enthusiasm—for dancing, for leaving, for everything—grew. I saw it. I watched, quietly. She gave her phone number to the new friends she met at the big barn dance bar, and the phone rang. Of course it rang; hadn't Madeleine met the whole world on the playground when the whole world had been kids? Everyone wanted to see her once more before she was gone; everyone wanted to hang with Madeleine, now that she was happy, and now that she was beginning to feel free again. It began to feel fun, like we were two people already in Montana, though maybe not quite there, and not quite together.

I worked, and I shopped, and I wrote, and I watched her: she danced, and she played, and she made friends who dropped acid. She stayed out all night and came home tired and drank beer in the kitchen at ten in the morning. She talked on the phone to an endless stream of new and old friends, which I noticed had started leaving her less and less time for talking with me. Weeks passed and I started to notice.

On the answering machine I heard: "Hey, Madeleine, what's up? It's Surfer Billy, wanna go canoeing this weekend?"

"Hey, Maddy, it's Dan, just wanted to say hi what's happening, come to the show Friday."

"Hey Madeleine, what's happening, I just called to say Hey."

"Hi Madeleine, it's Derrick. I guess I'll see you there."

Wherever there was. It seemed to make her happy.

Why did I begin to feel angry? I had gone with her a few times to the big barn bar, but I didn't like it; I thought it was an ugly New

Jersey place three times the size of the Blue Goose in Montana and not nearly as interesting. Just because it was big and loud and you could dance there, that didn't mean it was a good place. There were no gold miners there; you could not go outside and watch for meteors; the city lights wrecked the sky. What did it have that we needed? I couldn't imagine. After two or three times, I didn't go again.

"Hey Madeleine. Dan again. Call me later."

One Saturday I was standing at the screen door drinking coffee and thinking about Rapelje, Montana, and what on earth I might find to say about it for two thousand words. Sparrows chirped. I stood barefoot and sleepy and searching the clotheslines for inspiration and then she appeared before my eyes in a sun dress, pushing through the gate, rushing toward me. She is home, I thought with satisfaction. I raised the hook to unlock the door just as she hit the steps. She ran through, in more than her usual hurry, and she passed me. I said, "Hey, how was work?"

"Awful. Who cares. Screw work."

"Hey, so, I looked at our schedules and guess what? We're both off tonight."

"Off work. Screw work." She was running around the kitchen like she was looking for something.

"So you want to rent some movies and hang out?"

She said, "I have to go to sleep right now so that I can get up and go out in four hours. Where's my sleep mask?"

"You're going out in the middle of the day? What, like you have a doctor's appointment or something?"

She said, "I have a date."

"You have, you, a," I said. This was strange news. "Who could you date, I mean, on a Friday afternoon? Isn't the whole world busy at its soul-sucking nine-to-five jobs?"

"He's a drummer."

"Oh." Sparrows clung to thin branches above the alley outside, stupidly singing. I watched Madeleine maneuver through the kitchen. She had a date. I had never heard her say anything like this before and I did not know how to answer. Wouldn't she rather just be here with me? We could cook lentils.

"Who is this drummer?"

"Tad," she answered. She was dashing around, her sleep mask in one hand, now looking for an ashtray or something and racing to get to bed. I stood with my back to the painted screen door and my arms crossed.

"Where are you going on this, this, date?"

"We're going to the beach."

"But it's cold."

"We're just going to walk around."

The beach, off season. It was textbook. It was like screaming out "we are going to do something that could lead to sex." It seemed alarmingly foolish for a Montana-bound Bohemian to do such a thing because, well sure, we were supposed to love freely, because love after all was everything, love was the main thing, but this seemed so very . . . entangling. Why would she start a romance when we were about to leave? I quickly said what anyone would have: "Well, damn it, why won't you just stay home with me for fucking once and watch a stupid fucking movie?" With a horse-like bucking to my rear, I kicked the back door shut: slam.

Without slowing her cupboard rummaging or looking at me she inquired, "What's your problem?"

"My problem," I explained, "is that you go around dating drummers and meanwhile you can't find time for a lousy movie on our one night off. We're supposed to be going to Montana together but we can't even watch a movie and I never even see you. I don't like it."

Madeleine suddenly stopped opening and closing cupboards. She just stopped, and waited. Then she walked over to stand in front of me. Her eyes were ringed darkly, her face the clay shade of too little daylight. She said, "I haven't had a date since, since—"

"Since you've known me."

"That's right. Years. Don't you dare rain on my parade."

Her anger stung. We stared at each other and when she started to walk away I said, "I'm sorry. I just thought we could watch movies like we used to."

"We will watch lots of movies in Montana."

"Okay," I said.

"Okay."

"Maybe if you get home by eight or nine or something, we can still watch one movie," I said, after she had turned away.

"That's possible."

"Okay."

She was scanning the cupboards in a fruitless attempt to recall what she had been searching for, and failing that, she trotted off and disappeared behind her bedroom door.

And so I worked at the library all that day, trying to understand failure in Montana for my article as the deadline loomed, and thinking about Madeleine running around holding hands with some drummer. I rented movies on the way home from the library and stopped at the neighborhood liquor store where small cheap bottles of whiskey were lined up behind a dirty plastic, bullet-proof shield, and I found a bottle of red wine there to buy. I sat at the kitchen table and kept trying to draft a story about Rapelje. The clock on the stove said eight.

I drew an outline for my story, but six or so lines down the page I tore it off and crushed it and threw it to the floor. By 8:15 I had opened the wine and poured a glass. I stared at the yellow pad, with notes on it representing all that I thought I knew about William and Florence, and Rapelje, and doomed dreams.

Becoming the first family in a town in the dust of eastern Montana was a crazy idea, it was incautious and misinformed. It was a pipedream. But he did it. Why?

It was a business venture, my father had said. Had William really believed all that railroad hype? Wasn't he smarter than that? What was wrong with Case Machinery, anyway? You don't just leave good jobs. My grandfather had been described to me as a pessimist, the most negative person my father ever knew, someone who, by the time his fourth child came along, professed his clear certainty that everything that could go wrong, would. It already had. But would someone as grim as that have ventured to Montana? Or did Montana make him that way?

I considered this amid the mounds of dishes and the odor of unclean ashtrays in our Newark kitchen, in the orange glow that rose off the linoleum at night. And I wondered what Madeleine was doing, somewhere far away. Screwing a drummer in the sand? How sexually liberated of her. How free. Cheers to Madeleine. I poured another glass of wine.

Okay. In 1917 William and Florence emptied their Hoosier cabinet, canceled their magazine subscriptions, packed their Persian rugs, their floral china, their sterling silver, their lace curtains, and went west. A year later their piano arrived by train.

I drank more wine and slouched down, staring at the kitchen door. Losers! Who gives a fuck about these losers? Silence. What boring, stupid people. And I felt lonely, thinking about them, and wondering where Madeleine was. It all felt so pointless. I wanted something better for myself than that very moment I was in; I ached for something better, out there, somewhere.

When the answer came it struck my heart first and rose to my eyes. Tears appeared as if they had always been waiting. Of course: it was the ache. It had to be. My grandfather could not have stayed in Racine, Wisconsin, because he had been stricken with the yearning.

William went to Montana, he risked his whole life, because he was in love with this idea of Rapelje, so sure and crazy in love with it. But he never told anyone how he really felt, never said, never wrote it down. How could he tell? They'd all say he was wrong. So keep it safe, "just a business deal," just say whatever you have to say to make what you want seem okay. William made it seem like it was so perfectly normal, running to the dust, while in his heart he chased a wild ache believing it would make him happy. This was love.

And yet, in the end, his love was unrequited.

I fell back in my chair and pulled on my hair with both hands, and stared at the words "unrequited love" on the notebook.

Yes, of course: inside every adventurer's heart lurks a love begging to be returned. Before he even saw Montana, William understood that he belonged someplace different. Some would never understand; they would judge him. So he would not bother to explain his strange actions. Some desires defy explanation. This dream of Rapelje was his, and he would live it, because he believed in his heart it was right.

I scribbled frantic on my notebook: Montana's desert was my grandfather's great, doomed love. For William, the light in a strange land was Rapelje. But in the end, Rapelje would not have him.

I could see from where I sat, drinking wine in a kitchen in Newark, that until the end, until he could no longer stand it, my grandfather William believed in Rapelje; scared as he was to be there sometimes, strange and awful as locusts could be, and lonely as it so often was to stay there, it still seemed right, it had to be right because he felt it. He would do whatever he had to do to make this one right thing work because he did not believe there could ever be another so right for him. And he believed that if he worked long and hard enough, that place would one day love him back. His wish was so powerful that he stayed in the dust for twenty years, refusing to release it. He fought, and prayed, and even went dancing with Florence at the long hall in Wheat Basin, a town that was no bigger than a dance hall and a silo, a place only a few souls would ever chance to find before it was gone again, forgotten. The sun came up to light the roads home from their dances; even when fate turned its worst, he took the road home again to Rapelje, year after year, and waited for the time when the unyielding frontier would somehow want for itself all the great things that he wanted for it.

What William Soderlind finally had to live with in the ruin of his dream of Rapelje, was that, goddamn it, the desert did not want what he tried to give it. The desert didn't want him, and the desert never would.

"It's dust, William. All your love can't turn dust into a farm."

"But it seemed like a farm once, for a while," he says to me, when we are there in the dreamed world together, and the truth is briefly clear. "It sure seemed like farmland at first, when all that wheat was there."

"Anything can happen once," I say.

"Those farmers we recruited, they sure tried to make it work." Lifting a handful of pale dirt and watching it sift through his fingers, he says, "Maybe it is a farm, just too damn pig headed to admit it."

"Alright, so maybe somewhere, buried deep down in there, it is a farm, grandpa. But all we've really got here is what we see."

"Yes. All we've got is what we see," he says. "Well." He drops the last of the dirt; he removes a handkerchief from his pocket and wipes his hands, then wipes his round, damp head. He looks at me with blue eyes clear as water, paler than my father's, set in a rounder face. He is a loving man my father never explained to me fully and he says, "I suppose you've decided I'm a goddamn fool for this."

"No, grandpa," I tell him. "I would have gone with you."

"It might seem strange to you, but I really did love Rapelje. We had good times here. The best times. Never better anywhere, before or after."

"Yes," I say. "I know."

238

"Then it ended."

"Well, I guess you have to know when to let things go."

William Soderlind looks at me and his face suddenly brightens. "Ahh," he says. "Now you sound like a businessman. Good girl." He kisses my forehead, and I close my eyes.

I put down my pen and finished the bottle of wine. I reached for a cigarette but found the pack empty and tossed it across the table. I fell back against my chair and stared at the bounty of words I had scrawled.

The truth made me feel very small, for having misunderstood it as long as I had, believing more in what I wished for than in what I knew. You can't chase love. You can't do much with love, really, except feel it. You might have better success hiding from it, but that's no good after a while either. So that's the story. I had figured it out once again. I put my pen down.

At two in the morning in the murder capitol of the world, having finished a bottle of wine and two packs of cigarettes too, I grabbed my keys and scrambled out to get more, too shaken and restless to just sit with all that truth. So I climbed dizzy into the Ford truck in the driveway. I started the engine, and swung it around backwards, rounding the front end hard and fast into the garage wall. The big fender cracked loud against it. I stared across the hood at the wound. The Ford truck was now broken, too. I reparked. I walked back inside, locked the door, and went to bed.

Hangovers always made me vomit and once that started my hangovers didn't end for hours and hours and even days sometimes, oh god, the vomit, the sickness, the bashed fender, the bloated pasty face in the mirror and then I started to cough: I coughed a hacking cough and wheezed and then I couldn't even breathe and I thought I was dying, I was choking on thin air with a hangover that turned into bronchitis and Madeleine drifted in and out of my consciousness as

I lay in bed dying, choking, vomiting, hating myself and everything about myself because I was not so liberated, I was not so free; I
was angry and sad and my life did not contain love, only longing.
My life had the props of a fake freedom like boozy nights and Marl-
boros and jaded loser single friends desperate to find some kind of
meaning and now I even had some money to buy my freedom but
even that was not freedom, there was nothing free about it, because
I was so god-awful unhappy and I was lying in my sick bed alone.
Madeleine's cigarette smoke drifted in through my cracked-open
bedroom door and it choked me. "I'm dying," I croaked and she
said, "What happened to your truck?" and I couldn't answer because
I was dead.

I could not imagine smoking another cigarette ever again. I could
not imagine eating another bite, of anything, ever. I did stop smoking, then, in the ruins of everything, in the hangover that turned
into something like pneumonia, and then, on a roll, I also became a
vegetarian, overnight, because I did not want to eat blood, the idea
of blood made me vomit, it was ugly and mean, it was wrong, I
could do better dear god and I would if I just lived to try. Suddenly
it was obvious how hard I had worked to kill myself, for so long,
haunting dangerous places, doing harm to my lungs and liver and
heart and mind, or trying to drown like a puppy stuffed into the
rough sack of anxious unhappy days, so much good as dead for so
long but, no, I did not want to die. I really did not want to die. My
brother had died and I knew it was really possible to die but I did
not want to. I spent a few days in bed trying not to die and making
promises to myself about how different I would be if I survived. I
had to stop doing all the things that were killing me, and more than
that, I had to be able to see myself as someone else, some lost idea of
me that was now the key to recovering my life.

So, let's go. Let's go. This is not all there is, just what there is, so
go do something good and useful with your life. It's the sort of thing

you're supposed to learn from your grandparents, only, mine were dead when I was born so it took a little longer.

I felt better in a week or maybe ten days.

I sat in the kitchen with the door open, letting the afternoon air through the screen as I sat eating an orange, reading a magazine I had bought in New York to read on the train back to Newark. Madeleine came out of her bedroom in her pajamas at about four o'clock and said "Hey, you're up," and when she came closer, she said, "What happened to your hair?"

"Like it?" I asked. I had gone to Christopher Street in Greenwich Village, looking for lessons on how to be gay, and I found a barbershop with no line. So I went in.

She rubbed her hand over the bristles. "Who did it?"

"A barber in New York. Ten dollars. Do you like it?"

"It's short," she said, rubbing it.

"Try the bristles on my neck, they feel like a brush."

"You had pretty hair," she said.

"I cut it."

"Why did you do that?"

"I dunno. Wanted a change."

"Well," she stepped back and we looked at each other, and she said, "It's a good cut, anyhow." She went up into the bathroom and I heard the shower come on.

In the kitchen window shined the reflection of my face, my neck, my ears, the whole of my chin and jawbones, revealed. The distance from my earlobes to my shoulders seemed vast.

I sat at the table and stared down at the magazine. She came out of the shower in a robe with her hair wrapped up in a towel, eyes focused on the sharp metal instrument she was drilling at her cuticles as she marched across the kitchen. I said, "Uhm, Madeleine?"

"Yes dear?" she said.

"I am a lesbian."

241

She kept walking toward her bedroom without looking up from her nails, and I wondered if she had actually heard me. I stared at my magazine without reading anymore.

Then Madeleine came back in the kitchen and stood by the table. "Didn't we already know that?" she said, which is what most people, including my parents, would say when I told them.

"Well, yeah but, I think we're going to say it now."

She stood beside me and rubbed my bristly head again, slowly, then looked at the clock and said, "Oh, geez, gotta go." And she ran to her hairdryer.

Well. Now that we got all that straightened out, nothing left to do but pack up all our belongings, quit our jobs, forward the mail, and move to Montana.

In Newark, summer arrives full blast in spring so that by June, everything has come outdoors into a squalid frenzy: barefoot children, old women, men, flags of laundry, distorted music out of cheap car speakers, water out of hydrants, exhaust out of cars, garbage out of car windows or turned over garbage cans, McDonald's cups, beer cans, vodka bottles, stray dogs out and into the street and before long, it all starts to smell bad.

We were going to Montana, but we were having a little trouble saving the money we needed and tying up all our loose ends, what with my car needing a new fender and Madeleine's leaking oil ever since she hit a curb one morning while dozing at the wheel. We were in no hurry, after all, because we were young and free and we could do whatever we wanted to do with our lives, including waiting a few more months to move across the country. We agreed to delay our departure just until the end of August. Our lease, on the other hand, would end in July. Anyhow, we were tired of Newark. Newark was over for us. Some change was required immediately.

In late June, my mother and father offered us their house for the summer. They would be leaving for their lake house in Wisconsin. My father had successfully retired, and they would spend their long summers at the cottage now, up there until September sitting on a dock on a lake where there's no need to wear shoes and the phone hardly rings and it takes at least two weeks for the mail to catch up with them.

They had offered us their house, my childhood home, free of rent while they were gone. Their suburban colonial with a trim lawn: a place I thought I could never bear to live again, with all those carpeted rooms and specters of a girlhood spent in the wrong clothes, in the wrong cliques, in dancing school at the Short Hills Club with all those other girls whose shoelaces never broke (or, if they did break, who never tripped on them, or had trouble finding replacements for them, and made knots in them to make them last longer) and whose skin was flawless. I had wanted so badly to get as far away from this place as I could so that I could find all those other places where, surely, people did not lead sheltered, pointless lives. And even if I had not yet made it very far from the town I grew up in, at least I had tried; at least I had left. That seemed important, and I panicked at the thought of going backwards. Now I imagined smiling women parading with strollers through stripes of lawn and driveway, green, gray, green, gray, block after block in the suburbs where I could no longer even afford to live, had I wanted to; I was not welcome there, I had never fit there, I could not pay rent there.

And if I stayed there that summer, would I appear to be, as I knew I was, merely house sitting? Or would I be regarded as a thirtyish single woman, unsettled and unsuccessful, with nowhere else to go, now that her lease in Newark (of all shabby places) was up? I feared I would be judged. I thought of my mother, who had been brave enough to choose Short Hills at my age. She had not been able to teach me how to do it, to fit there, despite trying so hard. My mother, when last seen by me, had examined my hair with a mixture of worries: maybe for my resembling a boy, or for my being nearly thirty and so willfully unattractive to potential husbands, or just for being so unlike her that she did not know how to help me anymore. She put on her "I'm not going to say a thing" face, and did, in fact, say nothing.

In short, my hometown was not a place where I felt I could survive. But then Madeleine said, "Hey, it's air conditioned, right?" I wanted to flee all the rules of the world I was raised in, but Madeleine? She really didn't care. The rules of this place meant nothing to her. She'd still work all night and drink beer in the morning and leave the front door open for her friends to walk through. She'd set up her lawn chair on the driveway or wherever she pleased, ignoring local convention, and rules including the one that said no one should ever be seen on her own front lawn except when entering or leaving the house. And then I understood: free souls can live anywhere. Right? It's all a state of mind. In fact, what a gas: where better to prove yourself to be a rugged individual than at your mom and dad's house? Who could stop me from planting corn in the yard? Who could stop me from doing anything? The house was cost free; that's what mattered. We were so already gone from this whole dreadful state, the only question to ask now was, how will this new thing support my quest for Montana? We'd stay in Short Hills two months, save up, and then leave forever.

Decision made, we emptied the cabinets of our Newark kitchen, dismantled our bedrooms, stored away the stray doors and windows intended for the house we would build in Montana, and headed to greener pastures ten miles away. Madeleine was first to go, and I stood alone in our apartment, where not too long before I had come for the first time, seeking friendship. I took a long smell of that hair spray candle wax cigarette lemon dish soapy world to keep it stored forever: a memory of Madeleine as I had first known her, and me. I held this idea like a strange, beautiful object whose use was no longer known. I drove off with my truck fully loaded.

Madeleine was already in the house when I got there. She had kicked off her shoes and dug her toes into the clean pile carpeting. She breathed in the cold, recirculated air, and surveyed the tidy furniture: ten different rooms all cozily arranged. She was going to live in them all. She said, "Oh, I wouldn't mind this," and breathed, and wandered, touched things, fondled brass objects on the mantel, drifted through the rooms. She had never lived in a house this size. "Oh," she said, stepping onto the screen porch. "Nice."

In the breakfast nook, thinking out loud, she told me exactly how, if it were her house, she would modernize the kitchen. That's the key to feeling at home, she said. Remodeling. My family did not do such things; my parents pretty much accepted things as they were. But she stood in that kitchen and had a vision of how it could be different: she would knock out a wall to make a bright space. Add some windows. Not that she would actually do this in the time we would live there; she just saw all the possibilities. It was unlike anything I had ever thought, standing in that kitchen. It was very Montana.

"Oh, I have a good feeling," she mused. "I think this is going to be the Summer of Love."

Madeleine leapt barefoot across the pink pile carpet like it was a field of cotton candy. She set the central air conditioning at 64 degrees, despite my mother's note on the refrigerator that clearly stated "Air conditioner: set at 72." We turned the music on and left it on. This had never been a house with a stereo in the living room; this was the house of "Danny Boy" on the portable CD player, but now it was ours and it was different.

She unpacked her sleeping pills and claimed the master bedroom, the big one, with the cable TV and the king-sized bed and the bathroom. But I told her that I would not be condemned to my teenage bedroom, and she would have to fight me for the prime real estate. I offered a compromise: we could share the big bed in shifts, with no fear of disturbing each other, because we worked and slept at different hours and besides, that bed was so big, it was like having two bedrooms in one. It was absolutely possible to sleep without touching in that bed, married couples with big beds had surely managed this for years.

Madeleine said, "Nah, you take it," and slinked off to my old bedroom. We moved a TV in there; Madeleine had begun borrowing videos from the vast collection of a new friend, someone named Andrew, and with the help of cold air and the drone of bootlegged video tapes, she was able to sleep almost daily for a change.

Outside, it was hot. A heat wave was breaking records from all the way back to 1917, when people were dropping dead all over the East from heat. We drank a lot of lemonade. Madeleine bought little sundresses and bright sandals. I found a goldmine of flannel shirts in the closet and cut off the sleeves, nice and low so they exposed my newly growing underarm hair. I was developing a look to support my new radical feminist lesbian vegetarian neo-hippy western identity. I wrestled over tucking my T-shirts in or leaving them out. In, or out. In, out.

"What are you doing?" she asked, watching a fit at the mirror.

"Going out. Trying to."

"Where are you going?"

"Dancing."

"Oh," she said. "You're going to the big barn bar?"

"Uhm, no," I said. "Actually I'm going to the city."

"Oh," she said. "Where?"

"Uhm, it's, a women's place. Downtown. You want to go?"

"Oh," she said. "No. I got work and stuff later."

That July, I'd met someone at a club on Seventh Avenue. I didn't like the club. It was a lesbian disco. It had loud music selected by a

DJ, "she's homeless, she's homeless, la-da-dee, la-da-dah," it was not nearly as earthy and real as the Blue Goose seemed to me, it had flashing lights and edgy women who took about a half second to look me over head to toe and keep walking; it had mean women, and when I said things like, "Is this the line for the bathroom?" they'd say things like, "No, we just like staring at each other's backs. Jesus Christ." But still, it was the first time in my life I'd gone some-where with a genuine interest in meeting someone, which, it sud-denly occurred to me, was actually a huge part of why anyone went to any of these bars I'd haunted; I'd never thought of it before. So how could I resist it, feeling for the first time in my life that I might just like to meet someone? I went and stood with My People and felt awkward and dumb but I kept going because I had found no other way. And then I met Cindy. She was wearing a mood ring. "What kind of mood are you in?" I asked her at the bar. And bam, there we were back in Queens before I even knew what happened. Was this wild? There we were on her leather couch admiring the glass statue of a nude woman on her coffee table. A poster of a woman in vamp-ish pose hung on the wall. I held my beer bottle tightly.

"Who is that?" I asked, nodding toward the poster.

"Madonna," she said. "Yeah."

"Oh," I said. "Yeah."

Then without pause Cindy leapt on me. Just turned her body right around so that her knees straddled my lap and her little face was planted on my seemingly much larger face. Her mouth was on my mouth, and I thought to myself, "I'm kissing a woman. Thank fucking god I am kissing a woman." And it was the '90s, it was a bright cool moment to be gay and everyone seemed to be trying it, lesbians were everywhere, on the covers of magazines that asked, "Is Everyone Gay?" and for once in my life I wasn't afraid of the whole thing, it was just time and I was ready. Yes, there I was at last doing that thing that I had essentially been doing ever since 1973 and

247

summer camp and Arty, whose dripping nose hit my cheek as he aimed for my mouth, pinning me behind the arts and crafts hut. It was the same "I wondered about this" feeling, there on Cindy's leather couch. That same, squishy mouth, earnest but ultimately disappointed feeling.

But it took a few hours anyway and I stayed out all night without explaining, Madeleine didn't ask and I didn't tell because she was mine. Cindy was all mine. The phone rang. It was Cindy.

"Who was that?" Madeleine said.

"Just Cindy," I tossed off, returning to the mirror.

"Cindy?"

"Yeah."

"Who's Cindy?"

I didn't say.

"Oh-oh," Madeleine said. "Oh-oh, I know who Cindy is." She ran up to me and started laughing through her teeth, tsee-tsee-tsee. "I know who, don't I," she said. I smiled. "Well, when do I get to meet her?" she said.

"Uhm," I said. "Well, it's not like that."

Our worlds were colliding, right there inside the House of Revolution in the Summer of Love. I had Cindy, and I had Madeleine, and all I wanted was some other thing that neither was really providing. It was not like we were going to double date, maybe catch a Madonna concert with Cindy and this strange guy Andrew whose voice had mysteriously become the sole male voice appearing on our answering machine, and it said really odd things: "Uh, hey, this is groove-meister Andrew wah wah, Rosaline, Rosaline, she's my lover she's my queen, whoa boy I think I have to vomit. Hey I got the Monkees movie on tape. Cool?" Stuff like that. What did it mean? Did she know? She didn't tell me. He'd been to the house, too; when I wasn't there he'd been there. I could tell. There was a new kind of cigarette in the ashtrays. There were extra empty beer cans.

248

I would have to do something about Cindy before it got to the point of our friends actually meeting. Madeleine and I were moving to Montana. I told Cindy. I said, "I'm sorry Cindy I can't see you anymore. I am moving to Montana." She said, "Oh. Sure. Okay."

John called; he never stopped by. It was not like Newark where we were now, and even if Madeleine left the door open it didn't seem possible for him to visit a house he couldn't breeze into through the kitchen door. It didn't seem right to drop in some place with a door bell, no matter how much people told you to ignore it. This place was too strange for him.

The first time he called and I answered, he said, "Hey, so I hear you're a lesbian."

"Well," I said, "yeah."

"I knew it. I mean, I really knew. Let me ask you something," he said, lowering his voice. "Is this possibly a phase you're going through, maybe a past life memory?"

"I don't think that's it, John. But thanks for asking."

Then John said, Andrew this, Andrew that, Andrew is really into magic mushrooms and John hadn't done shrooms since before he had kids and is there any way we could get some?

I said, "I don't know John, whatever you want. Why don't you ask him."

"What's wrong?"

"Nothing is wrong."

"You sound like something's wrong."

"It's nothing. So you've met Andrew?"

"Well, no."

"It's just sort of funny how everyone talks about this Andrew all the time."

"Well, I've never actually met him, but . . . hey!" he said.

"What?"

"Hey, are you jealous? Hey, you aren't . . . I mean, you two, you're not, Madeleine and you never . . . never . . . did you?"

"John, come on," I said. "We're just friends. You know that."

"Well then what's wrong? It's the summer of love, man. Even my wife's extra happy."

On the screen porch overlooking the backyard that summer I'd sit into night, listening in the last of late daylight to the kids riding rolling toys down the short, short hills. Would those children grow up to leave, or stay? The house I had lived most of my life in seemed to me a shell, washed up on a beach in a neighborhood full of similar shells, with people moving in and out of them like crabs. I watched my parents' neighbors, the Murpheys: they cooked on the barbecue, they tossed baseballs back and forth in their yard. They had certainties: Meat. Money. Baseball. Home.

I closed my eyes, rubbed my stubbly hair; barbecue smells disturbed my effort to become a vegetarian. Falling asleep on my porch just as I had as a teenager, it felt safe there for now but I couldn't stay, I had to go somewhere, I would go to Montana. Long flat fields like my long flat body reclining on a chair. I could be anyone, I could go anywhere, I could raise barns with my new power saw, I could make wind chimes out of glass, and we didn't really need a shotgun, did we? I could live off corn, and berries in the woods, and I am not afraid ("No," John said, "Don't ever be afraid, if the Visitors sense your fear then they've got you"); I lay with a song in my head, La-da-dee, La-dee-dah, for this is all a dream we dreamed long ago, and the government wages war for profits and maybe John is an alien and I would quit my job, I would; my grandfather moved to Rapelje because I loved Madeleine. I turned, sleeping in the chair, wrinkling my cutoff camouflage pants. My body is a blank slate so paint it; we're here, we're queer, get used to it and I wonder about women, could I say I loved women, could I say I loved anyone but Madeleine? Did I still? I wanted that thing we both called Montana, I wanted it as my life, and she had come so close to going there with me. She was the closest of anyone. Slouched drowsy in the down-sliding cushions of a porch chair. It grew dark, it grew midnight, all of the neighbors had gone off to bed. The phone rang. I shook myself up. I ran inside to answer.

It was John.

"Hey, what's happening," he said.

"Same old," I answered, stretching. I stood in the kitchen, and I could see the clock above the sink: 12:30. I walked over with the phone and stood beneath the clock, leaning my back against the counter.

"Hey, did you mail order for tickets to the Dead shows?"

"No, John, I don't really do that stuff."

"Oh. I think Madeleine ordered. Did she?"

"She did?"

"Yeah."

John was drinking something while we were on the phone. He stopped talking and I heard ice cubes clink; in the stillness of the kitchen I noticed a squeaking sound overhead. I leaned my back against the counter and stared down at the floor.

"When are the shows?" I asked.

"There's nine dates, starting the end of August, like, the 29th, 30th, September 1st, September . . ." He trailed off and I could hear ice in his glass, him pausing to drink again. Nine whole nights of this obsession? Was anything worth following like that?

Squeak squeak squeak above me.

"Well that's really funny John because I think we ought to be half way to Montana by then, at least that's the plan."

"Aw, c'mahhn," he said. "Hey, I got this Cosmic Light news letter you have to check out. There's new proof that the government is collaborating with aliens to build a weapon in the desert but the bastards won't talk about it. Just bury the story and POOF, it disappears. Know what I mean?" Ice cubes clinked.

"Yeah, John," I said, "I guess I know what you mean but you know what? I'm just really not in the mood for this right now. Hey, how's Paula doing?"

"She's great she's great you should come up here and see her. Hey, is Madeleine there?"

"Yeah, I think so but she must be sleeping," I said.

"No, man, she told me Andy was coming over, they were going to watch the Monkees movie on video. Go get her."

"It's her night off, I can't wake her. She'd kill me."

"No no no, she's not sleeping, Andy is there."

His voice was a long-distance whine in my ear. Squeak. Squeak. Squeak, above me.

"Hey John, I'm not sure what's going on. If I see her I'll tell her to call and I gotta go now, okay?"

"Okay," he said. "Okay okay bye."

Squeak squeak squeak above me. I stood leaning back against the counter near the sink with the silent phone in my hand, only moonlight in the kitchen, and I realized that I was listening to Madeleine and Andrew, together in bed. Squeak, squeak, squeak. I had finally placed the noise overhead.

So: she had finally done it. I had not realized they had progressed this far. There had been no evidence, no condom wrappers in the garbage; I kept an eye out but I had found only smaller mysteries, like aluminum cans mixed in with the regular trash, and I sensed things were not right. Now I knew what had happened. The two of them were right then bare and embraced in air-conditioned darkness, cold enough at 64 degrees to put blankets on the bed, roll around with their legs locked, bumping hips and other places. Oh my god.

Squeak, squeak, squeak, in the room directly above the kitchen, in my childhood bed. What a nightmare: and here I had thought she was blissfully asleep on her night off. Wrong: she was upstairs fucking that son of a bitch while I contemplated quitting my job and leaving everything to live in the plains of Montana. We were not going to Montana if she was bedding down strangers and buying tickets to Dead shows and living who knew what kind of life without me. We weren't moving to Montana; of course we weren't. How could we?

Squeak squeak squeak. And you know what? I never wanted to go anyhow. I was just in love with some silly idea. And here she was all along not anything like my beautiful ideas at all; she is someone who would screw this disgusting groove-meister wah wah guy. Oh, the horror of it, the betrayal! The Creeps! Creeps! Heinous, dirty, copulating creeps!

In that squeaking I knew I'd lost everything I had dreamed of for years, because it was just not possible for Madeleine and me to stay together. Not here, not anywhere. It just wasn't going to happen. Maybe I'd always known that but it had taken me so long to stop fighting and accept it. Well: now I'd said it, at least to myself, and I knew it was done. I was going to hurt, and then I was going to move on, without her. And it didn't really matter where I went. It just mattered that I go.

"Oh damn them, why does it always come down to who you fuck?" I said out loud, and kicked the cabinet behind me with my heel.

Squeak, squeak, squeak, the box springs flawlessly repeated.

But even as I stood there feeling hurt, I also understood that Madeleine had lost her best friend, and that she had also been hurting. She would have liked things not to change. Maybe she was still hoping for a future that would give us back our past. She loved me, but even she must have known we couldn't do this together. Why not? It was not for me to say. Why couldn't I love Bob? Why couldn't Fred do it with me? Maybe Fred was gay.

Squeak squeak.

Holy shit, I thought, it's been ten minutes, is she ever going to come? Come on already, let's get this over with. Come, you sons of bitches, come!

That's what I was thinking just then. I was listening and thinking and staring straight ahead, incessant squeaking above me, when Madeleine appeared. White wisps of her summer pajamas glowed in the doorway. My eyes met her eyes. Squeak squeak squeak, overhead.

In the same instant I realized the rhythmic squeaking was coming from the kitchen clock above the sink, where I was leaning. In that moment I realized that the clock had always squeaked that way, as each second passed, but I had momentarily forgotten.

"What are you doing, standing around in the dark?" she said, and smiled, rubbing her eyes.

"I was, I was just thinking."

"Yeah?" she said quietly, yawning dramatically. "What about?"

"You want some milk or something?"

"Water."

"You alone up there?"

"Of course I'm alone."

"No Andrew?"

"Ha! Andrew?" Then I saw her catch on: her eyes got wide and then narrowed down and her little smile bunched to the side of her face. She shook her head and she said, "You know, I had sex last week, but I was dreaming at the time."

She stepped into the kitchen without turning the light on. I loved the way she moved, like a cartoon character drawn just a little bit too large, firm, sturdy; she changed the balance in a room, everything shifted toward her. I opened the refrigerator and stared into the light, moving things around slowly inside. I wished then, with a longing sprung from the fairy tale feeling of summer nights and long friendship, that this big carpeted colonial really had been our house, that we lived there together bound in some real and unalterable way, for life, with kids and jobs and the town swimming pool each summer. Like a family. And this place could be our Montana. I wished that at least she could be my sister. She was not. And I knew that I would keep reliving my moments of truth over and over, until I got one right; and then, I would lose her. I took a deep breath.

"I've been thinking," I said, "about going to Montana."

She said nothing; she drank her water. The kitchen was still linoleum and brown stove, clock squeaking as seconds passed by.

"We can't do it," I said flatly.

"Well," she replied. "I've been wondering about that too. I guess not."

"You agree, huh?"

"Yeah."

"You're not mad at me?"

"No," she said. "Not mad."

"You could still go, you know."

"Well, I dunno. Montana . . ." she trailed off.

In three weeks, Madeleine would be offered a new job, in upstate New York, not far from where John lived, and it would be too perfect, too hard to resist, and she would take it. She would move away, not to the Rockies but to the Catskill Mountains. I would not go there with her; I would have to find my own way. But just then, we didn't know what would happen. It is easier to dismantle than to rebuild, and sensing that, I said with sudden dread for my wide-open future, "God must hate my guts. I can't get anywhere."

She said: "Oh, brother. I'm going to bed."

But when she got to the hall she turned around and said, "You know, you've traveled a lot farther than Montana since I've known you. Do you know what I mean? So much farther. It's just not the right thing, for us to go. That's all."

"Yeah," I said. "But it's hard."

"Only when you fight it."

She glowed in her gauze, in the moonlight, maturity and genes and years of German beer rounding her hips and breasts into a woman-sized pearl.

"You're a survivor," she told me, not gently but as a matter of fact. "You know this is not the end of the world."

And then Madeleine left, absorbed as if by moonbeam back up the stairs.

I ran, jumped time and space barriers, did every kind of mind trip game I knew how to do, and there was nothing I could do. . . . I had to change myself.

Steven Gaskin, hippie,
from *Haight Ashbury Flashbacks*

U.S. DECLARES WAR, PACIFIC BATTLE WIDENS Unity in Congress

Only One Negative Vote as President Calls to War and Victory

MISS RANKIN'S IS SOLE 'NO' AS BOTH HOUSES ACT IN QUICK TIME

The House adopted today, 388 to 1, the resolution declaring war with Japan forty minutes after it was presented, and would have done so sooner but for speeches by a few members who pledged unity of action by this nation in winning the war. The only member voting "no" was Miss Jeanette Rankin, Republican of Montana, who, over a span of twenty-four years [has served just two terms in Congress and], kept her record of "no war" consistent. Miss Rankin was one of several in 1917 who voted in the negative when the war resolution was passed.

New York Times, December 8, 1941

In Columbus, Montana, a woman named Mildred was angry with me. She said I got the whole story wrong.

She opened up her pressed lips and said: "You didn't get it at all. We loved Rapelje. We had parties. We had dances. We used to dance in those days until dawn. There wasn't any way to get home, in the dark. You couldn't see to go anywhere so we just stayed. There used to be a dance hall in Wheat Basin, and everyone would come, and oh they'd lay the babies on the piled up coats and take turns watching them, sweet little things, and all the children came and everyone was happy."

She said, "You didn't tell anything about that. All the things you wrote made it sound so sad there."

"Well," I told her, "maybe that's because I was sad."

"Well you were wrong."

I went to visit Mildred because she had written me a letter. After my article ran in *Montana Magazine,* about a dozen people, mostly elderly women, had written me letters. They had stories of their own about how their families had ventured west in the last frontier boom days, lured by promises that hadn't come true. Some had lost everything; some made it back; some had lost it all over again. Some of the women wrote letters about Rapelje; some wrote about other places that had dried up and nearly died, like Molt, Montana, a little farming hub with a stop on the spur rail line to Rapelje where people still live, but only a few, and just in a zip code, not an actual town because the town is gone; you can stand there where Molt once was and look out at the plains and wonder what went wrong. Or maybe, you could stand there and look into space and be grateful for everything that happened, exactly as it had. Some letter writers had settled down in little crannies in the Rocky Mountains where "California people" had recently invaded. California people act like Christopher Columbus, all of them thinking they found the place first and viewing any living remnants of that pioneer time like they were prehistoric objects of fascination. Marvelous cattle grates. Remarkable leathery hands on a man. A woman from Divide, Montana, told me her family's ranch near Butte was suddenly worth more when they went to sell it because the broker realized the land held a grave: her kid brother had been buried right there after he died in some childhood accident, maybe around 1915. Her dead brother's plot was an authentic pioneer grave site, and the California people like that sort of western authenticity. They pay good money for it. The ones who wrote me letters about living in Rapelje all said they just loved that place. They really did: they loved it, even if they hated it at first, when they got off the train and realized they'd been sent to some kind of arid hell. Mostly those letter writers liked my article, because it reminded them of all they had loved, and lost, and they understood that feeling, and it made us all a little sentimental to remember those things for a while. But some of them, like Mildred, didn't buy it.

Cousin Bill called me up when my article was published in *Montana Magazine*. He said people raised a real fuss about it at the Stillwater County 4-H Club Fair. Apparently a bunch of Rapeljeites cornered Aunt Jean and really let her have it. "Was that some relative of yours, wrote those things about us?" they wanted to know. "She called our homes ramshackle," said one, and, "She called my husband 'aged,'" said another. "She entirely neglected to mention our state champion school basketball team."

"They're madder 'n hell," Bill told me. "Damn near run my mother right off the fair grounds."

"But I meant to say I love it there . . ."

"Aw, never mind," he said. "People round here just don't get it when you say things like 'endless achin' mystery.'"

So I guess the story I told was not the truth as everyone saw it.

As our Summer of Love crashed into September, Madeleine heard about a job in upstate New York and we were suddenly throwing all our energy into that, trying to get her to what seemed like the best next place. I proofread her application, helped her pick out photographs to send, and not long after she applied for the job she found out that she got it. It happened so fast. She started making lists of things to do and things to pack and all the stuff she'd have to take care of before she moved up to live in a town near John and Paula, getting started on a new adventure and a job that would not require her to stay up all night alone in a New York City office building. We got so busy making plans for that big move, and I got so busy helping her pack up and go, it was like someone just came in and changed the subject, and we weren't talking about Montana anymore.

We weren't talking about much at all, really. Not real talk, not about anything that mattered. We didn't ever get past the surface of things anymore. We weren't talking deep, or hanging around drinking beer and dreaming about some other better place that we would find out about together, some day; when she was all packed and ready to go, she did not have any visible moment of reconciliation with all that had happened, or not happened, between us. She had not had any apparent moment of remorse, or shown any signs of loss, nor had she come to find me sitting quietly on the screen porch wondering if anything means anything or if we should all just say "fuck it" and stop wishing for anything in our lives besides money. Then, she did not give me a sly look as I slouched there, a look that said she had understood everything, perfectly; she did not kneel down beside me and take my hand off the arm of the folding porch chair that I had slumped down in, and never did she press her mouth onto the rubbery palm of my hand, slowly, then bend my fingers slowly closed, and she did not say to me, then, "You are the most important person in my life and you always will be. If the world could only be the way you dream it is, I know we would be happy." She never stroked her hand against my forehead. She did not look hard into my eyes before she stood up and went away forever.

And I didn't say anything either.

I was done. I had loved Madeleine and she loved me and when people love each other whole new worlds exist suddenly, full of potential, lively and infinitely expanding until someone withdraws from the project. Then eventually you both do, if you're lucky, and it's just gone. It was all gone, just like that, the possibility of Montana left us like a quick relief, not unlike the process by which, she once told me, you could fend off demons: Madeleine told me that if a sycophantic spirit ever approached and tried to countermand my soul I should just stand up and thrust my hand out and shout "NO!" Just like that. The soul-sucking vampire spirit molester would go away. They can't have you if you don't let them take you. There was no point in telling Madeleine for once and for all that I had once wished I could be happy forever, loving her; she must have known. What I'd been through, in the end, was not about her anyhow; it was about finding a life. And I still wanted the life I had imagined for myself all along, even after she was finally gone and Montana was gone with her.

In that summer when we did not move away together, with my parents about to reclaim their house, it seemed like I had about a day to decide what to do with the rest of my life. Madeleine was making her lists on paper (call U-Haul, call realtor, change oil in car, forward mail) but I had a list of my own in mind: find new place to live, find new friends, select course for future, consolidate gains in personal growth, carry on the dead revolution, figure out how not to lose heart. Madeleine was packing up her stereo and her drum set and all of her clothes, loading it all into her Honda, and I was watching her from the living room, sinking my bare toes into the pink pile carpet. What could I do? I had no idea. There had always been such a big gap between what I wanted and what I had. I still wondered if some secret world existed somewhere that I had not yet heard of, the place where all the diehard idealists, the vegetarians, the back to the land people, the struggling artists, the smart women, had gone off to, to live better lives. Why had they not sent me a postcard?

I would continue to watch for the invitation, but meanwhile it was pretty obvious to me, at last, that if I wanted the sort of life I had dreamed of so earnestly yet vaguely, then I couldn't wait for it to appear. I would have to start making it myself.

I got in the passenger seat of a Saab driven by a real estate broker named Jahn who I met through a local women's social network, a group I'd found locally hoping to make some friends. We'd just been talking generally about interest rates and things, and I was unmoved by the discussion, but Jahn carried forth about property investments with her big red smile plastered on tight. She said she had something to show me, just for fun. "Now this place," she said, "you should really just see it. When I walk through that front door, I think, 'Italian Villa.'" Her car pulled up in front of an old ratty house in my hometown, about two miles away from my parents' house. This dump had holes in the walls and ceilings. There was a fireplace that did not work in the foyer. There was lead paint peeling off the windows. I walked around for a few minutes and I decided to buy it.

What else was I going to do? I had all that Montana money saved up, and a variety of power tools and house parts, too, and the job I never wanted was paying me enough to handle a big mortgage. I decided I would do what my Cousin Bill calls "gettin' western with it." I decided I would start rebuilding the house by myself despite the fact that I had no idea at all how to do that. It just struck me as the perfect place to start making something for myself.

I saved all the letters that the old women in Montana sent me after they read my Rapelje article, and in my freshly painted study in my own house two years later I pulled the letters out of a file drawer. Something was still missing. Maybe it was the exhilaration of empty plains. Maybe it was the thrill of abandoning familiar things in search of ideas you could not be sure were even real. Maybe it was just that I needed more time. But sometimes, I wondered if I'd made a mistake, and just been so big a fool over Madeleine that I'd missed the whole point: that I really did need to move to the state of Montana, the actual state that is the fourth largest of our fifty U.S. states and not just the ecstatic state I conjured up sometimes while insulating my own damn attic, feeling "western."

Madeleine didn't call me much anymore but when she did we still fell into the familiar talk of good old friends. One spring I told her that I wanted to go interview those ladies who sent me the letters, soon, before they all died and took the secrets of Rapelje, Montana, and every other western mistake with them. I'm not sure what I really wanted from them, but I'd start by just asking what I'd never asked anyone: Why? Why did they go to Montana? What is it about that place that they had wanted so badly that no other possible world would ever do? I decided I could try to write a new article out of these interviews. I called Madeleine and asked her to go with me, just for two weeks, because I wanted her to take pictures. We knew how to work together. I thought maybe, even, we could drive out there in the hot sun and drink beer and hang out with our friends like a family beneath the sky full of a billion stars. But things are never the same the second time you do them.

We flew into Billings and rented a car. I had scheduled all our interviews in a circuit around the state. We drove and worked by a fairly rigid plan. Our first stop was in Missoula, also known as the "Peace City" because Congresswoman Jeanette Rankin had lived there. Jeanette Rankin had had the quirky fate of joining Congress twice, winning races twenty-three years apart, each time just as the nation entered major combat, as if it were her whole cosmic destiny to show up in time to vote "NO" to world wars. What a determined soul. We paid homage to her on our way to see Mydas, the woman who had been the school teacher in Rapelje when my family lived there.

Mydas was ninety-three years old. Square hips, green plaid polyester, white hair in a tight bun: she sat with taut posture on the edge of her seat, talking, clutching a wooden cane in front of her. The knuckles on her hands were just as round as her flat blue eyes. She told me she had arrived in Rapelje when she was twenty-six years old. The first thing she did when she got there was cry.

"Oh, it was a nothing little place," she said.

It had sounded like an adventure: better than California, where she lived, and better than the offers she received from schools in other places. She graduated from Berkeley teacher's college and was hired away by a Montana boomtown. It was not what anyone expected her to do. Mydas Capps, sorority sister, founder of the girls' Latin club and class valedictorian, was bound for big things. She mystified her friends and family as she said good-bye. "Good-bye, friends and family, I am going to Montana." At last her train stopped at the end of the spur line out of Billings, and she stepped onto the platform. It was 1927, and Rapelje was barely a collection of a hotel and a few stores and houses. The rest was a dry moat around a castle in little danger of attack. All the children came to greet her; she saw them all standing on the train platform looking up at her and out there beyond them she saw nothing. She cried.

But then, Mydas fell in love with Reuben, the other teacher at the local school in Rapelje. Apparently they fell so giddy in love that the school children spied on them, hoping to catch a glimpse of some amorous transaction; that's what my Aunt Shirley remembered. After they married, they moved to Missoula; when I visited Mydas there, she said Reuben had recently died. And I wondered about being ninety-three years old, with memories of loves that lived and died already, and of places that once dotted the map but can't be found any longer.

We talked for a while and when there was little left to remember she stood up. She walked slowly out to the kitchen door with me and Madeleine and looked over the five acres of yard on which Reuben had kept a small farm. Booming Missoula had started closing in around it. Mydas invited us to stay for meatloaf, but we didn't.

In the car I told Madeleine, "Maybe we should have, you know?"

"Nah," she said. "You don't eat meat, remember?"

"Well, yeah. True." We went to a bar to hear music instead.

The next day we went up to Butte, and then to a small town south of that city to find a woman named Nancy, who made dolls and who spent her days in a remote quiet place, alone. The only home she had ever known was the West, where her parents had come seeking adventure. Once a year she traveled, she said, but she always came home to Montana. Nancy made dolls, and told stories, and read magazines. She'd read my story in the magazine and she liked it, she said. Madeleine took her picture. I took notes, but Nancy didn't say much.

Then we drove back toward Bozeman. We stopped in a town called Manhattan, named by some homesick Dutch men who went west to grow hops for beer. We visited a woman named Dorothy, who, after she finished the eighth grade at the Rapelje school, had taken a job cleaning house for Florence and William Soderlind. That's what she told me in her letter. She said Florence was a good woman, very clean. Dorothy confirmed a story I had heard about my grandmother: that she made her children's friends take a bath when they came for sleepovers at her house. Children from the farms didn't always have bathtubs. They didn't have windows either; some didn't have shoes. Florence was just trying to help by drawing those baths but the kids were never happy about it.

Dorothy's family had moved west from Chicago in 1919. In Chicago her father sold vegetables he grew in a tiny yard, barely making enough to care for his family. How much could he grow if he had 160 acres? That's what you got in Montana. All that land for free. It was beyond imagining. If you had asked him why he went some place so far away, unseen, he would say there was no choice, not really; his family had nothing. They were assigned a homestead north of Rapelje. They packed up and left. It turned out that the

267

entire back end of their dusty quarter lot was a coulee—a big hole—with a couple trees growing on the bottom. The treetops almost reached the ground where Dorothy remembers standing as a girl, looking down. Now and then a cow would wander out across the pasture to the coulee and fall in.

Meanwhile, on a train barreling across the northern plains bound for Oregon, the youngest son of the Ypma clan came down with scarlet fever. The conductor put the whole family off the train: mother, father, and all six of their kids, out with their luggage in the dirt, a Swedish family new to America, stranded south of Rapelje. They never reached their intended destination farther west, just settled where they landed, finding work on local farms.

Dorothy married a young Ypma and left Rapelje for Manhattan, Montana. It was such fertile ground compared to Rapelje. Grain grew in the valley there. The Ypmas bought land and farmed it for fifty years. By the time I met Dorothy she and her husband had stopped farming, sold their land for what must have once been an unthinkable sum of money, and then watched it get carved up into housing lots, gobbled up in Bozeman's sudden sprawl. By the mid-1990s, so many people were moving to Montana that the land was starting to fill up. This brought McDonald's, strong coffee with steamed milk, certain upscale ice cream franchises, bagels, and other things beside food that seemed to have no real place in the frontier.

Dorothy took us for a drive past all the subdivisions, past the farm that she and her husband had worked, and she stopped in the parking lot of a large grocery store with a windmill on top. It was a Dutch store with real Dutch things to serve all the Manhattan immigrants, she said very softly. Inside, we walked back to the cooler aisle where she showed us the imported Dutch cheese. We nodded. I shut my notebook right about then. Madeleine put away her camera. The story was escaping us. We went back home with Dorothy to eat cheese and smoked trout on crackers.

The last stop, in Columbus, was Mildred. She was not very happy to see me.

"It was good, then," she said. "It was a world you'll never know. You sure didn't capture it in that story you told." She turned to Madeleine, who was finishing up her last roll of film: "That's enough pictures," she snapped. She turned to me: "You didn't even know your grandmother. I knew her. Oh, such a lovely woman. And never sad, believe me."

Mildred cranked up an old Victrola with tin records dated 1919; the song she played was called "Love's Dream." The hammer moved over little dents in a metal disk, and music like ice cream truck chimes wept distorted through the room. It still played behind us as Mildred walked with Madeleine and me up the street, to the house near hers where she said William and Florence lived in 1936, the year they left Rapelje and tried to start their lives over.

"Over here," she said, "on the corner of 23rd Street, that is where William and Florence moved. He came here to open up another bank. They didn't stay long before they moved to Billings."

Twenty-third Street: it sounds so grand, like there must be at least twenty-two others. Maybe there are. But the blocks of small houses in Columbus fade away after a short distance and not much appears beyond them. It was a small town, though still large compared to Rapelje. Mildred let Madeleine take one picture, of me and her standing on the whitewashed stone steps of that house on Twenty-third Street, the last place she could remember seeing my grandmother.

Back in New Jersey much later, when I showed that picture to my father, he looked down hard but then said he didn't recognize the house at all. "Nope. That's not the one," he finally said. "Unless I'm crazy, but I don't think I ever lived there." He stared at the photo, then handed it back to me, shaking his head, and he told me Mildred was wrong. We looked at each other, and we shrugged our shoulders.

Madeleine and I said good-bye to Mildred and then we drove back to Billings to spend the night at the Holiday Inn. In the morning we would board a plane for New Jersey, but for now she was stretched out on the bed clicking channels on the TV. We had a few hours left in Montana, and I decided that I would use them. I decided to go for a drive. I asked Madeleine if she wanted to go, but she preferred watching basketball, calling room service, and making a mess for the housekeeper to clean in the morning. "Have fun, be careful," she said.

I drove off, alone. I started on the highway. After a while, I turned off and got onto the unpaved back roads. I decided to look for Rapelje one more time, using only old roads that were nothing but faint dashes on my rent-a-car map and which seemed to criss-cross the plains for no purpose. There wasn't much there.

It was Father's Day 1993. As I drove I consumed one of six Rainier beers purchased at the Town Pump in Park City, feeling for a moment decadent and lawless and defiant again, proving at the same time that it's possible for me to understand every mistake I have ever made and make them all again anyway. But it was so remote out there in the hot flat land beyond the well-traveled path, and I guess I just figured it didn't matter. Nothing seemed to matter. And that felt pretty good, after all.

For hours—for *hours*—I saw no other human as I drove, just a century of ruined houses in the weeds. Rusted windmills stark in feral fields, blades unable to turn any longer. Abandoned roads. And every so often I came to an intersection and a wooden sign that made a promise, like "Molt-Wheat Basin." Dust rose behind my car like a flag. What was I looking for? In time the ecstatic feeling finally returned. A scrap of paper in my travel log says, "big, big, bigger than life for the wonder of it all—pure freedom, exhilarating freedom, to live or die on the plains." It's something like that, but not that exactly. I drove, and around me I felt the power of all the things

I could not see: the past, and dinosaur bones, and waiting missile silos buried in that gorgeous dirt. All the old monsters are buried there still, and I felt them, even though they seem to have been silenced forever.

I drove the dirt roads past homesteading shacks, an abandoned church and schoolhouse, a grain elevator in a place that was once Wheat Basin. There was no longer a dance hall. The road was the same one my grandparents once used to drive: a crevice in a vacant land, making turns for no apparent reason.

It was a long time before I found a sign that said Rapelje. At 9 p.m., I hit the eastern edge of town. It was not fully dark; the sky was shades of violet. Lights bunched up in the center of town. I sat there in my idling car for a moment, but there really wasn't much to see. All that seemed to matter was that it was still there. Having confirmed that, I pulled up to the mailbox by the Post Office trailer and left the motor running as I stepped out to mail a Father's Day card. Three people stood nearby talking and ignored me, an intruder, someone just passing by as if anyone could ever just be passing by Rapelje. I mailed my Father's Day card from Rapelje, Montana, for the postmark. Then I left, northbound, past the four grain elevators and the old railbed, and in another twenty miles I found a highway and a fast route back to Billings. From there, it was an easy drive back to the motel.

Up in the room, Madeleine was in bed but not sleeping. In the dark, I held up five cans of warm beer from the six pack I'd bought many hours before. A little light through the drapes gleamed off the cans and I asked her if she wanted one, but she looked at me like I was crazy. "You weren't out there drinking and driving, I hope," she said, as if such an idea had never, ever occurred to her. I said, "Of course not, I'm not stupid." I undressed and slipped into my own bed and lay there for a while. Such a long trip, and still no answers. Maps, pictures, stories, interviews, miles on the car, books full of notes, and to be honest I still wasn't even sure what I was trying to find. Just something. I stared out the split in the heavy motel drapes to see the fluorescent lamps glow in a near-vacant parking lot. I closed my eyes.

I was getting used to finding nothing. And nothing is alright, really. Nothing is its own kind of beautiful.